THE NIXON THEOLOGY

★ ★ ★

THE
NIXON
THEOLOGY

★ ★ ★

Charles P. Henderson, Jr.

HARPER & ROW, PUBLISHERS
NEW YORK, EVANSTON, SAN FRANCISCO,
LONDON

ACKNOWLEDGMENTS

The author gratefully acknowledges use of copyrighted material from the following publishers and publications:

From *Six Crises* by Richard M. Nixon. Copyright © 1962 by Richard M. Nixon. Reprinted by permission of Doubleday and Company, Inc.

From *Witness* by Whittaker Chambers. Copyright © 1952 by Whittaker Chambers. Reprinted by permission of Random House, Inc.

Some of the material in this volume has been adapted from an article appearing in *The Nation* in September, 1970.

The author also wishes to thank the Reverend Frederick E. Fox for permission to reproduce a short quotation from his personal letters.

FIRST EDITION

STANDARD BOOK NUMBER: 06-063860-5

LIBRARY OF CONGRESS CATALOG CARD NUMBER: 76-183642

To J.P.H.

Contents

★ ★ ★

vii

Introduction

★ ★ ★

This book was conceived during the events following Richard Nixon's announcement of the invasion of Cambodia, April 30, 1970. As a chaplain at Princeton University, I was caught up in the apocalyptic fury of protest that followed hard upon the President's television address. As soon as he had signed off the air, the campus erupted. Within minutes hundreds of students, joined by significant numbers of faculty, poured into the university chapel to express their outrage over what appeared to be a sudden and dramatic escalation of the war. Soon there were more than two thousand packed into the dimly lighted sanctuary. The rally was barely under control as a self-appointed steering committee struggled for order. Scores of people swarmed around the pulpit, demanding an opportunity to speak. There were several speeches, but as time passed the audience began to demand decisive action. Several voices shouted out, insisting that the assembly call a strike. Few had any clear idea of what it meant to strike a university, but the shouts grew more intense: Strike! Strike! Shut it down! Shut it down! Someone called for a vote, and an overwhelming majority roared in approval. Princeton University was unofficially On Strike! It was the first of more than two hundred colleges to give voice to this unprecedented defiance, much of it directed against the person of Richard M. Nixon.

The prevailing mood of the student body was one of moral indignation and outrage. Nixon's decision to widen the war was seen by the Princeton students as the final atrocity of a man long noted for his duplicity. But this response was diametrically opposed by the welcome which Nixon received at his first public appearance following the Cambodia speech. Sharing the dais with evangelist Billy Graham during his crusade at the University of Tennessee in Knoxville, Nixon addressed an audience of enthusiastic youth. He spoke grandly of the nation's "spiritual sources" and specifically of Billy Graham, who, he said, had the one message which this country needed to hear in its time of trouble. Here stood Richard Nixon alongside the man who represents for so many the very personification of religion and morality. To that audience in Tennessee, Nixon appeared as sincere in his righteousness and religion as he appeared diabolical to the majority of students at Princeton.

It is phenomenal that, after two decades of exposure to a national audience, Nixon still manages to elicit such diverse reactions. Despite his long years as Congressman, Senator, Vice President, leader of his party and now President, he still remains an enigma. Fascinated with the contrast between the conflicting images he projects, I began my own "Nixon watch" in earnest. Cued by his remarks at the East Tennessee Crusade, I began looking for further evidence of his piety. Was what he said at that Billy Graham rally calculated to dampen the moral outrage prevalent on many college campuses —were his words politically motivated—or did they reveal a more genuine and perhaps deeper conviction, a personal faith more significant than most observers had previously noticed? To my surprise, I discovered that when Nixon is pressed to justify a particular policy or decision, he regularly draws upon his religion. Called upon to defend his foreign policy or his conduct of the war, he most frequently invokes his training as a Quaker. Asked to explain his domestic programs, he often refers to the influence of his "protestant ethic." Though he does not have the charisma one would expect of a religious leader, Richard Nixon evidently takes his moral and theological convictions seriously. He seems to believe that his brand of Christianity is not only the prevailing factor in his own life, but equally the irreplaceable core of American culture.

Nixon vibrates to the rhythms of American folk religion. He perfectly illustrates the curious inbreeding of patriotism and piety, the protestant ethnic and liberal pragmatism that has been so pervasive in this nation's history. Nixon combines in one personality the major strains of American religiosity, even those that prove contradictory. My first inclination, therefore, was to treat him as yet another example of that combination of sentiments, instincts, and ideas that make up the "civil religion" common to the American majority. Still, as I explored the public record, reading his speeches, reviewing his own book, poring over biographies, editorials, and newspaper and magazine articles, I began to perceive that Nixon held to his religion in a rather uncommon way.

As I traced through the critical moments of his career, I discovered an overriding concern that his decisions and acts should be not only sound, but righteous. Nixon seems to be compulsively motivated to justify his actions and cement his ideas in the certainties of his own conscience. There have been many instances when he has been called upon to defend his character, but beyond the demands imposed upon him by a suspicious public, Nixon consistently takes a vindictive stance. He seems to be driven by a deep need to prove his integrity. As my study continued, I began to see that his entire life may be viewed as an attempt to reconcile his religion with the contradictory facts of his experience, to harmonize his moral convictions with the necessities of his career.

When he spoke in his inaugural address of the crisis in America as a crisis of the spirit, he unintentionally revealed the central dilemma in his own career. It is my contention that the persistent confusion and controversy about the "real Nixon" reflect a prevailing insensitivity to what may well be the single most important factor in his life. The continuing importance of Nixon's contacts with churchmen and church organizations, his propensity for the pious and moralistic in public debate, his circular appeals to conscience in almost every major address, suggest not the settled convictions of a man who has integrated his beliefs with action, but rather the compulsions of one caught up in a profound perplexity. Nixon's book, *Six Crises*, is aptly titled. In it he attempts to outline the "lessons" he has learned from his most critical and trying moments. What the book actually illustrates, I will argue, is that his fundamental crisis is unresolved. In addition to the overt debacles of his career, there is the far more basic crisis of *his* spirit. It is this phenomenon that the present volume seeks to explore.

Since Nixon's religion plays an important part in his underlying quest for identity, and since his religion is so illustrative of the conflicts in American culture as a whole, I first set his religion in context, revealing its historical and cultural roots. I then examine the presidency itself, suggesting that the responsibilities and role of the President sharpen and intensify Nixon's personal dilemma. Finally, I follow his biography and his career from childhood to the present, pointing out the peculiar stresses and prevailing tensions of his character. In the final chapters, I have tried to explore the wider implications of Nixon's crisis, suggesting that in a very real sense it is a problem we must resolve as a society. *The Nixon Theology* is at once an attempt to define the root assumptions and beliefs of the nation's thirty-seventh President and to suggest that his personal predicament reflects a more far-reaching crisis of national identity.

THE NIXON THEOLOGY

★ ★ ★

⋆ I ⋆

The Inaugural

On January 20, 1969 Richard Nixon walked from the Capitol building down the long flight of steps to the reviewing stand where he would take his oath of office. At last he found himself on center stage, prepared to assume the awesome responsibilities of the presidency. Now Congressmen and Supreme Court justices, generals, statesmen, and clergy would look to him for signs of the leadership he would offer the nation in the next four years. The video cameramen and commentators stood watch behind the glass windows of the communications tower, ready to report his words by satellite around the world.

While the act of swearing in a new President is stark in its simplicity, the attendant ceremony is orchestrated for maximum impact. Members of the Inaugural Committee use the most potent symbolism, the most suggestive images at their command. For they know that in this one act they must dramatize the metamorphosis of party politician into Chief of State. On Inauguration Day the President-elect must appear far more awesome than his abilities, his power, and his constitutional authority will in fact make him. He must take on the transcendent aura of the presidency.

In the case of Richard Nixon it was particularly critical that this change in role be convincingly demonstrated, for as he prepared to assume his powers he still projected an image tarnished by twenty years of combat in the arena of partisan politics. More than any President in recent history, he was recognized as a politician pure and simple. His two immediate predecessors had come to power as a result of their own calculated efforts, but neither Kennedy nor Johnson had crystallized in the public mind as a creature of the political system in which they both fared so well. It was generally believed that Kennedy had been elected on the strength of his charisma and Johnson, despite unsavory memories of his political adolescence in Texas, by the tragic circumstances of the assassination.

Moreover, Nixon took office at a time when the nation was deeply anxious about the viability of the political process. Americans were morally exhausted by the assassinations, the riots, and the war, the rising crime rate, and a continuing crisis in the cities— all of which seemed to imply that the system itself was functioning badly, that perhaps it was already beyond repair. The inaugural was Richard Nixon's prime opportunity to introduce himself as a leader who would transcend old party rivalries and unite the nation in renewed confidence, even a sense of mission.

Nixon was probably as sensitive to the difficulty of this task as his most hostile critics. He knew that if he were to make a convincing impression as a man who would redeem the nation, he must summon up the most powerful and moving symbols in the popular mythology. Consequently, as he prepared his inaugural address he secluded himself in his study, reviewing the words of all his predecessors. As he later reported the experience, he scanned the paragraphs written by Washington and Adams, Jefferson, Madison, Monroe. . . . Despite the changing circumstances and varying opinions of other Presidents, he discovered a "single theme common to all the Inaugurals . . . that was that each President, . . . in his own way, recognized the spiritual heritage of this nation, and asked for the blessing of God on this country." Nixon had gone looking for the key to a national reconciliation, and found it in the "spiritual heritage" recorded in past inaugurals.

Though not recognized as a deeply religious figure, Nixon was anxious to present himself as a man of faith. While composing his

2

speech and considering plans for the inaugural ceremony, he found abundant opportunity to express his deepest beliefs. For the inaugural is, by tradition, an affair of profound theological significance. More than any other event in the life of this nation, it calls forth that mixture of piety and patriotism which is so much a part of the American consciousness. The ceremony includes all the ritual and regalia of this country's two-hundred-year history.

Yet while the occasion is designed to express the nation's most sacred traditions, it also betrays some of our more serious faults. There is an element of satire in the affair. Priests in liturgical vestments contrast with souvenir vendors, while marching soldiers mix with high-school majorettes; there is a rich flavor of irony in the interplay of prayer and politics, cannon and candied apples, flags and frills. In 1969 there was a Lincoln float which set forth the Emancipator's words in papier-mâché and gold foil: A HOUSE DIVIDED AGAINST ITSELF CANNOT STAND. In the streets, war protesters wore ghoulish masks with a striking resemblance to the new President, and even as Nixon spoke of his hope for a new era of peace, the subterranean garages of Washington's government buildings were filled with armored personnel carriers and troops on riot alert. Secret service agents were scattered through the area in unprecedented numbers, their eyes combing the crowd for the first signs of the violence that had been so widely predicted. And yet, for most of the spectators the event was full of traditional solemnity. It was a time when the country's most powerful leaders and her most ordinary citizens gathered in the streets to wave their flags, glimpse their new President, and show reverence to the God of their fathers.

Worship played an unusually large part in the inauguration of Richard Nixon. The Religious Observance Committee worked for months in advance to set a spiritual tone for the occasion. In the closing weeks of 1968, the committee issued a call for spiritual renewal, requesting all churches and synagogues of America to unite in prayer for the new President, for the government, and for the country. On Inauguration Day, the committee arranged for three minutes of national worship "to commemorate with joyful reverence this peaceful transfer of authority and to proclaim to all the world our faith in God and our spiritual rededication."

The committee also distributed a collection of prayers, Bible readings, and famous quotations. A passage from I Peter echoed the law-and-order sentiments of the recent campaign. "Be subject for the Lord's sake to every human institution, whether it be to the emperor as supreme, or to governors as sent by him to punish those who do wrong and to praise those who do right." A prayer by George Washington sought the help of God in cultivating "a spirit of subordination and obedience of government." Ten thousand specially printed cards showing a pair of hands in an attitude of prayer were distributed for display in store windows and public buildings. On the cards were the words: THANKSGIVING, BLESSING, DEDICATION, GUIDANCE, *and* Richard Nixon's campaign slogan: FORWARD TOGETHER.

During the ceremony, the Mormon Tabernacle Choir joined the United States Marine Band in the Star-Spangled Banner and a selection of music, both martial and devotional. The nation's most popular religious leader, evangelist Billy Graham, opened the service with a typically hard-hitting invocation, more a sermon than a prayer:

Our Father and our God . . . we recognize on this historic occasion that we are "A Nation under God." We thank thee for this torch of faith handed to us by our forefathers. . . . This faith in God is our heritage and our foundation. Thou has warned us in the Scriptures, "If the foundations be destroyed, what can the righteous do?"

The whole world is watching to see if the faith of our fathers will stand this hour. Too long we have neglected thy word and ignored thy laws. Too long have we tried to solve our problems without reference to thee. Too long have we tried to live by bread alone. We have sown to the wind and are now reaping a whirlwind of crime, division and rebellion.

And now with the wages of our sins staring us in the face, we remember thy words, "If my people who are called by my name shall humble themselves and pray and seek my face and turn from their wicked ways, then will I hear from heaven and will forgive their sin and will heal their land."

It may seem extraordinary that such a sharply evangelical prayer could be included in an event of such secular significance. Yet Billy Graham rose to the podium and in no uncertain terms told the American people that they must be "born again" through a simple faith in Jesus Christ. His words echoed the message he had preached to more people than any evangelist in history. It was the message of his great crusades, and it was delivered at the direct invitation of Richard Nixon.

The presence of Billy Graham on the inaugural dais signaled the fact that revival had finally made its way to the capital and to the White House itself. Graham has been, for twenty years, a close friend and adviser to Richard Nixon and the religion which they share would be much in evidence, not only at the inaugural, but throughout the tenure of the nation's thirty-seventh President.

The evangelist was joined in prayer by clergy representing Jewish, Protestant, Roman Catholic, and Greek Orthodox traditions. There was also a full-scale ecumenical service in the West Auditorium of the State Department—the first of its kind in history. These plans were made in full consultation with the President-elect; never before had so much prayer been invoked to place this nation's Chief of State in office.

And religion was not limited to the prayers. The inaugural address itself was replete with references to God and the Bible, the American spirit, the spirit of Christmas, our virtues and vices—

even the angels. Contrasting the economic crisis which tormented the nation during the depression years with the looking-glass version facing us in 1968, Nixon said:

Standing in this same place a third of a century ago, Franklin Delano Roosevelt addressed the nation ravaged by depression, gripped in fear. He could say in surveying the nation's troubles: "They concern, thank God, only material things." Our crisis today is in reverse . . . we are caught in war, wanting peace. We're torn by division, wanting unity. We see around us empty lives wanting fulfillment. We see tasks that need doing waiting for hands to do them. To a crisis of the spirit we need an answer of the spirit.

And then the President went on to describe those spiritual resources which, he asserted, would give the nation confidence during the 1970s. "When we listen to the better angels of our nature, we find that they celebrate the simple things, the basic things—such as goodness, decency, love, kindness."

Nixon spoke also of more material concerns: full employment, better housing, rebuilding the cities, protecting the environment, enhancing the quality of life. But the speech was lofty; it continually pressed out beyond the bounds of the immediate and the topical to the realm of dreams and visions. "The American dream does not come to those who fall asleep." (His play on words was not intended; this was an earnest, even emotional appeal to the American people.) No, we must pursue the dream actively, relentlessly—marshaling "the energies of our people" to "build a great cathedral of the spirit—each of us raising it one stone at a time, as he reaches out to his neighbor, helping, caring, doing." He particularly wanted to convey his sense of caring, his concern for the people, *all* the people. For Richard Nixon is not the one-dimensional politician that many of his critics have made him out to be over the long years of struggle for the presidency. Among his most deep-rooted convictions is the universalist teaching of his Quaker past, his belief that men are born with an infinite capacity for good. It was this

6

idealistic strain in his own character that Richard Nixon hoped to project in his first speech as President.

As he turned to the question of the war, Nixon borrowed the syntax of St. Francis of Assisi, echoing his classic prayer for peace. "Let us take as our goal where peace is unknown, make it welcome; where peace is fragile, make it strong; where peace is temporary, make it permanent." The President envisioned a beneficent America, willing to cooperate with any people who would help "to strengthen the structures of peace, to lift up the poor and the hungry." He closed his address with a lyric passage from Archibald MacLeish, a reference to the Apollo astronauts and their Christmas Eve prayer from the moon, and finally his own statement of faith:

Our destiny offers not the cup of despair, but the chalice of opportunity. So let us seize it, not in fear, but in gladness—and "riders on the earth together," let us go forward, firm in our faith, steadfast in our purpose, cautious of the dangers but sustained by our confidence in the will of God and the promise of man.

Since the President so self-consciously patterned his speech after those of his predecessors and made such a special effort to recognize the nation's spiritual heritage in his plans for the inaugural, we would do well to take careful measure of those elements in American culture and history which he seeks to emulate.

When Nixon took his oath of office, he placed his hand on the two family Bibles that bear the record of his ancestry in this country. The record extends beyond the Revolution to 1690, when the first Milhous, a Quaker arrived in Chester County, Pennsylvania, in pursuit of religious freedom. On his father's side James Nixon was the first to settle in North America; he arrived from Ireland at Brandywine Hundred, Delaware in 1753. From the beginning, Nixon's genealogy follows the broad outlines of American history as it might be recorded in a high school text book. After fighting in the Revolution, his ancestors set out toward the frontier. As they moved westward they became farmers and preachers, helping runaway slaves in the underground railroad and fighting in the Civil War. The Nixon and Milhous families preserved their Protestant traditions, remaining for the most part Methodists and Quakers. As they moved, they carried their Bibles with them, faithfully inscribing all the important dates between the covers of the family Scriptures.

Though President Nixon still claims the Quaker birthright inherited from his mother, it is important to note that the Quakers were profoundly influenced as they went west by the prevailing patterns of American religion. It was during the nineteenth century that the Milhous family severed its ties in the East and followed the tide of migration toward Ohio, Indiana, and eventually California, finally settling in the Quaker town of Whittier, thirteen miles from Los Angeles. But as the Quakers migrated toward California they were caught up in the most powerful movement of nineteenth-century religion, namely revivalism.

As the country grew and the population moved west, the states were swept by wave upon wave of revival. In the established congregations of New England and tent meetings of the frontier, the fever spread, affecting the entire people. In the East, Timothy Dwight, president of Yale and grandson of Jonathan Edwards, emerged as the militant leader of the awakening. In one year (1802) a third of the student body at Yale was converted to his "positive Christianity."

On the western frontier the revival took even more dramatic forms. Where there were no churches, circuit riders and itinerant evangelists organized camp meetings. They became masters of emotionalism—praying, preaching, wailing; their sessions were often marked by violent emotional outbursts, the converted sometimes falling into fits of ecstasy, barking, yelling, and rolling over the sawdust floor. From the stately campus of Yale to the wild fields of

Kentucky and Tennessee and as far west as the white man had gone, Congregationalists, Presbyterians, Methodists, Baptists—and Quakers— were fired to a pitch of fervor.

The revival movement was not limited to preaching and praying, however. A network of voluntary societies was established to carry out a variety of missionary, educational, and reform causes. The goal was not only the conversion of individuals to the Christian faith, but the transformation of a whole society. Citizens of the "benevolence empire" fought for temperance, prison reform, education, peace, and the abolition of slavery. The movement included members of all denominations, thus again softening the theological differences and divisions that had been so striking in the colonial period. Most important, revivalism contributed to the emergence of those broad and widely shared convictions that may appropriately be termed a national religion.

Filled with zeal and active in works of charity, Christians across the nation saw their movement as the manifestation of an American destiny. Many believed that the fulfillment of history was at hand, that the thousand-year reign of Christ was about to be set up—by and for the people of a triumphantly Christian nation. Lyman Beecher, one of the most famous preachers of the century, articulated these sentiments:

If it had been the design of Heaven to establish a powerful nation in the full enjoyment of civil and religious liberty, where all the energies of man might find full scope and excitement, on purpose to show the world by one great successful experiment of what man is capable . . . where should such an experiment have been made but in this country! . . . . This light of such a hemisphere shall go up to Heaven, it will throw its beams beyond the waves; it will shine in the darkness there, and be comprehended,—it will awaken desire, and hope, and effort, and produce revolutions and overturnings until the world is free.

Such convictions flourished in a nation which constantly reminded itself that state and church, though separate institutions, were the twin supports in the symmetry of the American Republic. Revival was necessary, not only to nurture individual souls but to infuse into the entire culture a common sense of mission. In the absence of an established church, or even a union of disestablished denominations, the revivalists attempted to preserve their Protestant background by sheer force of persuasion.

(Ironically, while Americans cultivated the conviction that the United States was to play a unique part in God's plan for mankind, these very beliefs were evidence of the most primitive of human instincts. The basic myths of tribe, nation, or race are those that assert a superiority and a special relationship to the gods. While Americans were convinced that their nation represented something radically novel in history, they were also articulating a primeval human myth.)

As the camp meetings and crusades were aimed at individual conversion, as the works of charity were carried out on a voluntary basis in the private sphere, so the prevailing ethos was individualistic, activist, and often chauvinistic. Binding the destiny of the nation to the success of their own crusades, the revivalists appealed at once to emotions of piety and patriotism. Rephrasing the older Puritan concept of a covenant between man and God, they saw in American history convincing proof of a divine guidance and blessing. Ideas once tied to specific theological formulations now became the general currency of a popular piety. Though Puritan theology had emphasized the continuing sinfulness of man and the imperfections of American culture, politicians and preachers promoted a more mythical concept of American history. Out of the record of names and places, of conflict and compromise, was drawn the simpler story of the nation's saving mission. Even the crude realities of war were transformed into graceful patterns of a transcendent justice.

By the time Chicago businessman Aquilla Pickering established Whittier as a "Quaker city" in 1887, the Friends of the West and

Midwest had adopted much of the theology and most of the practices of evangelical Christianity. In fact, the town soon became the center of a Quaker revivalism that spread throughout southern California. The evangelists of the California Yearly Meeting preached their gospel at tent meetings; the services of the Whittier Friends included sermons delivered by professional clergy, as well as congregational singing and spoken prayers. Frontier revivalism had gone far toward closing the gaps between the denominations. Even the pacifism characteristic of Pennsylvania Quakers had been seriously compromised. When Frank Nixon, a Methodist, married Hannah Milhous, a Quaker, it was not surprising that he was willing to join his wife's congregation and give their children a common Quaker upbringing. He knew that they would receive virtually the same instruction in the Sunday school of the East Whittier Friends Meeting as was given in the conservative Methodist churches of his own childhood.

It was this general background which President Nixon reflected upon in June, 1971, when he visited his mother's birthplace at Vernon, Indiana. "My roots are here," he affirmed, and he went on to suggest what "mother would want me to say." In addition to being "very proud of your country, she would also want to say to this group: Keep your religious faith." But it is misleading to say that Nixon's roots are in Indiana. For though he had come to dedicate a plaque in honor of his mother who was born there in 1885, the family homestead had burned to the ground, and there were no known relatives of the President in this town of 500 persons. So the plaque was placed somewhere along Highway 50, the main route running west from Cincinnati. The Milhous family had followed the frontier west to California; and Nixon has continued the classic search for a new frontier. He has chosen to live not in the enduring towns of middle America, not in Vernon, Indiana, but in those places where novelty is supreme: New York City, Washington, D.C., southern California, and sunny Florida. In choosing the novel

11

over the orthodox, Richard Nixon is characteristically American. Complementing the religion of revival that prospered in a land of seemingly unlimited growth, we have evolved a politics of revival. The political history of this century can be written around our frantic search for renewal as we constantly hope to recapture the magic of a New World, the promise of the Revolution, the opportunity of the West. Like the evangelical preacher, our politicians promise a radical transformation of society in the image of a mythic past.

One feels this in current practice. On October 27, 1969, President Nixon appeared with Billy Graham at a breakfast meeting in the State Dining Room of the White House. They met with a group of Congressmen and Senators to celebrate the National Day of Prayer, and their remarks on this occasion clearly demonstrate the persistence of a mythical concept of American history. The President again reflected upon the accomplishments of his predecessors. "As we look back over our Presidents through the past 190 years . . . I think all of us realize that at times of great challenge . . . particularly in this century . . . there had to be something more than honesty and more than wisdom in the leadership of this country. . . . There had to be, we believe, some call to destiny."

Nixon now led his audience in a "moment of silence" to ponder his words and then introduced Billy Graham, who presented the same themes in more detail. Graham, in fact, gave a short survey of American history, pointing out what he took to be the four major turning points of the American spirit. The first, he said, was at Valley Forge when George Washington knelt in prayer and "out of that turning to God came the solution to the problems of the Revolutionary War, and ultimate victory." The second crisis, he claimed, was the Constitutional Convention, which found itself at a point of irreconcilable conflict, when "Benjamin Franklin reminded them of the nation being founded by men who believed in God . . . and out of that prayer meeting [came] . . . our Constitution." In Graham's view, the third crisis of American history was the Civil War, and

12

there he saw "Abraham Lincoln . . . how time after time he turned to God, calling the Cabinet to prayer, kneeling in prayer with a woman who [had] come to visit him. . . ." And finally: "I wonder if the fourth crisis is not the present crisis. I wonder if the time hasn't come for us to look . . . to the supernatural power of God that I believe has intervened in American history before. . . . Our President has said, 'Ours is a crisis of the spirit.' The great problem in America today in my knowledge is a spiritual problem. It is a spiritual problem and until we face it and attack it from that point of view, I think we are in for more trouble."

When the President and his evangelist call for a recovery of this country's spiritual heritage and insist that the nation address its problems from the perspective of an historical faith, they are pointing to a specific phenomenon in American religion. They are recommending a return to the nationalistic religion of their common Protestant origins. Theirs is a religion which sees a perfect harmony between faith in God and in the nation and which identifies the will of God with the welfare of the state. As Nixon put it in 1970: "America would not be what it is today, the greatest nation in the world, if this were not a nation which has made progress under God."

There are a number of problems associated with this mixture of patriotism and revivalist religion. In the first place, the call to revival (or to political reform) can be killed by the monotony of repetition. In the nineteenth-century there was an area in New York State that was called the burned-over district because its people had been kindled to revival so often that even salvation had become a habit. An incessant call for renewal can be self-destructive when the rhetoric becomes a substitute for the reality of change. The dilemma of Richard Nixon is that so many people now feel that his promise of a New Revolution is simply rhetorical. In such a climate only suspicion and fear will grow sometimes festering into hate. It has happened before.

The darker side of nineteenth-century religion expressed itself in a distrust of immigrants, dissenters, nonconformists, and Catholics. In 1844 the city of Philadelphia was rocked by riots, an incident which clearly illustrates the sinister consequences of a religious and nationalistic fervor turned to hate. The conflict began over the use of the Protestant Bible in the public schools. On Friday, May 3, a crowd of "Native Americans" rallied in a public market. A small scuffle sparked open rioting, and the crowd swelled into a mob, raiding Irish-Catholic homes in the neighborhood. Several days of riots followed, with houses burned and bullets flying. The Pennsylvania militia was called out to quell the disturbance, and the final toll revealed seven dead, thirty-seven wounded.

The nation would again experience the bitterness of a stale revival in the McCarthy era of the 1950s; we would feel it in the campaigns of George Wallace and in the extremes of the student movement; we would sense it in Campaign '70. Fear has been a constant companion of faith in America, for the revivalists have consistently preached their message in response to a perceived threat to their culture and religion. Behind the rhetoric is often a clot of fear, not simply for the nation but for the special interests of a specific group or class. As the religion of Richard Nixon echoes a particular phase of Protestant history, we shall see that it also reflects the interests of a particular constituency.

In 1857 still another wave of revival began, this time in New York City, when a midday prayer meeting sparked a burst of enthusiasm and drew nationwide attention. As never before, leaders in the business and financial community provided the organization and backing. This revival was a harbinger of things to come: the new alliance between business and big-time evangelism would prove a powerful force in the twentieth century.

More than any politician in recent history, Richard Nixon has captured the loyalty of the "Christian businessman." Typical of this constituency and true to the spirit of 1857 is W. Clement Stone, chairman of the Combined Insurance Company of America and president of Religious Heritage of America. The latter, a private corporation, tries to "sell America to Americans" by promoting our "Judeo-Christian heritage." In 1968 Mr. Stone fulfilled his stewardship to this country by donating $201,000 to the campaign war chest of Richard Nixon (in a campaign which was outspending the Democrats by more than two to one); in 1970 he voted to elect his President "Churchman of the Year."

Beyond the generalities about a Judeo-Christian tradition, the constituency that Mr. Stone represents banks on the nineteenth-century alliance between the protestant ethic and laissez-faire economics. The revival of 1857 and many that followed promised to liberate the individual so that he could use his abilities within the free enterprise system, translating godly grace into the symbols of worldly success. The rise of industrial magnates in the mold of Andrew Carnegie served to confirm the thesis that free enterprise and competition were the perfect conditions not only for the evolution of a superior economy, but equally for the emergence of a superior character. The corporate philanthropist—hard-working, confident, aggressive, but also concerned for the poor and the underprivileged, became the prevailing Protestant ideal. Despite the shocks of the Civil War, the utopian hopes that had flourished at the turn of the century were now fanned by the dynamism of American industry and the accomplishments of the new technology. The association between Christianity and corporate enterprise which had been cemented in 1857 thrived in the land of free competition.

In 1971, speaking to the United States Chamber of Commerce, Richard Nixon would flatter his audience with sentiments drawn from the nineteenth-century alliance: "I want to do something to help people," he said. "Let's look at the facts. Here is the simple truth: there is no government agency and no philanthropy, no foun-

15

dation, no voluntary organization that has done as much to help people as the private enterprise system. . . . What we need today is to take a lot more pride in the system that makes it possible for us to be the most generous and the most compassionate nation, not only to our own people, but to other people on the face of the world." If this explanation of the relationship between free enterprise and the virtues of generosity and compassion sounds somewhat mythical, it nevertheless exemplifies a major element in Nixon's thought. Despite the logic of a mind sharpened by training and practice in the law, he is apparently drawn to the simplicities of a mythic imagination ("Here is the simple truth . . .").

Certainly Nixon has not been alone in asserting the righteousness of this country. The hopes of a national religion, the promises of American mythology have been put forward by every President in recent history. Here is Woodrow Wilson tripping down the list of national virtues: "Nowhere else in the world have noble men and women exhibited in more striking forms the beauty and the energy of sympathy and helpfulness and counsel in their efforts to rectify wrong, alleviate suffering, and set the weak in the way of strength and hope. . . . The feelings with which we face this new age of right and opportunity sweep across our heartstrings like some air out of God's own presence." Wilson was not overstating his convictions. His own religion and a tradition of piety in the presidential office enabled him to say with complete sincerity that he saw God's own presence in the spirit of the American people.

The Presidents of this century have expressed the national religion with a conviction equal to that of their predecessors. During his inaugural Warren G. Harding affirmed his belief in "the God-given destiny of our Republic." Calvin Coolidge closed his address with an evangelical appeal to world mission: "America seeks no earthly empire built on blood and force. No ambition, no temptation, lures her to thought of foreign dominions. The legions which she sends forth are armed, not with the sword, but with the cross.

16

The higher state to which she seeks allegiance of all mankind is not of human, but of divine origin. She cherishes no purpose save to merit the favor of Almighty God."

Franklin Delano Roosevelt put forward a full statement of the American religion in his carefully written third inaugural. He spoke in cosmic terms of the soul of America, the faith of America, the spirit of America. "The faith of America . . . is the product of centuries. It is . . . no mere recent phase in human history. It *is* human history." "In the face of great perils never before encountered, our strong purpose is to protect and to perpetuate the integrity of democracy. For this we muster the spirit of America, and the faith of America. We do not retreat. We are not content to stand still. As Americans, we go forward, in the service of our country, by the will of God."

The postwar Presidents echo similar sentiments. Even as some contemporary theologians announced the death of God and the advent of the secular city, our Presidents have not hesitated to invoke the Almighty, to quote from the Scriptures, to pray and to preach. The crusading spirit proved a still vital force in the fifties and sixties. In fact, the language of the crusade, the techniques of revival, and the myths of American religion were uniquely suited to the period in which Richard Milhous Nixon emerged on the national scene. As we have seen, his inaugural is steeped in the traditions of our national faith. And not only the inaugural. His concept of the presidency, his personal identity, his very being, are shaped and stamped by the weight of his Protestant past.

It is important to understand Nixon's religion, not because his beliefs are unusual or unique, but because they have a peculiar bearing upon his personality, his political style, and his conduct of the presidency.

17

★ II ★

A President's Public Faith

When President Nixon attempts to distill American culture to its essence and to define its contribution to the world, he frequently resorts to a simple dictum: "America was a good country. America stood for spiritual and moral values that far transcended the strength and wealth of the nations of the Old World." And Nixon believes that these Great Truths of the past are still valid in the seventies: "There is a great deal of goodness in this country, a great deal of moral strength and fiber left in this country, and that, in the end, is what really matters."

Nixon has expressed these sentiments at the National Prayer Breakfast, an event held annually in Washington, D.C. under the sponsorship of International Christian Leadership, a group of clergy and laymen who believe that Christianity can be infused into the nation's politics by gathering her individual leaders in corporate worship, not only in Washington, but in all the centers of power in the land. The movement is patterned after the revival of 1857, with much of the organization coming from members of the business community.

It has met with astounding success. There are now congressional prayer breakfasts, governors' prayer breakfasts, and prayer breakfasts in all 50 states and a thousand cities. In February of 1971 the *New York Times* reported: "More than 3,000 persons attended the breakfast at the Washington Hilton Hotel in what has become one of the biggest events of the year in this city." President Nixon,

Chief Justice Warren E. Burger, and evangelist Billy Graham presided at the head table as leaders of the nation mixed scrambled eggs and prayer, Bible readings, and sermonic assurances that this country was still the greatest in all the world.

The President seems to delight in the popularity of these meetings. He has been one of the most regular and faithful supporters of the movement since its inception in 1953. In fact, he has attended these functions more consistently than the services of any denomination, including the Friends. He seems to thrive in the informal atmosphere of a civil religion, and his enthusiasm overflowed as he addressed his audience of three-thousand that February morning. Scanning his audience, which included many of Washington's notables, Senators and Supreme Court justices, political, philanthropic, and corporate VIP's, the President said: "Perhaps it would be impossible to find any audience in America in which more power, in the best sense of the word, was gathered in one room than here at this Prayer Breakfast this morning." More power . . . in the best sense of the word. That religion plays an important part in public affairs Richard Nixon is proud to assert; that it is a vehicle of power, of raw political clout, as exemplified by the guest list for the National Prayer Breakfast—this presents an array of difficulties to the politician anxious about his image. Power is a word of many connotations, not all as bland as those commonly associated with our nation's spiritual heritage. And so the President backed off a bit from his enthusiasm for the power represented at the Hilton Hotel. It was power in the "best sense of the word" that he would respect in his prayers; power that would enable the United States not only to be "very rich and very strong, but more important, [to be] a good country and the hope of the world."

Nevertheless, the President had not resolved the dilemma which he stumbled into when he linked the nation's "spiritual strength" to its power. He had accidentally touched upon one of the most important yet poorly conceived aspects of American political life. Though the majority of Americans view religion as an asset, perhaps even a requirement for those who hold political office, the actual effect of a politician's religion upon his opinions and policies is seldom considered in depth. And though the President is expected to be a man of faith, there is little consensus concerning the proper relation of religion to the conduct of his office.

When we explore the many realms of government, we discover an abundance of evidence to suggest that Americans demand public and official expression of their faith. There is prayer in the halls of Congress, spoken by chaplains paid out of the federal treasury; there is a nondenominational chapel in the Capitol building—with an open Bible on the altar, and standing nearby, the national flag. Freshly cut flowers are placed on either side of a stained-glass window depicting George Washington at prayer. Public buildings are inscribed with biblical quotations, prayers, and pious pronouncements. Prayers and sermons are delivered on the decks of U.S. ships at sea and at every military outpost. Now there are full-scale worship services on Sundays in the White House. Our coins and dollars bear their proclamation to every market place in the world: "In God we trust." The astronauts have even preached the gospel in outer space, reading Scripture as they orbited the moon.

The abundance of symbols notwithstanding, there is little sensitivity to the ways in which politicians use religion to mold public opinion. Perhaps the chief reason for this lack of awareness is the continuing interrelation between patriotism and piety. When President Nixon speaks of spiritual resources which he believes are so important to the very survival of the nation, it is difficult to determine whether he refers to a specific set of religious beliefs, moral values, or simply a deep (and therefore spiritual) love of country.

A brief selection of opinions expressed by friends and members of the Nixon administration illustrates the deep confusion of moral, theological, and political factors. Secretary of Defense Melvin Laird was recently involved in a public dispute with the American Civil Liberties Union over the Army's Character Guidance Program. According to Department of the Army publications, Character Guidance is a program designed "to strengthen in the individual the basic moral, spiritual, and historic truths that undergird our nation's heritage." Although the Character Guidance materials are designed to be "nontheological and nonsectarian," Army chaplains are responsible for directing the monthly training sessions required of military personnel. The Civil Liberties Union has objected to this program, charging that it represents a violation of the First Amendment's separation of church and state. Secretary Laird replied by defending the language of the Army publications in question, and went further to assert that chaplains should be free to use "God, faith, and similar terms" at will. He concluded by arguing that, while the military services "consistently have adhered to the position that espousal of religious dogmas or particular sectarian beliefs is not the purpose and has no place in the Character Guidance Program," nevertheless "references to these terms are appropriate." We are left with the paradoxical predicament that military chaplains, called to their profession out of a deep belief in God, must give compulsory courses in America's spiritual heritage from a nontheological point of view. Upon Army order, they are asked to teach the one opinion that their several faiths would deny: that you can have your "spiritual heritage" without your God. The severity of this predicament is softened somewhat by the Defense Secretary's illogical conclusion that while belief in God may not be taught, it may be mentioned.

While the Secretary of Defense was arguing for a continued alliance between church and state, the Vice President was urging a stricter separation. Early in his term, Spiro Agnew boldly attributed the nation's moral decadence in part to clergymen who are more interested, he said, in rescuing the Florida alligator than in the proper spiritual concerns of their calling. The Vice President could not understand why Christian leaders had strayed out of their spiritual realm to question the appointment of Water Hickle as Secretary of the Interior. Thus, in one instance we have a government spokesman advocating the use of religion to support the programs and purposes of government, while in the next we find another insisting that there is no relation between issues of conscience and the affairs of state.

It was still another understanding of religion that White House adviser Billy Graham had in mind when he expressed his certainty that world leaders look to this country more for her spiritual quality than for her gadgets and technology. He had just come from an interview with Golda Meir, who was in this country hoping to secure a new shipment of supersonic Phantom fighters. Reported the Evangelist: "I talked with Mrs. Golda Meir the other day, and I don't think she would mind me quoting her. She said, 'America must not lose its spiritual strength.'"

As evidenced by these examples, "spiritual" is a word of wildly varying connotations, in each case raising far more problems (and controversy) than it resolves. If we are to understand the relation between religion and politics—that is to say, religion and power— we must analyze more carefully the elements involved. At the most basic level there is a consensus that the government has a moral responsibility, that officers of government should exert moral leadership far beyond the requirements of the Constitution or of law. The state is seen not merely as a neutral bastion of order; it is an active agent of social justice. Likewise, elected officials should not only preserve, protect, and defend the established order; they should exert their power to move society toward morally desirable goals. Hence, every government official is involved in rendering value judgments, expressing his opinion, and applying his power to advance values of his own choosing.

This fact is demonstrated most powerfully by the President. As

Chief of State he is seen to have an all-embracing responsibility as a promoter of the nation's supreme values. And since there is no neat agreement as to what those values are, his position is uniquely precarious. While the country is divided on the most fundamental moral issues, the President is expected to speak with the clear and resounding voice of conscience.

Richard Nixon has received his share of exhortation, counsel, and advice. He has been cajoled by church groups, commentators, self-appointed prophets, and the most prestigious federal commissions. The Scranton Commission on Campus Unrest concluded: "The most important aspect of the overall effort to prevent further campus disorder—indeed, the most important of all the commission's recommendations—rests with the President. As the leader of all Americans, only the President can offer the compassionate, reconciling moral leadership that can bring the country together again." Speaking for the Leadership Conference on Civil Rights, Bayard Rustin said during a television interview in July 1971: "It is the responsibility of the President to set the moral and political tone that will open housing outside the ghetto to poor people and black people. He must take a moral position. Until he offers the moral leadership, then the other people are not going to act at all." Says Yale Professor David Barber: "The President is expected to personify our betterness in an inspiring way, to express in what he does and is (not just what he says) a moral idealism which, in much of the public mind, is the very opposite of 'politics.' He ought to keep us safely in his care. He ought to get the country moving. And he ought to inspire our higher selves with an example of principled goodness."

When we piece together the responsibilities thus pinned upon the President, we find that he must exhibit characteristics that would qualify him for canonization: he must offer compassionate, reconciling leadership, he must inspire the public will, and exhibit goodness and truth in his every act. It is a strange twist of American opinion that, while distrusting its politicians, the public looks to the President as a primary source of moral inspiration.

Richard Nixon defines his role in the same high-minded terms used by his critics. During the 1968 campaign he delivered a major radio address on "The Nature of the Presidency." This was one in a series of low-key, high-content statements designed to answer the charge that the Republican candidates were not confronting the issues. It represents the most thoughtful presentation we have of Richard Nixon's views on the presidency. Toward the end of it he invoked the pastoral concept of his office:

> The President cannot stand alone. Today, more than ever in modern times, he must reach out and draw upon the strength of the people.
>
> Theodore Roosevelt called the Presidency "a bully pulpit"; Franklin Roosevelt called it pre-eminently "a place of moral leadership." And surely one of a President's greatest resources is the moral authority of his office. It's time we restored that authority—and time we used it once again, to its fullest potential—to rally the people, to define those moral imperatives which are the cement of a civilized society, to point the ways in which the energies of the people can be enlisted to serve the ideals of the people.
>
> What has to be done, has to do done by President and people together, or it won't be done at all.

The President does not disagree with his opponents on the extent or the importance of his moral responsibility. But he may draw differing conclusions as to which policies it is his duty to defend. To attack him for not taking a moral stand on civil rights, for example, clearly overlooks the fact that his own position may well express his best judgment as to the relative responsibilities of local, state, and federal governments in carrying out integration. If his opposition to bussing as a means of achieving a racial balance reflects a calculated appeal for southern votes, then his position is unethical. But his vice is in the deception, not in the policy. There is nothing intrinsically evil in the opinion that federally imposed bussing regulations are an improper means of integrating southern schools. One may hold that opinion and still passionately believe in the value of integration, the equality of the races, and the urgency of a national reconciliation.

The problem is that there is no clear or simple connection between moral principle and public policy. Those who denounce the immorality of the President's policies will most often be found in a differing political camp. Their judgments often betray a prior choice of strategy, party affiliation, or public constituency.

The Vietnam war offers ample illustration of this point, since both the President and his critics have used morality to defend their positions. Both sides in the debate have proven so facile in asserting the absolute righteousness of their own cause that the considerable dilemmas involved are often obscured by a simplistic and self-serving rhetoric. The public has been so frequently caught between the sweet resonances of a presidential press conference and the bitter denunciations of a peace march that it fails to catch the dialectic of conscience involved in either position. In large part, public cynicism about the political process reflects the fact that the fundamental moral questions are so seldom debated in the depth or with the objectivity they deserve.

As we shall see throughout this volume, neither Richard Nixon nor his rivals are careful to distinguish their moral judgments from decisions of pure expedience. In fact it is typical of American politics to supply moral exhortation where reason is lacking. In this regard, Nixon has proven to be a chief offender. Far from ignoring the moral authority of his office, he has shown himself a master of the didactic style. Whether in complete sincerity or by cynical calculation, his characteristic appeal is to the conscience.

If it is difficult in the American environment to sort out the expedient from the ethical, the confusion is greatly magnified by a third factor common to our political milieu: religion. The casual and often irrational interplay of church and state makes a clear

25

separation between the religious and the secular realms almost impossible. Here again the President plays a unique role. Because he is regarded in the popular mind as the very personification of the state, he is expected to exemplify not only the deepest patriotism but also a piety consistent with the nation's religious roots. His list of official duties only hints at the extent to which he is regarded as a sacredotal figure. He is expected to issue proclamations of national prayer and religious celebration, is called upon to lead the nation in worship at moments of public trial or triumph, to mourn the passing of the country's heroes. His office is flooded with invitations to speak at religious conferences, meetings, and ecclesiastical assemblies. The President routinely sends congratulatory messages to religious organizations celebrating important anniversaries and letters of condolence to individuals in time of need.

Eisenhower's White House chaplain, The Rev. Frederic E. Fox, who acted as a liaison between the President and the religious community, recently described the position of the President:

The longer I worked with the President, the more I felt his duties were essentially pastoral. He is shepherd of the sheep, nearly 200 million of them. And by his "pastoral duties" I do not mean simply his dealings with the private charities and anxieties of the American people. I mean his concern for the whole of public life, economic, diplomatic, and military—everything he talks about in his annual State of the Union Address.

The President is "Honorary Chairman" of many of our national charities. He is expected to bless almost all of America's voluntary groups—civic, business, and cultural—over 6,000 organizations which people may join if they wish, including religious ones. . . . While in the White House I also corresponded—over the President's signature or on his behalf--with thousands of individual citizens who were sick, bereaved, or ridden with fears and anxieties. The cares of these citizens came naturally to a man of my background (a Protestant minister). As a pastor of a church, I had dealt with these for years. . . .

26

The people . . . asked the President the same questions they used to ask me.

Shortly after his inauguration, Richard Nixon described his own reactions to the mail that came to his office. Though he could not read even a significant percentage of the letters addressed to him personally, he reported that "each evening at the end of the day I try to read a few, to get a feeling of the country, so as not to get out of touch—in that Oval Room—with all of the deep feelings that people around this country have about the Presidency and our nation."

The President discovered in a majority of these letters more evidence of a "deep religious faith." As he said during the Seventeenth Annual Prayer Breakfast at the Sheraton Park Hotel, Washington, D.C.: "In these days in which religion is not supposed to be fashionable in many quarters . . . over half of all the letters that have come into our office have indicated that people of all faiths and of all nations in a very simple way are saying: 'We are praying for you, Mr. President. We are praying for this country. We are praying for the leadership that this nation may be able to provide for this world.' "

In addition to the general feeling that somehow the President will be an agent of divine guidance, he is also called upon by custom, by Congress, and by the unique requirements of current events to act as high priest in the civil religion. After the death of former President Eisenhower, for example, Nixon was naturally expected to lead the nation in its rites. He declared a national day of mourning and issued a proclamation of prayer. By order of a joint resolution of Congress, the President must set aside Memorial Day as a time of national prayer. All such proclamations are accompanied by the President's personal eulogies or exhortations.

While the public expects that the President will fill these pastoral

27

responsibilities as a matter of course, Richard Nixon has taken up his sacral role with deep conviction. For he seems to believe that there is a semiofficial, national religion which is essential to the unity and survival of American culture. There is abundant evidence to suggest that he sees this country not as a pluralistic society, but as a nation rooted in a common heritage and sustained, even in the 1970's by a common religious vision.

Among a collection of presidential statements sent me by White House press secretary Ron Ziegler is the following:

We have the manpower and the material resources to enter now on the greatest period of growth any nation has ever known. The question is whether we have the will and the moral drive to take charge of our destiny once again. We have lost some of our vigor and some of our confidence. Only if these are restored can we meet our moment in history; *only true religion can help each of us restore them* [Emphasis mine].

Only true religion can help. But what is the nation's true religion? The President has never systematically expressed his own theology, and though his affirmations of the national faith are resounding, he leaves us with little definition of what he means by our spiritual heritage. "I have a profound conviction," he will say, "that the whole national experience of our people . . . is evidence of . . . a widely shared religious faith." Yet when he applies his faith to specific issues, the resulting controversy reveals not the unity of a common faith and culture, but the deep divisions of a period characterized by change and polarization. For example, in attempting to explain his opposition to liberalized abortion laws, the President referred to his belief in the "sanctity of human life." His remarks were immediately and severely criticized by leading members of his own Society of Friends. Likewise, when he announced his support of increased aid to parochial schools, partly because they represented "a specific view of human life," he was instantly assailed by

28

Protestants who were convinced that the Roman Catholic view of life is antithetical to their own.

In view of the bitter conflict the President has witnessed over the "religious issue" (including the controversy which played such a large part in his 1960 defeat), one wonders that he can still maintain that religion represents the nation's "fundamental unifying strength." As we follow him in the presidency, there is mounting reason to suspect that an understanding of his religion and the ironic role it has played in his life may well be the single most important factor in unraveling the complexities of his political career.

One of the early signs that Richard Nixon would place special emphasis upon the pastoral functions of his office was his announcement that, instead of attending a prominent Washington church, he would initiate private services of his own in the White House. Press Secretary Ron Ziegler announced that Billy Graham would play a leading role in the selection of preachers, while former Oklahoma University football coach Bud Wilkinson would be responsible for the necessary arrangements.

Predictably, Billy Graham was chosen as the first of the White House preachers. The evangelist recalled the President's proclamation: "To a crisis of the spirit we need an answer of the spirit." Graham added the flattering observation, "I don't think I've ever read a passage that so pinpointed the problems of our generation in America and throughout the world." He went on to proclaim that "only a personal relation with God" would provide the resolution to the nation's problems.

The second White House preacher was Dr. Richard Halverson of the prestigious Fourth Presbyterian Church in Bethesda, Maryland. Halverson is vice president of International Christian Leadership, the organization which sponsors and organizes the prayerbreakfast movement. He has also been a leading contributor to *The Presbyterian Layman,* a publication of the Presbyterian Lay Committee. This offshoot of the United Presbyterian Church is funded by a group of prominent businessmen who seek to discourage the more liberal involvement of denominational leaders in social issues. Characteristically, Presbyterians of Halverson vintage have resented the pro–civil rights, antiwar stance which their denomination has taken in recent years and would reverse this trend by a more evangelical emphasis upon simple salvation.

It is not surprising that liberal Protestants were suspicious that White House services would be dominated by conservative clergy, who would lend an aura of sanctity to the President's policies on civil rights and Vietnam. Theologian Reinhold Niebuhr charged that the White House rites undermined the First Amendment provisions for the separation of church and state by giving semiofficial status to religious practices which were void of social criticism. He argued that the President's sponsorship of Christian worship represented the establishment of a "tamed religion." "By a curious combination of innocence and guile, he has circumvented the Bill of Rights first article. Thus, he has established a comforming religion by semi-officially inviting representatives of all disestablished religions, of whose moral criticism we were naturally so proud. . . . It is wonderful what a simple White House invitation will do to dull the critical faculties."

Dr. Norman Vincent Peale, who has preached favorably of Richard Nixon for many years, again came to his friend's defense: "His is a very deep and simple faith. In holding services in the White House, the President is only doing what comes very naturally just as he has done all his life. The White House, after all, is Mr. Nixon's residence. And if there's anything improper about a man worshiping in his own way in his own home, I'm at a loss to know what it is."

The theologians, of course, had not questioned the President's right to private prayer. Their concern was that *public* worship sponsored by the Chief of State represented a violation of constitutional principle. They had further argued that the White House services were suspect if the preachers were to be chosen primarily because of their sympathy for the President. Rather than address himself to these questions, Peale chose to defend Nixon on purely personal grounds. In so doing, he echoed an individualism typical of nineteenth century revival.

Subsequent White House preachers have been drawn from more varied theological positions. The independence of Billy Graham has been balanced by the orthodoxy of Terence Cardinal Cooke of New York; the positive thinking of Peale has been supplemented by the more critical reflections of Dr. Edwin Espy of the National Council of Churches. There have been Congregationalists and Lutherans, black Baptists, even a scattering of rabbis. White House celebrants have represented Protestant, Catholic, and Jewish communions, yet spokesmen from the more radical and nonconforming sects have been studiously ignored: Seventh-Day Adventists, Jehovah's Witnesses, and segregrationist Baptists. On his left the President has avoided the Quaker pacifists and popular activists of the major denominations: Malcolm Boyd, William Sloane Coffin, Daniel Berrigan, and Father Groppe.

There is nothing in the White House preaching that would challenge the principal convictions of Richard M. Nixon. Despite the advice he receives from Bud Wilkinson and Billy Graham, the services are preeminently the creation of the President. In fact, he orchestrates the program, regularly introducing the preacher, praising the choir, welcoming the congregation. He opens the services, casting himself in the role of host, moderator, and master of ceremonies.

As in selecting his preachers, so in bestowing all his blessings, the President must be careful to favor a wide variety of sects and communions. For example, the White House recently publicized a list of twenty-one "distinguished Americans" whom it had chosen to honor for contributing to voluntary action. Among recipients of the presidential citation were four clerics—a Roman Catholic Cardinal, a Greek Orthodox primate, a Jewish vice-president of the Synagogue Council of America, and an executive officer of the American Baptist Convention. Others honored were Bob Hope, Art Linkletter, Danny Thomas, Walter Reuther, H. Ross Perot, Laurance Rockefeller, and Whitney Young. The list perfectly conforms to the contours of American culture; the clerics were included precisely because they are comfortably situated in the broad center of American society.

In a similar vein the President's religious itinerary is orchestrated to cover a range of opinion, while normally avoiding contact with groups or individuals critical of his policies. Here Nixon's own instincts are reinforced by the requirements of his office. He must appear deeply religious, yet neutral on the important issues of ethics or theology. His piety must transcend the divisive interests of organized religion. Given the variety of denominations, sects, and traditions that prosper in the favorable climate of American culture, this task involves a high degree of risk.

Uniquely problematic to Richard Nixon is his relationship with the various factions of his own Quaker faith. Though he has affirmed a passionate concern for peace and has maintained his membership in the East Whittier Friends Church, his relationship with the pacifist denomination remains awkward and often strained. He has invited the Quaker pastor of his home congregation and the Quaker president of Whittier College to preach at the White House, but has ignored the Washington Friends Meeting and rebuffed several delegations of Quakers who have attempted to consult with him.

Washington correspondent Drew Pearson followed the intricate preinaugural maneuvers. He reports that the Friends Committee on National Legislation first tried to arrange a conference between the Quaker candidate and key leaders of his denomination. Dwight L.

Chapin, Nixon's appointments secretary, answered with a polite refusal. Later, editors of the *Friends Journal,* a Quaker magazine, asked for an interview for a possible article on the candidate's religious views and affiliations. In reply, Herbert Klein referred them to an outdated and fawning biography published eight years earlier. In November, after the election, Philadelphia Yearly Meeting, the foremost Quaker group in this country, decided to seek a "pastoral visit" with the President-elect. This is a Quaker custom, calling for visits by the Friends to a member of their faith who is about to undertake an important venture or who may need spiritual counsel. A letter sent on November 20 proposed a meeting with five or six Quakers; it suggested that they might consult with the President-elect concerning ways to strengthen and support him at such a critical moment of responsibility. In reply Chapin telegraphed: "Richard Nixon regrets that present demands upon his time will not allow him to schedule the requested appointment."

Since this early exchange, the Quakers have openly opposed the President, periodically disavowing his brand of pacifism and scoring his conduct of the war. In like fashion, Nixon has studiously avoided the Washington, D.C. Friends, who are particularly critical of his policies. Seldom have relations been so cool between a President and the brotherhood of his own church.

Interestingly enough, Nixon is more communicative with other religious groups. In March, 1970 he met for three hours with Billy Graham and ten black Baptist clergy, including Dr. E. V. Hill of the Committee of Concerned Ministers for Evangelism. In June he addressed the annual meeting of the Greek Orthodox Archdiocese of North and South America, telling the assembled prelates: "Your church continues to instill the enduring wisdom of the ages in men's minds, and in their hearts, the faith which is the bulwark of all greatness." In July he traveled west to Salt Lake City to visit the Mormons during their annual Pioneer Day. He spoke from the steps of the Mormon church office building, noting that it was the pioneer spirit that sent the first settlers to Utah and the astronauts to the moon.

The President's staff is careful to arrange his religious schedule to emphasize his support of those groups once regarded as disadvantaged minorities, but now firmly rooted in the values of the majority. There was no mention by the President or his Mormon hosts at Salt Lake of the hatred and persecution of Mormons by those very frontiersmen who exemplified the "pioneer spirit." In July 1970, the Mormons of Salt Lake could share in the President's myth of the old frontier, for now they were firmly committed to the values of the New Revolution.

In a similar vein, Nixon has been most anxious to pursue his Roman Catholic contacts. During his first trip abroad, he flew to Rome for a private audience with the Pope. Secretary of State Rogers and White House adviser Kissinger joined him at the Vatican, consulting with top church officials. On his return to Washington, he expressed the view that ties with the Vatican should be kept open, especially on matters of foreign policy.

In February 1970 he issued an unprecedented invitation to top Roman Catholic educators, calling them to the White House for discussions of ways in which the federal government could come to the rescue of parochial education. He later announced the appointment of a special commission to study the possibilities. The commission has since reported back, affirming the President's pledge to assist private education. In June, Nixon appointed Henry Cabot Lodge as his personal emissary to the Vatican. A White House spokesman commented: "It is important to have the benefit of the Vatican's information and views on a continuing basis and to exchange views on a continuing basis." Later Nixon met with seven officials of the United States Catholic Conference to discuss the problems faced by the "forgotten" American who belongs to an ethnic minority.

Nixon reached into the ranks of the Catholic clergy to select the new head of the Civil Rights Commission, opting for Notre Dame President Theodore Hesburgh, whom he had earlier commended for his stern guidelines on campus demonstrations. And in January, 1971 the President met with Terence Cardinal Cooke of New York to hear his report on a Christmas visit to Vietnam. Cooke is the Catholic church's "military vicar" to the armed forces. He told Nixon that he had witnessed "tremendous progress" since his last visit in 1969. He also asserted that despite the reports of drug addiction among returning veterans, morale was high and he was "very impressed" with all that the U.S. Government is doing for the Vietnamese people.

Ironically, Nixon has gone much further in expressing his favor toward the Catholic Church than John Kennedy. It would have been fatal for Kennedy to advocate federal support of parochial education or to assign a personal emissary to the Vatican, even had he desired to do so. Coming from a Roman Catholic President, such action would have confirmed the bitter warnings of those who had opposed him on narrow religious grounds. Yet now, largely because of the contribution which Kennedy made to ecumenical understanding, a Protestant President can advocate policies politically impossible ten years earlier.

In July of 1969 the nation was caught up in an event that sparked an outpouring of its deepest patriotism and pride. Astronauts Neil Armstrong, Edwin Aldrin, and Michael Collins returned from the first manned expedition to the surface of the moon. In the ecstasy following their return and a safe splashdown in the Pacific Ocean, all the stops were pulled out in a celebration of far-reaching religious significance. In the festivity that swept the nation we see the President as the chief celebrant, acting in his priestly function to lead a common thanksgiving.

As soon as the astronauts had been safely sealed in their isolation booth on the decks of the carrier Hornet, they were greeted by a worshipful and ebullient Chief of State. As he stood looking at the spacemen through a plastic partition, he asked the Hornet's chaplain, John Piirtot, to offer a prayer. Astronauts and President bowed their heads as the chaplain intoned: "Lord, God, our heavenly Father, our minds are staggered by the magnitude of this mission. As we try to analyze the scope of it, our hearts are overwhelmed. . . . " Colonel Collins, holding a microphone inside his sterile compartment, closed the prayer with a strong "Amen!"

The chaplain had taken a fair measure of the nation's feeling in his prayer—the hearts and minds of the people were overwhelmed. So was the President. "This is the greatest week in the history of the world since the Creation!" he exclaimed. He went on to say that he had received over one hundred letters of congratulation from heads of state throughout the world. Pope Paul was among the world leaders to telephone the President while still on board the Hornet. The pontiff gave "thanks to God for the safe return of the explorers of the moon."

Richard Nixon's exhilaration was echoed across the country as church bells rang in town squares in every state. A replica of the Liberty Bell standing in the Iowa State House was officially sounded for the first time since its installation in 1950. Dr. Werner von Braun, who had designed the Saturn V rocket that carried the Apollo capsule, was given a hero's welcome in Huntsville, Alabama. At St. Patrick's Cathedral in New York, Terence Cardinal Cooke offered a Mass of thanksgiving. People of every denomination in every section of the nation seemed to respond to the sentiments of Colonel Aldrin, who had said just two hours before touchdown: "Whoever you are and wherever you are who are listening to this great event—we ask you to give thanks in whatever is your own way." Denominational differences seemed to dissolve in the euphoria over this triumph of American technology.

President Nixon apparently views his nation's space program as an expression of national character; it was a testimony to her moral fiber, even to a transcendent spirit that could work miracles around the world. "Our current exploration of space makes the point vividly," he had said in June to the graduating class at the Air Force Academy: "The journey of the Astronauts is more than a technical achievement; it is a reaching out of the human spirit. It lifts our sights; it demonstrates that magnificent conceptions can be made real. They inspire us and at the same time teach each of us true humility."

On his return from a triumphant world tour in August, a trip which included a visit of eastern Europe and Romania, the President said: "As I stand here today I really feel in my heart that it is that spirit—the spirit of Apollo—that America can now help bring to our relations with other nations. The spirit of Apollo transcends geographical barriers and political differences. It can bring the people of the world together in peace." In Romania he had told President Ceausescu that the people of the United States and of communist countries were all part of "a human family whose similarities and common interests far outweigh the differences." As I shall argue below, these words were not inconsistent with Nixon's root beliefs, though they were surprising to many who still viewed him from the perspective of his anticommunist record. In fact, his trip to Romania prefigured the later, more startling announcements of journeys to China and the Soviet Union.

Yet it is ironic that the President spoke so optimistically in the summer of 1969 of the growing concord of the human family. For soon after his return to this country, the differences among the American people, momentarily obscured by the Apollo moon walk, began to reemerge. Father Hesburgh released the unanimous report of his Civil Rights Commission; the priest whom Nixon had so lavishly praised for his moral courage now joined the six members of the commission in assailing the Nixon administration for "a major retreat" in desegregating the South's public schools. The spirit of Apollo would not transcend a national politics in which the southern strategy, law and order, the Vietnam war, crime, poverty, and civil disobedience made for continuing divisions.

In his euphoria following the splashdown, the President had said to a group of foreign students: "Any culture which can put a man on the moon is capable of fathering all nations of the earth in peace, justice and concord." In addition to the lapse of diplomacy involved in making such a chauvinistic statement in the presence of foreigners, Nixon's remark betrayed one of his most critical weaknesses. He seems so certain that the values of this country are universally binding that he could find even in the technological success of the moonshot the symbol of a transcendent mission. How the Apollo space program could "father" justice and peace around the world is a mystery beyond explanation. The conclusions that Nixon draws from his faith in America are often credible only if one allows for an element of miracle in world affairs. That his own country would not be united even by the "miracle" of the moonshot was a fact powerfully demonstrated in the bitterness of a revived peace movement and the stifling climate of Campaign '70.

During his first few months in office many activists in the civil rights and peace movements waited in patience while Richard Nixon formulated his policies for peace in Vietnam and unity at home. By the fall of 1969, however, the quiet would no longer hold. He faced his first wave of nationwide protest.

Increasingly, members of the religious community played an active part. Father Groppe of Milwaukee was arrested in Madison, Wisconsin for leading a group of welfare-rights protesters in a takeover of the state legislature. Eleven members of a peace group called Quaker Action were arrested on the steps of the Capitol in Washington for reading the names of American casualties in Vietnam. A Roman Catholic priest was cited for contempt at the Milwaukee trial of twelve war protesters alleged to have destroyed draft records at a Selective Service center. Leaders of the United Presbyterian Church USA meeting in San Antonio, Texas called on the President to restore diplomatic relations with Cuba and lift trade embargoes against the Castro regime. The Episcopal Church's House of Bishops urged that amnesty be granted to draft resisters who have acted out of convictions of Christian conscience. The United Church of Christ went on record urging that the Congress enact "drastic revisions" of the Selective Service Law to protect individual freedom.

It was now obvious that the protest was not the exclusive product of the extreme left. Across the country, Roman Catholics and Baptists, Presbyterians and Jews deliberated over the agonizing problems of the war and draft reform, poverty and race. American involvement in Indo-China had shaken the religious community, accelerating a far-reaching reassessment of the role of religion in society. The major issues that divided the country as a whole were seldom more hotly debated or more thoroughly discussed than within the assemblies of the organized church. Though there was little consensus over specific policy recommendations, it was increasingly clear that no politician could insure the support of organized religion simply by repeating the traditional appeals to conscience.

Yet even as the streets of Washington filled with shouts of protest during the October and November demonstrations, the White House continued to express its faith through the most routine formulas of piety. The President's October proclamation for a national day of prayer declared that "at a time in our nation's history when the power of prayer is needed more than ever, it is fitting that we publicly demonstrate our faith in the power of prayer."

Often there was a profound irony in the official prayers issued by the White House. On the day of the incursion into Cambodia, while United States soldiers joined the South Vietnamese in a sweep of the sanctuaries of the Parrot's Beak and Allied forces initiated policies which were to result in thousands of enemy and civilian casualties, the White House press secretary issued still another in the series of religious proclamations. "By the President of the United States of America—A Proclamation: One of the cruelest tactics of the war in Vietnam is the communists' refusal to identify all prisoners of war, to provide information about them, and to permit their families to communicate with them regularly. . . . Now, therefore, I, Richard Nixon, President of the United States of America, do hereby designate Sunday, May 3, 1970, as a National Day of Prayer for all American Prisoners of War and Servicemen Missing in Action in Southeast Asia. I call upon all of the people of the United States to offer prayer on behalf of these men, to instill courage and perseverance in their hearts and the hearts of their loved ones and compassion in the hearts of their captors."

The President, of course, could not be held guilty of the irony involved in simultaneously sending out prayers at home and soldiers into the field, nor could he alone be blamed for a one-sided concern for American victims of a war in which the enemy was being killed at a ratio of more than ten to one, for the Congress had voted for its day of prayer on April 28, and on that day few Congressmen were aware of what the Commander in Chief was planning for Cambodia. It was only the latest in a series of ironies that would have the President plead for the enemy's compassion on the morning after his announcement of a new offensive in the war.

Neither Congress nor the President has since learned restraint in the use of piety to score political points. In 1971 the White House extended its Day of Prayer, expanding it to become a "Week of Concern for Americans Who Are Prisoners of War or Missing in Action." The preamble, written by public relations officers in the White House, chastised the enemy in even more strident terms for "callous indifference" and a "barbaric attitude" toward the prisoners. In content, this did not differ from administration pronouncements on the American position in Paris, at the United Nations, or before the world press. The government's instructions on how to pray were couched in the same moralistic language it had used toward the Vietcong.

And yet Richard Nixon's efforts to communicate his religion have not gone entirely unrecognized. In June of 1971 he was designated as Churchman of the Year by Religious Heritage of America. Outgoing RHA president W. Clement Stone commended him for "carrying his deep religious commitment into the Presidency." The newly elected leader of this quasi-religious organization, Lisle M. Ramsey, announced that he had received "a call from the White House" urging him to join a group of lay leaders who would initiate a volunteer effort to "remove the tensions from our college campuses and inner cities" by encouraging peaceful discussion of the issues and renewing an "appreciation of the country's spiritual values." Among the plans drawn up by Ramsey was an essay contest for high-school students on the theme, "What Our Religious Heritage Means to Me." There would also be meetings of students with government leaders in Washington, distribution of the national flag, bumper stickers, buttons, and flyers carrying such messages as: I LOVE AMERICA—LET'S SELL AMERICA—IN GOD WE TRUST—GOD BLESS AMERICA—ONE NATION UNDER GOD—and HAVE YOU PRAYED TODAY? The official slogan for this campaign would be BUILD AMERICA TOGETHER.

It was clear that for the men of RHA, patriotism and piety are not only closely related, they are identical. That their campaign was encouraged by "a call from the White House" raises a question as to the President's own convictions. Is he persuaded by this maudlin substitution of advertising for religion? Is his also a national god who appears on bumper stickers and whose followers can be effectively reached by billboard slogans: HAVE YOU PRAYED TODAY?

As we follow his public appearances, a partial answer begins to emerge. Note his choice of platforms for a first showing after his venture into Cambodia. Following weeks of disorder on the nation's campuses, the President surfaced at a Billy Graham rally at the University of Tennessee on Youth Night, that special evening common to all Graham's crusades when the audience would be stacked with the young. While several hundred demonstrators gathered outside, the youthful delegations from distant churches of West Virginia and Alabama, Arkansas and North Carolina, poured their thousands through the portals of the giant "Volunteer Stadium." The President began his remarks by attempting to identify with the aspirations of his audience: "I can tell you my life is dedicated to the cause that I know you are dedicated to, all of you. I want this nation to be at peace, and we shall be. I want the air to be clean, and it will be clean. I want the water to be pure, and it will be pure. I want better education for all Americans, whatever their race or religion or whatever it may be, and an equal opportunity for all, and that shall be." He had ticked off all their causes, and he simply promised that, yes, these problems would be resolved.

It was that simple. In fact, it was hardly worth discussing these mundane concerns, for the country can achieve all these goals and "yet have a sterile life unless we have the spirit . . . a spirit that will be represented by the man who follows me. . . . If we are going to bring people together as we must bring them together, if we are going to have peace in the world, if our young people are going to have a fulfillment beyond simply those material things, they must turn to those great spiritual sources that have made America the great country that it is." Here the President linked the chief objectives of his administration—peace abroad and unity at home—to the program of a Protestant evangelist. It was quite clear that this President took his Christianity seriously.

On that night in Volunteer Stadium the "Spirit of America" was none other than the Third Person of the Christian Trinity. But as we follow the President's speeches, we find that his definition of the national spirit is highly plastic. On Patriot's Day, April 19, 1971, while Vietnam Veterans Against the War were gathering at the Capitol to turn in their medals and testify to this country's crimes in Southeast Asia, the President addressed the Eightieth Continental Congress of the Daughters of the American Revolution. After discussing some of the chief policies of his first two years in office, after congratulating the ladies of the DAR and praising the wives of the American prisoners, he concluded his speech with a short anecdote about "the flame of the American spirit." He described the visit of a lady from Virginia who brought him a gift, a 3' × 5' American flag she had made by hand. He had accepted her gift, commenting on the difficulties of making such a flag. His visitor was prepared for such a query: "Yes, Mr. President, it was a lot of work. There are 78,000 stitches in that flag. But it was all worthwhile, because to me every one of those stitches just stands for something that is right about America."

And so this evening, I would only say that I am deeply thankful that such a spirit of love for this country is still alive in America today. It was in that lady's heart, it is in all of yours, and it is in millions of hearts across this land.

With that kind of patriotism, that kind of love of country, we shall never lose sight of the American dream. And with that spirit, we shall make that dream come true.

Here was a purely patriotic conception of the "spirit of America," an uncritical patriotism that concentrated exclusively on the virtues of the country, as if in answer to the protests raised on that same evening by the Vietnam Vets.

The President would use a very different concept of the national spirit in a speech delivered at the dedication of the Arkansas River Navigation System in Catoosa, Oklahoma. This 1.2 billion project would make Tulsa, Oklahoma a "seaport," connected to the Gulf of Mexico by the Mississippi and Arkansas Rivers. "This region can become a new magnet for people seeking the good life," said the President to his audience of twenty thousand. "You have demonstrated once again the vitality of the American tradition of daring great things and achieving what we dare. In an era when some voices urge Americans not to aim so high, to turn from the pursuit of greatness to the cultivation of comfort, it is valuable for our youth, our future leaders, to have before them this dramatic example of the young spirit still at work building our nation. . . . Let us all stand taller and say we're proud to be Americans." As the audience yelled its approval, a half-dozen lonely protestors were spirited away by the Secret Service.

The Arkansas River Navigation System was built over a period of eighteen years, with bipartisan support from both parties in the Congress; it is among the most expensive public works projects ever undertaken by the federal government, far exceeding in cost the Panama Canal or the St. Lawrence Seaway. Regardless of economics, however, it is a paradox of recent political history that a Republican President should enthusiastically commend such a vast expense of federal monies as a symbol of the American spirit.

On Patriot's Day the President identified the spirit of America as a simple love of country; at the East Tennessee Crusade he called upon a Protestant evangelist to preach the spirit. Public works, patriotism, or piety—how do we sort out the tangle of sentiments that make up Richard Nixon's version of the American dream? Is the God of Billy Graham really a critical factor in the President's life, or is his religion simply one in a long list of vague feelings that drift in his subconscious? Is it a deeply rooted driving force, affecting his personality and policies in important ways, or is it largely a matter of image, a calculated response to all those letters that pour into the Oval Room with their earnest prayers and petitions?

There is some evidence to suggest that the President is more concerned about his religious image than for the substance of a personal faith. Early in his campaign for the presidency one of his leading speech-writers, Ray Price, wrote out a memorandum on

44

general strategy which was intercepted by Joe McGinniss, who reproduced it in his book, *The Selling of the President, 1968.* The memo includes the following thoughts on the religious dimensions of popular attitudes toward the presidency.

We have to be very clear on this point: that the response is to the image, not to the man, since 99 per cent of the voters have no contact with the man. It's not what's *there* that counts, it's what's projected. . . .

Politics is much more emotional than it is rational, and this is particularly true of Presidential politics. People identify with a President in a way they do with no other figure. Potential presidents are measured against an ideal that's a combination of leading man, God, father, hero, pope, king, with maybe just a touch of the avenging Furies thrown in. They want him to be larger than life, a living legend, and yet quintessentially human; someone to be held up to their children as a model; someone to be cherished by themselves as a revered member of the family, in somewhat the same way in which peasant families pray to the icon in the corner. Reverence goes where the power is; it's no coincidence that there's such persistent confusion between love and fear in the whole history of man's relationship to his gods. Awe enters into it. . . .

Selection of a President has to be an act of faith. It becomes increasingly so as the business of government becomes ever more incomprehensible to the average voter. This faith isn't achieved by reason; it's achieved by charisma, by a *feeling* of trust.

And so the media people set out to create that feeling of trust, to compel the leap of faith, the reverence and awe that a presidential hopeful must attract.

In the presidency, as well, Nixon has used the media to convey the impression that he is a deeply religious figure. In 1971, as the polls began to show serious erosion in his popularity, he sought to repair his image. He arranged an unprecedented series of personal interviews in which he focused attention upon his family background, and particularly on the religious influences that have shaped his life and policies. He met first with Peregrine Worsthorne, a British journalist, and followed up the interview with a personal memorandum, linking his domestic policies to a family upbringing rooted in the puritan ethic. Then, in an interview with C. L. Sulzberger of the *New York Times*, he explained his Vietnam policies as an expression of his Quaker background and the pacifist convictions of his mother. Appearing on the "Today Show" with Barbara Walters, he spoke of the ferment among the nation's youth, explaining their attitudes as reflecting a deterioration of religious faith combined with a superabundance of material wealth.

Clearly Richard Nixon is aware of the public expectations of piety in the presidential office. He is conscious of the political advantage to be gained by successfully projecting an aura that invites reverence and trust. Therefore, if we are to get a true impression of the depth and sincerity of his faith, and the role it actually plays in his politics, we must look more carefully at the man, sifting through the events of this childhood and early life to find patterns of personality and behavior that may reveal his deeper convictions.

★ III ★

Politics as a Vocation: Childhood and Early Career

In 1952, a mere six years into his political career, Richard Nixon stood before the delegates at the Republican National Convention to receive his party's nomination for the vice presidency. Sweeping victories in contests for Congressional and Senate seats, capped by the spectacular conviction of Alger Hiss as a communist spy, had propelled him to this place of acclaim. He had fast become a leading attraction at party functions and a powerful advocate of Republican hopes for victory in the national elections. Now as he stood with General Eisenhower, a hero whose reputation transcended party rivalry, he asked his audience in a style that betrayed his youth, "Haven't we got a wonderful candidate for President of the United States?" Only a few hours before, the warmly smiling General had delivered his call: "I want to make this campaign a crusade. Will you join me in such a campaign?" California's junior Senator would be "proud and happy" to oblige, for he had been primed by his political adviser, the aggressive Murray Chotiner: "Dick—you'll never amount to much in politics as Junior Senator. For you, it's a question of going up or out—there are no other alternatives." As Chotiner had it figured, Senator Knowland, who held seniority over Nixon both in the Senate and among California Republicans, would inevitably overshadow his junior unless Nixon took this risk for the vice presidency, circumventing Knowland and moving directly into presidential terrain. As at all the major junctures of his life, Nixon found here an element of inevitability, perhaps even of a destiny beyond his comprehension. When he stood at the lectern to receive the ovations of his party that fortunate evening in 1951, he is reported to have thought: "Here by the Grace of God go I."

At least those are the words which his friendly biographer, Ralph De Toledano, reports were in his mind. Others were less convinced that his rise bore evidence of a providential agency. Soon the young candidate would be caught in a desperate struggle to preserve his reputation (and his position on the Republican ticket). The press had unearthed the makings of a major scandal. Banner headlines declared: SECRET RICH MEN'S TRUST FUND KEEPS NIXON IN STYLE BEYOND HIS SALARY.

Reactions to Richard Nixon have always been polarized. At one extreme, are members of his Republican congregation who elect him Churchman of the Year; at the other, infidels who see him as the archetypical politico, the Plastic Man who will sell out any principle, even his own honor, to insure election to a higher office. Theodore White, who has followed Nixon closely in his series, *The Making of the President,* presents a revised version of the latter opinion. In 1960 White perceived a fatal "weakness of philosophy," a "lack of over-all structure of thought, of a personal vision of the world that a major statesman must possess." But in 1968, by a curious alchemy of his prose, White transforms the flaws of the younger candidate into virtues. This transformation began in November of 1967 when Nixon surprised White by sitting down beside him on the New York–to–Washington shuttle. During their conversation White noticed that his companion earnestly queried the stewardess on all the techniques used to convert an untrained girl into an efficient and pleasantly postured hostess. He also questioned White relentlessly on his writing habits, his tax deductions, his theories on Isaac Newton and the human mind. During this quiz

White observed: "Nixon was professional now and the professional lawyer's mind was incisive—probing, stabbing, reaching into point after point. . . . It was a new view of the Nixon personality—in which the trait uppermost was a voracious, almost insatiable curiosity of mind, a hunger to know, to learn, to find out how things work, to understand and explore in detail."

"At this passage in our acquaintance," he wrote, "I came to believe that one must respect this man. . . ." And then, at the conclusion of his book, he called upon his years of observation.

Richard M. Nixon is still an unfinished portrait. His victory in 1968 can be discussed *ad infinitum* in terms of plans and programs, organization and tactics, strategies and media. Yet his greatest struggle was always with himself, within his personality. His greatest adversary was always a past Richard Nixon whose image stained the minds of millions of Americans; his greatest victory since 1960 has been his ability to learn, to persist, to master what it was he did not know, and then, finally, to understand himself.

Nor is the process yet finished. No more plastic President, none more open to suggestion and ideas, none more willing to admit mistakes or learn from error has sat in the White House in recent times.

This is Plastic Man turned hero, and it is Theodore White, abandoning his search for the over-all structure of thought that he once thought necessary to all statesmen. Stories and recollections of Nixon's youth provoke similarly disparate and inconclusive results. His high-school debating coach recalls, "He had this ability to kind of slide around an argument instead of meeting it head on, and he could take any side of a debate." Of such observations whole theories are conceived about his slippery tactics in campaigns fought decades later. A college dramatist reports, "I taught him how to cry in a play by John Drinkwater called *Bird in Hand*. He tried conscientiously at rehearsals, and he'd get a pretty good lump in his throat, and that was all. But on the evenings of performance tears just ran right out of his eyes. It was beautifully done, those tears."

So the candidate cannot be trusted, he becomes a master of pretension. Or his football coach will reminisce, "He was a second-string man. Weeks would go by and he wouldn't even play a minute, but he'd hardly ever miss practice, and he worked hard. He was wonderful for morale." Said one of his teammates: "Boy, was he an inspiration!"

But must this be the final explanation of the President for those of us who can accept neither the shining attributions of his friends nor the paranoid inventions of his worst enemies? Several authors have recently tried to apply psychoanalytical tools to his personality as a youth. Borrowing the technique from Eric Erickson's treatment of Gandhi and Luther, analysts have plumbed the presidential psyche and surfaced with highly speculative conclusions. Here is MIT Professor Bruce Mazlish taking off from the fact that Nixon's mother had to leave home for a period of two years to care for the older Harold, who had contracted tuberculosis and needed the drier climate of Arizona (Arthur is a third Nixon son):

"How old was Richard when his mother 'deserted' him? If Arthur was seven or so at the time, it would make Richard about twelve or thirteen. What effects did these 'traumatic' events have on him? We can only speculate. First there is the strong possibility that he unconsciously perceived his beloved mother's leaving him for two years as a 'betrayal.' Consciously, he obviously understood the necessity. If I am right about the unconscious feeling of 'betrayal,' this might affect his later attitudes on the subject of 'traitors' in high places, preparing him emotionally for such a belief."

There is a possibility that . . . if . . . we might . . . he might . . . yes, we *can* only speculate. That is the problem. For all the material written about him, we have only the sketchy images, the bare facts, and the weighted anecdotes: There is Richard sitting on the bench . . . boy, was he an inspiration!

The one recurrent motif in his childhood, obscured by biographers and critics alike, is his religion. And it is too persistent a factor in his life to be ignored. Much of Nixon's childhood was spent at the East Whittier Friends Meeting House where a small Quaker congregation prayed and sang hymns, and heard sermons, four times on Sundays and on week nights as well. This was a California Quaker church, more akin to free-church fundamentalists than to the quiet pacifists of the East. As Richard Nixon recalls it: "Our little community church was the center of our lives. On Sundays we went to Sunday School and church in the morning and to Christian Endeavor and church at night. On Wednesdays there was prayer meeting, on Thursdays there was a choir practice. The annual Sunday School picnic was an event we always looked forward to." Nixon's first successful campaign resulted in his election as president of Christian Endeavor, the interdenominational youth group of the time. When he returned home from law school, he taught a Sunday school class at the East Whittier church. He has since spoken at Christian Endeavor meetings and maintained his membership with his home congregation even during the presidency. The church was the center of his life, and yet his family religion was sharply split between his mother's humble piety and his father's rocking, socking evangelism.

Hannah Nixon became the neighborhood confessor as she presided over the family store. "I remember," said a family acquaintance, "at the Ambassador Hotel, when Richard lost the nineteen-sixty election, everyone else was in tears, but Hannah was calm. She just said a prayer when she heard the bad news. She was a very strong woman."

The Milhous women were strong in their faith, and Nixon acknowledges the deep impression left on him by his grandmother. "My grandmother set the standards for the whole family. Honesty, hard work, do your best at all times—humanitarian ideals. She was always taking care of every tramp that came along the road, just like my own mother, too. She had strong feelings about pacifism and very strong feelings on civil liberties. She probably affected me in that respect. At her house no servant ever ate at a separate table. They always ate with the family. There were Negroes, Indians, and people from Mexico—she was always taking somebody in."

Hannah Nixon did not have servants; she had to work at the store, bake pies, mind the children, and care for the sick. And there was deadly sickness; she spent two years in Arizona with her oldest son Harold, looking for a cure for his tuberculosis. She stayed with him at a nursing home, paying for the board by cleaning floors, cooking, and serving the food. While they were away, her youngest son Arthur contracted tubercular meningitis and died within a week. "It is difficult at times to understand the ways of our Lord," Hannah told an intimate friend, "but we know that there is a plan and the best happens for each individual."

The long stay in Arizona had not cured Harold, however, and his condition gradually deteriorated. One morning he asked Richard to drive him into town—it was Hannah's birthday, and he had saved to buy her a present. Reaching out as best he could for a token of appreciation for her years of devotion to him, he chose an electric mixer, a new invention, that would make her work in the kitchen somewhat easier. Richard took Harold to the store and then headed off to school. When he walked into his classroom, the message was already there: "Come home, your brother has died."

Always Hannah stood up to these shocks with her unshakable conviction that behind all the suffering, all the sickness, and the apparently vain struggle to protect her children, there was nevertheless a plan. If anything, the hardships intensified her conviction that God, in his mysterious ways, would work for the good of each member of the family. She would gather her young around the breakfast table every morning to say their prayers and Bible verses. She would take them to church to hear the promises of a positive gospel. Have patience in the face of tragedy, and if there is suffering, have hope in the ultimate triumph of the good.

Richard Nixon was to echo these convictions even in his analysis of secular affairs. "Crisis is a recurring theme in American history," he wrote in the preface to his book, *Six Crises*. "In 1776, Tom Paine titled a series of pamphlets, *The American Crises,* and every schoolboy is familiar with its most famous line: 'These are the times that try men's souls.' Not every schoolboy is familiar with another line from *The American Crises:* 'Not a place upon earth might be so happy as America.' " Here were the Quaker convictions of his mother translated into a theory of American history: "That counterpoint of sacrifice and optimism is built into the discussion of every crisis in this book, and every crisis America faces today." It was an all-encompassing theodicy, allowing for every defeat, yet always seeking a favorable destiny in the next turn of events.

During the winter of 1967–68, as the opportunity for a second shot at the presidency grew more certain, Nixon called upon Billy Graham for a word of counsel. According to Dr. L. Nelson Bell, editor of *Christianity Today* and father-in-law of the evangelist, Nixon invited Graham to join him in Florida. "The Evangelist, though ill, obliged, and the two spent long hours reading the Bible together, praying and discerning the future as they walked the sandy ocean beach. At that time, Graham doubted that Nixon could win, but urged him to run anyway." When Nixon finally made his decision to run, he wired his counselor and told him that his influence had been the deciding factor.

Dr. Norman Vincent Peale also registered his reading of Nixon's destiny, and in the summer of 1968, as candidate Richard Nixon sat in the impressive Marble Collegiate Church in New York City, Dr. Peale took to his microphone and told his congregation that no goal was too great to be within reach of those who would apply the power of prayer—even the presidency of these United States.

In an updated preface to *Six Crises* written for the '68 campaign, Nixon speculated upon the meaning of his return to political life. "I wish I could analyze the workings of American democracy and the mystery of public opinion that took a man from "finished" in

1963 to candidate for the Presidency in 1968." "No man, not if he combined the wisdom of Lincoln with the connivance of Machiavelli, could have maneuvered or manipulated his way back into the arena," wrote the candidate. Richard Nixon *knows* that his best efforts could have failed—he had confronted unfavorable turns of fate in his own childhood and in his career, disastrously in 1960 and again in 1962. And so: "Only time will tell what course destiny will take in this watershed year of 1968."

Nixon seems to believe that the results of a presidential election are determined by forces beyond human understanding and control. He apparently sees, not merely the workings of an impersonal fate, but even the direct intervention of a benevolent God. At the Republican National Convention in Miami he drew upon a theology which sees the hand of God in the nation's politics. He attempted to evoke a sense of historical crescendo as he quoted Lincoln's parting words to the people of Springfield, Illinois.

Today I leave you. I go to assume a greater task than devolved on General Washington. The Great God which helped him must help me. Without that great assistance I will surely fail. With it, I cannot fail. [And Nixon continued,] The next President of the United States will face challenges which in some ways will be greater than those of Washington or Lincoln, because for the first time in our nation's history an American President will face not only the problem of restoring peace abroad, but of restoring peace at home. Without God's help, and your help, we will surely fail. But with God's help, and your help, we shall surely succeed.

There are a number of problems associated with this message, especially as delivered in such a partisan setting. It is not clear whether it is the success of the Nixon-Agnew candidacy or simply of the nation as a whole that depends upon divine intervention. As we shall see, there is evidence to suggest that Nixon believes his own political interests are in line with the will of God. His is an optimism rooted in the unshakable faith of his mother that, however tragic a situation may appear, the good will finally triumph. This is the positive gospel of Norman Vincent Peale: "This world is somehow built on moral foundations. This . . . is the one lesson history teaches. . . . The Good never loses."

The other side of the Nixon family faith is represented accurately by his father. Frank Nixon did not bow in humble acceptance of his fate. He harbored an evangelist's indignation at the sins of a corrupt human race. When he came to California, he had difficulty finding a permanent career, or a home. He had worked as a glass blower, house painter, potato farmer, sheep rancher, telephone linesman, and motorman. In California he met and married Hannah Milhous and worked for a while as foreman on the Milhous ranch. But soon he was off again, seeking his own fortune. At Yorba Linda, California, he planted a lemon orchard on a barren hillside, but the orchard failed to provide an adequate income. So he tried Whittier again, now buying a plot of land on the main road to Los Angeles. He pumped gas and eventually set up the Nixon general store, which did provide a meager income, enough to keep him in Whittier. Stories circulated, perhaps of Frank's own authorship, that soon after he bought his plot of land oil was discovered in the lemon grove, enough to have made him wealthy.

Frank Nixon's consciousness of wealth so narrowly missed was intensified and transformed into righteous fury with news of Teapot Dome; the theft of government oil reserves through a conspiracy of officials in President Harding's administration touched off his wrath. He turned livid with rage as he railed against the "crooked politicians" and "crooked lawyers" who had manipulated the theft of public property. Hannah remembered Richard telling her soon afterward, "I'll be an old-fashioned kind of lawyer, a lawyer who can't be bought."

Whatever the truth of these family myths and memories, it is clear that Frank was a man of sultry disposition. One friendly observer described his relationship to his children: "Frank's rigid and uncompromising attitude, not only toward politics but toward life in general, made life hard for his family." Adds Hannah: "He would not hesitate using the strap or rod on the boys when they did wrong, although I don't remember that he ever spanked Richard." If Richard avoided the spankings that were frequently given his brothers, it was by his own design. Very early he learned how to mollify the anger of his father: "Dad played no favorites with us . . . when you got into mischief, you had to be pretty convincing to avoid punishment. . . . He had a hot temper, and I learned early that the only way to deal with him was to abide by the rules laid down." Obey the rules, work hard, do well at school. Richard Nixon found deep gratification in obeying his father's moral laws: "I was determined not to let him down. My biggest thrill in those years was to see the light in his eyes when I brought home a good report card."

Frank Nixon's was the morality of reward and punishment, of right and wrong. His universe was ruled by a righteous God. Years later Richard would recall his father taking him to Los Angeles, where he committed his life to the evangelical faith: "I remember vividly the day just after I entered high school, when my father took me and my two brothers to Los Angeles to attend the great revival meetings being held there by Chicago evangelist, Dr. Paul Rader. We joined hundreds of others that night in making our personal commitments to Christ and Christian service."

Christian service— Though he has never expressed an interest in the ordained ministry, Richard Nixon sees his political career as a fulfillment of that call to service and the ambitions his father was never able to pursue. His sense of vocation is intimately bound up with his father's puritan ethic. In contrast to the patience and long-suffering of his mother, he learned from Frank Nixon that "crooked politicians" have got to be fought. In a passage strongly sympathetic toward his father, the younger Nixon once wrote: "He loved the excitement and the battles of political life. During the two years he was bedridden before his death, his one request of me was that I send him the *Congressional Record*. He used to read it cover-to-cover, something I never had the patience to do. I have often thought that with his fierce competitive drive and his intense interest in political issues, he might have been more successful than I in political life had he had the opportunity to continue his education." And yet Richard Nixon seems to feel the tension between his mother's pacifist assumptions and his father's love of combat, although their polarity was long ago absorbed into his personality. Writing after his defeat in 1960, he explained: "The last thing my mother, a devout Quaker, wanted me to do was go into the warfare of politics. I recall she once expressed the hope that I might become a missionary to our Quaker mission fields in Central America. But true to her Quaker tradition, she never tried to force me in the direction she herself might have preferred."

In his book the one recurrent metaphor for politics is militaristic: Politics *is* warfare, and while war appears on the surface to be opposed to religion, a deeper understanding, we are told, discovers the hidden relation between faith and the power struggles of a politician's trade. The following Nixonian analysis reveals the strained logic of this secret alliance: "Coolness—or perhaps the better word is 'serenity'—in battle is a product of faith. And faith, apart from that which stems from religious heritage and moral training, comes to an individual after he has gone through a necessary period of indecision, of doubt and soul-searching, and resolves that his cause is right and determines that he must fight the battle to the finish." Coolness, serenity, and faith come with the certainty that the cause is right. But what is the criterion for making such an important value judgment, if not religious and moral training? So then, serenity in battle is a direct reflection of faith in a higher purpose. Nixon continues his thoughts on the psychological symmetry of aggression and faith: "A man who has never lost himself in a cause bigger than himself has missed one of life's mountaintop experiences. Only in losing himself does he find himself. Only then does he discover all the latent strengths he never knew he had and which otherwise would have remained dormant."

Nixon used his strength-through-faith reasoning to reconcile his decision to take a combat role in World War II. Here, too, the Quaker pacifism of his mother was pitted against the crusader's mentality of his father. Arguing for increased expenditures for the military in 1950, he said: "It is not easy for me to take this position. It happens that I am a Quaker; all my training has been against displays of strength and recourse to arms. But I have learned through hard experience that, where you are confronted with a ruthless, dictatorial force that will stop at nothing to destroy you, it is necessary to defend yourself by building your own strength." Only a few years later he argued for a massive invasion of Vietnam and a preventative attack against mainland China. From the beginning his Quaker religion had included elements of a militant evangelism. And in the sultry air of the revivalists' tent at Los Angeles, he was confirmed in a faith that could easily justify a policy of massive retaliation. Ironically, he also fulfilled his mother's dream of him as a missionary for peace; it became part of his political ambition to preach the idea that peace can only be guaranteed by a constant preparation for war. In the paradox of a nuclear stalemate with the Russians, he found the resolution of the opposite poles in his training. Having passed through his period of "doubt and soul-searching," having resolved that his cause was right, he threw himself into the fray of political combat prepared to "fight the battle to the finish."

The warfare that was Richard Nixon's life began in the competitions of high school and college as he struggled, against sickness and sometimes also the more agile minds of fellow students, to gain the academic victories he believed were so important. And he often won. . . . In intramural debate, in campus politics, and in academic competition he frequently took home the prize. At high school he won the constitutional oratorical contest three times and upon graduation received the California Interscholastic Federation Gold Seal Award. In college he won the *Reader's Digest* Southern Conference extemporaneous speaking contest and the Southern California intercollegiate extemporaneous speaking competition. At Duke Law School he was elected to the Order of the Coif, a national honorary society; made a position on the *Law Review* staff, was president of the Duke Bar Association, and graduated third in his class. Said a classmate at Duke: "Dick was there for only one purpose, and that was to train himself to be the best lawyer in the country." When he arrived on the campus of Duke, he had no idea how he would fare in the fierce competition for scholarships and the coveted top ranks in the class.

"I'm scared," he confessed to an upperclassman late one night in the library. "I counted thirty-two Phi Beta Kappas in my class. I don't believe I can stay up with that group."

"You needn't worry," an older student reassured him. "The fact that you're studying so late shows you're not afraid of hard work. You've got an iron butt, and that's the secret of becoming a lawyer."

His compulsion to excellence sprang from very deep roots. Imagine the first-year law student counting the prize winners in his class to size up the competition, or picking the brains of an upperclassman for the secret of becoming a lawyer—not only a *good* lawyer, but the best in the country!

Yet Richard Nixon was also a product of the East Whittier Friends Meeting and Whittier College. He had been taught in the classrooms of Sunday school and college that worldly success alone would not satisfy the deeper human needs. Whittier College, by charter, is dedicated to the Quaker ideals and to George Fox's personal vision of "Christian democracy," and it was here that the moral impulse appears in his style of leadership. Within a month after Whittier's freshman registration he had joined a clique of students who formed a new fraternity, the Orthagonians, or Square Shooters. Nixon and his friends wanted to set up an alternative to the Franklins, a staid group favoring the heirs of Whittier's wealthier families, who on occasion sported evening clothes and black ties. The Orthagonians adopted sweaters and open collars as symbols of their informality. Nixon wrote the club song and collaborated in producing their first play. True to the humanitarian convictions of his mother, he fought to have William Brock, a black football star, admitted to the fellowship of his Square Shooters. Said Brock: "I really get mad when I hear Democrats or anybody accuse Dick of bigotry. That sort of thing is fantastic. Dick was my buddy in college years before he or anybody else figured him to become a politician." Nixon was elected president of the fraternity.

He also won the presidency of his class in his freshman year, and as a senior was elected head of the entire student body. His most outstanding achievement as a student leader was to move successfully for a change in the college prohibition against dancing on the Whittier campus. He took his case before the board of trustees, arguing that it would be more wholesome for the students to hold their dances on the campus than to seek the "dens of iniquity in Los Angeles."

Throughout college and law school, Nixon apparently was regular in his worship. At Duke he attended Quaker meetings in Raleigh or services at the University Chapel. Classmates remember him as friendly, but austere, and named him Gloomy Gus. Nixon and his two roommates rented a small room at the back of a farmhouse a mile from campus. They pursued their studies relentlessly, apparently setting the pace for their entire class. Nixon finished third; his roommates stood first and second at graduation. They did not often indulge in the pastimes of a university campus. Les Brown and Johnny Long led popular and professional orchestras at Duke for dancing and parties. "Old Nixon used to like to hear them play," one roommate recalls, "but he'd only hang around maybe fifteen minutes and then he'd hit the books again." Nixon occasionally played handball, but he rarely dated. "Dick wasn't allergic to girls," said another friend. "He liked them, as all of us did. But we just didn't have the money, and the dates were few and far between."

The comment is typical of the evidence we have about Richard Nixon. We know most of the facts: his family background, his school record, letters of recommendation—all the names and places are there, but few echoes of his most intimate experience. He liked girls, "as all of us did." But beyond that revelation, we know virtually nothing of the deeper emotions of loneliness or love, of sexual desire or fantasy, or even of doubt and the soul-searching he tells us is such an important part of the public life. To be caught up in a cause bigger than oneself—this, he says, is one of life's mountaintop experiences. But the man remains an abstraction. He simply does not open up the world of his private imagining, either to his friends or perhaps even his family.

Nixon's compulsive sense of privacy plays a decisive role in his personality and is clearly critical in shaping his public image. Here again he uses his religion to explain his behavior. The Quaker perspective, he says, has shaped his determination to remain silent concerning his personal feelings—to conceal his innermost convictions. When asked by Garry Wills what effect his Quaker background had upon him, he answered: "Oh, I suppose it is the stress on privacy. Friends believe in doing 'their own thing,' not making a display of religion. That's why I never use God's name in speeches, or quote the Bible." (But he does, in fact, use God's name rather abundantly.) "I suppose Quakerism just strengthened my own temperament here. I'm an introvert in an extrovert profession."

Actually, Nixon's sense of privacy is reinforced by his profession.

Politics may require constant exposure to the public (it is in this sense an extrovert profession), but it also requires extreme caution in tailoring one's image to the limits of popular opinion.

Billy Graham believes that Nixon privately holds a more profound evangelical faith than he will admit in public. When I asked the evangelist why the President does not state his convictions more explicitly, Graham answered, "This has been rather difficult for him with his Quaker background. He has been extremely reticent to speak out on his personal faith for fear that people will think he is using it politically." No evaluation of Richard Nixon would be complete without a recognition of the extent to which he does keep his deepest convictions to himself. It is a major thesis of this book that he does not project deep emotions and beliefs that are ruling factors in his life. Because he is not explicit, many observers conclude that he has no inner substance, certainly no deep religious faith. Ironically, his Quaker sense of privacy, a religious conviction that has formed his behavior from earliest childhood, now accounts in large part for his reputation as a one-dimensional celluloid personality.

The impression that he lacks depth and spirituality is increased by the fact that he has so often spent his energies in achieving external goals. It is hard to find in his efforts to win a debating championship or high standing in his class at law school convincing evidence of a profound quest for meaning. Yet there is something in his pursuit of the mundane that suggests a deeper, more compelling motivation.

His admirers look to his success and find evidence of the most straightforward virtues. H. Claude Horack, Dean of Duke Law School during Nixon's graduate years, wrote to J. Edgar Hoover recommending him for a post with the FBI: "Some time ago you suggested that I might refer to you an exceptional young man who has an interest in the work of the Federal Bureau of Investigation. I have such a man in mind who is to graduate in June. . . . Richard

Nixon, one of the finest young men, both in character and ability, that I have ever had the opportunity of having in my classes." After changing his mind about the FBI and trying unsuccessfully for employment with several prestigious New York law firms, Nixon returned to Whittier, where he went to work for Wingert and Bewley, the town's oldest firm. His first assignment was to handle divorce cases, and he at once applied to his work the moral precepts of his Sunday school training. Writes biographer Toledano: "Quaker-born and Quaker-bred and living a life in which the temptations of the flesh played little part, Dick Nixon was acutely embarrassed by the details of marital discord, adultery, and personal complications that lead to the breakup of marriages. The intimacies of the bedroom confided by his female clients frequently made him blush —and to this day he frowns on those of his friends who become involved in litigation before the Domestic Relations courts." It is understandable that the young man who had always lived up to the letter of the law would feel uncomfortable in the lawyer's confessional, but his continuing dislike for colleagues who work in domestic relations betrays a deeper reaction. It suggests that when he makes a moral judgment, he then carries out his decision with uncompromising conviction, seeing in the most ordinary pursuits the dimensions of a crusade.

After only one year with his firm, Nixon was made a partner and sent out to establish a branch office in La Habra, California. He was appointed town attorney in La Habra, then assistant city attorney and police prosecutor in Whittier. In this capacity he enforced the law by closing a local café which had become a nuisance to the people of Whittier—complaints were registered that patrons staggered out into the street even in broad daylight. Nixon ordered the police to wait outside and arrest anyone who appeared to stagger. So many of the clientele were arrested that the owner was forced to move his business to Los Angeles.

One of the strangest events in the President's life was his courtship of Pat Ryan. Nixon met her at a tryout for a play sponsored by a theater group in Whittier. That same evening he proposed, and pursued the matter unremittingly until he convinced her the marriage would work. He stopped dating anyone else; he waited around her house when she went out with other men; he even drove her to Los Angeles when she had a date there, and waited to take her home. He approached the delicate challenge of courtship in exactly the same style as had proven so successful in other areas of endeavor: having made his decision, he followed it up with the single-minded determination of a zealot.

Pat Nixon's description of their social life gives us a rare image of her husband at play.

Our group used to get together often. Of course, none of us had much money at the time, so we would just meet at someone's house after skating and have food, a spaghetti dinner or something of that type, and then we would sit around and tell stories and laugh. Dick was always the highlight of the party because he has a wonderful sense of humor. He would keep everybody in stitches. . . . Sometimes we would even act out parts. I will never forget the night when we did "Beauty and the Beast." Dick was the Beast, and one of the other men dressed up like Beauty. This sounds rather silly to be telling it now, but in those days we were all very young, and we had to do home entertainment rather than go out and spend money. . . . It was all good, clean fun, and we had loads of laughs.

This is an unusually charming portrait of Nixon's personal life and pleasures. As his career advances we find sharply diminishing evidence of his spontaneity and humor. Pat's description of the incident sounds almost apologetic in retrospect: "This sounds rather silly . . . but . . . it was all good, clean fun." When she speaks of their more recent experiences, she reflects the austerity of her husband: "Neither Dick nor I care a bit for the creature comforts." Like the President, Pat is motivated to pursue the more subjective rewards of a higher cause. Throughout his long career she has been at his side, throwing herself into the campaigns she initially opposed, bearing with him in defeat, facing the slander. Her sacrifice has been considerable. Like all the Nixon women, she has a patience which insists, despite defeats, that the good will finally triumph.

The tenor of Pat and Dick's early years was interrupted by the surprise attack upon Pearl Harbor. Immediately Richard Nixon set out for Washington. Even without a prospect for employment, he knew that he must thrust himself into the mobilization, and eventually the war. He first got a job in the tire-rationing division of the Office of Price Administration, but soon grew impatient with this federal bureaucracy. So he waived his Quaker deferment and signed up with the Navy. After training, he was sent as a supply officer to Green Island, the first in a series of assignments in the Pacific. His record in the Navy was more distinguished for extracurricular activities than for any direct part in the fighting. As a supply officer he had access to certain luxuries: bourbon whiskey, hamburger, and fruit juice, which he distributed—often free of charge— to his fellow officers and men. This *ad hoc* operation came to be known as Nixon's Hamburger Stand. He also taught a course in business law, and learned to play poker. He so thoroughly mastered the odds of the game that he returned with savings of $10,000, much of it won at Green Island poker tables.

Nixon used his military record in his first campaign for public office. In the summer of 1946, the Republican candidate for Congress from the twelfth district of California issued typical flyers and leaflets. Among them, one spoke of a "clean, forthright young American who fought in defense of his country in the stinking mud and jungles of the Solomons." The flyer went on to castigate the incumbent Democrat who, it said, had "stayed safely behind the front in Washington" while others were dying in defense of their country. The Republican repeatedly referred to his exploits at war, promising in his literature and in debate with his civilian opponent "to preserve our sacred heritage in the name of my buddies and your loved ones, who died that these might endure." One would not have guessed that the candidate who was making such effective use of his military record would later become the country's second Quaker president.

★ IV ★

Politics and the
Anti-Communist Crusade:
Beginnings

Richard Nixon's peregrinations toward the presidency began on December 4, 1945, when he formally accepted the endorsement of the Republican Committee of One Hundred, a group of party leaders who had organized to hunt for a candidate capable of unseating Jerry Voorhis, popular five-term veteran of the New Deal. He had written to Republican district chairman Roy O. Day that his campaign would be fought forcefully, but on the issues. Party leaders, however, preferred the professional advice of a Beverly Hills campaign manager—Murray M. Chotiner—who was to style Richard Nixon's maiden effort according to his own steam-roller tactics. Advised Chotiner: "There are many people who say we want to conduct a constructive campaign and point out the merits of our own candidate. I say to you in all sincerity that, if you do not deflate the opposition before your own candidate gets started, the odds are that you are going to be doomed to defeat." Figure the percentages, cut and paste the candidate's image, kill the opposition—here was the mechanical formula of a party theorist who would reduce politics to a war game. Chotiner's hatchet tactics prefigured the worst excesses of a later era, when the advertising and media experts would conspire to sell a President. The tactics of the

'46 campaign were less refined but similar in style. Richard Nixon opened his attack in Whittier. "I want you to know," he said, "that I am your candidate primarily because there are no special strings attached to me. I have no support from any special interest or pressure group. I welcome the opposition of the PAC [the CIO Political Action Committee], with its communist principles and its huge slush fund." This charge became the critical issue in the candidate's first public debate and eventually the key to the election. Nixon charged repeatedly that Voorhis was endorsed by, and therefore by implication associated with, a communist-dominated affiliate of the CIO. He dramatized his point during the first debate when Voorhis denied the charge. At this point Nixon leaped up and stalked across the stage, waving a document that he had pulled from his pocket. It was a subcommittee report from a local PAC chapter recommending that the national office endorse Voorhis. Nixon thrust his paper in the Democrat's face and held it up for the whole audience to see. Here was documentary evidence. Evidence, yes—but of what?

Nixon's over-all strategy was to suggest that Voorhis could be counted among those "lip-service Americans" and elected officials "who front for un-American elements, wittingly or otherwise, by advocating increasing federal controls over the lives of people." This charge was repeated by Nixon—and his Republican organizers —with varying degrees of overstatement. Un-American could mean, in different contexts, a New Deal Democrat, a reformed Socialist, or a communist spy. This was the domino theory of domestic politics: endorse the most innocent-sounding program for federal aid and you set up a chain reaction that inevitably leads to communist control. There was an implied cause-and-effect relationship between Jerry Voorhis and Soviet victory in the cold war. In discussing the Eisenhower administration we shall examine in some depth the anticommunist theology that would make this mythical analysis plausible to a majority of Americans in the years following World War II.

In fact, Jerry Voorhis was a widely respected Congressman who, at the time of his contest with Nixon, was moving to the right politically. Graduating Phi Beta Kappa from Yale in the twenties, Voorhis plunged into the mêlée of reform politics. He worked as a laborer, joined the Socialist Party, organized a school and home for orphans. Fired by a romantic idealism, he called himself a "Christian Socialist." After the depression he became convinced of the necessity of working through major party politics. By 1936 he had become a Democrat and a follower of Franklin D. Roosevelt.

Given Voorhis's background as a Congressman there was little room for doubt about his anticommunist credentials. He sat on the House Committee on Un-American Activities and had sponsored the Foreign Agents Registration Act, one of the most stringent antisubversive devices passed prior to World War II. Yet he had several liabilities. His romantic instincts occasionally led him to support policies that were foreign to the mind-set of a postwar electorate. Federal control of tidelands oil—even nationalization of the oil industry—may be proposals worthy of debate; yet to the constituency of California's Twelfth District they sounded irresponsible or even subversive. Nixon simply pointed to similar recommendations made by Voorhis, often years earlier, and he succeeded in making his opponent appear to be a dangerous radical.

"What is the difference between legitimate attack and smear?" wrote Murray Chotiner. "It is not a smear, if you please, if you point out the record of your opponent. . . . Of course, it is always a smear, naturally, when it is directed to your own candidate." Chotiner's ethics are clearly articulated in his own speeches. For him, telling the truth simply consists of the careful selection of the most unfavorable facts about your opponent; you then hammer away at them in the attempt to make his worst ideas appear typical. Conversely, the image projected of your own candidate must be carefully cleansed of all possible stain: "We never put out the complete voting record for our candidate, vote by vote, in spite of the demands from people within our organization. The reason is— even if your candidate has voted 99 per cent right according to the person who reads the record, the one per cent will often turn the prospect against you." Says Chotiner, in sum: "We come to the question of ethics in the campaign. I cannot overemphasize the fact that truth is the best weapon we can use." This is the single reference to ethics in a lecture of some fourteen thousand words which Chotiner gave for the Republican National Committee during a nationwide tour in 1955. Despite his involvement in a 1956 Congressional investigation of influence peddling (and a period of exile from Republican circles), Chotiner has been a chief Nixon strategist since the original campaign in 1946. He has survived the years of defeat and infamy, finally to be included in the ranks of the White House staff.

Nixon's 1946 opponent had another fatal weakness: Voorhis could not mount a sufficient counterattack. He seemed a more cautious personality, inhibited by occasional periods of self-doubt and introspection. As soon as he left the platform after a joust with Nixon in their first debate, he withdrew for solace to his campaign manager.

"How did it go?" he asked.

"Jerry," his adviser replied, "he cut you to pieces. He had you on the defensive all the way. He picked the battleground, and you let him fight on his own terms." Politics is warfare.

Nixon met success in this first campaign, ending the career of Jerry Voorhis in a sweeping victory at the polls. He won by a vote of 65,586 to 49,994, and later defended his campaign with the single description: "Voorhis lost because that district was not a New Deal district. Our campaign was a very honest debate on the issues." Picture candidate Nixon striding across the stage with his document proving the existence of a Voorhis-CIO-Moscow troika. In the aftermath of the election, it was noted by dispassionate observers that Voorhis had never in fact received the endorsement of the controversial PAC at either the regional or the national level. The image of Nixon standing before his audience with apparently irrefutable proof of all his arguments reflects both the force and the weaknesses of his early career.

As a freshman Congressman in 1947, Richard Nixon was assigned to the House Education and Labor Committee and the House Committee on Un-American Activities. Though rookie Representatives normally remain backstage during their first term in office, within two years Nixon had parlayed his contacts and opportunities on these committees into a national reputation. His closest associate on the Labor Committee was Charles Kersten of Wisconsin, a devout Roman Catholic. The two young Congressmen shared a deep concern about the peril of international communism, particularly the challenge it posed to their common Christian faith. They educated themselves on the issue; Kersten introduced Nixon to Monsignor Fulton Sheen, who was writing a book on the subject, and Father John Cronin, who was working for the National Catholic Welfare Conference. Cronin had established himself as an expert in communist infiltration of the labor unions.

Nixon was thus convinced that the anticommunist cause was essentially religious, and his convictions were shaped in the course of contact with Roman Catholic associates. Fulton Sheen gave the two Congressmen his book, *Communism and the Conscience of the West*. They read it together and spent several hours discussing its conclusions. Sheen argued that the confrontation between Russia and the United States was more than a power struggle between two nations, it was a contest between the two ideologies of the West, the one essentially materialistic, the other theocentric. Sheen be-

71

lieved that the religious dimension of the conflict was of first importance; the church would play a critical role by providing an ideology diametrically opposed to that of Karl Marx. If the noncommunist countries abandoned the truths of religion, he argued, they would lose the struggle by default. For Sheen, the distinguishing characteristic of the noncommunist West was not its political or economic systems, but a common Christian tradition.

If Monsignor Sheen provided the theory, Father Cronin supplied the practical clues that put Nixon on the trail of Alger Hiss. During Cronin's investigations into organized labor, he had established contacts in the FBI. Through these sources he obtained information about communists in government; among the names that passed along this route to Cronin and thence to Nixon was that of Alger Hiss. Nixon thus knew that Hiss was a suspected communist at least a year and a half before Whittaker Chambers mentioned his name at an HUAC hearing. When Nixon took the initiative in the investigation of Hiss, he could check his own leads against classified information supplied through these unauthorized channels.

Whittaker Chambers appeared before the House Committee on Un-American Activities on August 3, 1948 to testify to his knowledge of communist infiltration into government. He told of his career in the Party from 1924 through 1937, and of his contacts with members of the communist underground. In this first round of testimony Chambers did not say that his colleagues were espionage agents; they were merely members of a "study group" which sought to "infiltrate" and influence government policy by legal means. Among the four individuals he named was Alger Hiss, a graduate of Johns Hopkins University and Harvard Law School who had served as clerk to Supreme Court Justice Oliver Wendell Holmes and had practiced law privately in Boston and New York. Hiss had been a State Department official involved with President Roosevelt at the Yalta Conference and an organizer of the charter meeting of the United Nations in San Francisco.

As soon as Chambers' allegations were publicized, Hiss wired the committee offering to defend himself and deny the accusations. On August 5 he appeared, and told the committee: "I was born in Baltimore, Maryland, on November 11, 1904. I am here at my own request to deny unqualifiedly various statements about me which were made before this Committee by one Whittaker Chambers the day before yesterday. I am not and never have been a member of the Communist Party. I do not and never have adhered to the tenets of the Communist Party. I am not and never have been a member of any Communist front organization. I have never followed the Communist Party line directly or indirectly. To the best of my knowledge none of my friends is a Communist."

So persuasive was his testimony that the committee was nearly unanimous in feeling that there should be no further hearings, and that its files should be turned over to the Department of Justice and the matter forgotten. The committee was unanimous with the exception of Congressman Richard Nixon, who argued that the Department of Justice could not be trusted to pursue the case. Chambers had made his allegations known to the FBI two years earlier, but the Justice Department, Nixon suggested, was simply not interested. The Truman administration was so concerned to "get along with Stalin" that it could not see the enemy in its midst. Moreover, Nixon had private sources of information confirming his opinion that Chambers had told the truth, while Hiss, despite his credentials, had lied. Though none of his colleagues had detected anything in Chambers' testimony that would confirm this judgment, Nixon commented: "I did not feel that it was an act. . . . On the contrary, I felt he indicated deep sincerity and honesty." Nixon was so convinced, in fact, that he prevailed upon Karl Mundt, HUAC chairman, to appoint him as head of a subcommittee that would question Chambers again. Characteristically, Nixon records his decision as one of heroic proportions. "My stand, which was based on my own opinion and judgment, placed me more or less in the corner of a former Communist functionary and against one of the brightest, most respected young men following a public career. Yet I could not go against my own conscience, and my conscience told me that, in this case, the rather unsavory-looking Chambers was telling the truth, and the honest-looking Hiss was lying."

From this point until Hiss's final conviction of perjury in 1950, Nixon pursued the dictates of his conscience with unflinching dedication. First, he subpoenaed Chambers to meet with him in executive session only two days after Hiss's devastating appearance; the interrogation lasted nearly three hours. Convinced that Chambers did know Hiss, but still not satisfied that he had clinching evidence, Nixon drove from Washington to Chambers' farm in Maryland. "It was the first of many long and rewarding conversations I was to have with him during the period of the Hiss case, and through the years until his death in 1961. Like most men of quality, he made a deeper impression personally than he did in public." Ralph de Toledano reports that Nixon frequently drove out to see Chambers on his farm: "At times of stress, even when he was Vice President, Nixon would drive to Westminster for a visit, informing only friends such as myself and the most reliable members of his staff. It was not only counsel that he sought from the older man, but a kind of intellectual replenishment and emotional stability. . . . Nixon, never one to open his heart or his mind unstintingly, came as close to this with Chambers as he did with any other man."

What Nixon found in Chambers was a passionate, even frantic Christianity, a devotion to the anticommunist crusade, an imagination which saw the world as caught up in a cosmic struggle between light and darkness, God and the Devil. In Nixon's words: "Here was a man of extraordinary intelligence, speaking from great depth of understanding; a sensitive, shy man who had turned from complete dedication to communism to a new religious faith and a kind of fatalism about the future." In Chambers Nixon discovered a Quaker whose imagination was sparked by the symbolism and mythology of the cold war; and when his own psyche needed inspiration, Nixon would feed upon those fiery visions of a cosmic encounter with the powers of darkness.

That Nixon so quickly identified with Chambers, that he was willing to stake his career on Chambers' testimony, that they should strike up such an intimate and lasting friendship—these facts call for a more serious analysis of the anticommunist faith that was their common bond.

Chambers opens his book on the Hiss case with a foreword in the form of a letter to his children. He describes his pilgrimage from his years as a dedicated Soviet agent, through the agonies of repentance, conversion, and ultimately to the suffering that was his expiation for earlier sins. He saw the Hiss trial as his own martyrdom, a martyrdom undertaken by the direct command of God and reflecting a perfect imitation of Christ. "At heart," he wrote, "the Great Case was this critical conflict of faiths; that is why it was a great case. On a scale personal enough to be felt by all, but big enough to be symbolic, the two irreconcilable faiths of our time— Communism and Freedom—came to grips in the persons of two conscious and resolute men. . . . Both [men] knew, almost from the beginning, that the Great Case could end only in the destruction of one or both of the contending figures, just as the history of our times . . . can end only in the destruction of one or both of the contending forces." It was communism and freedom, Whittaker Chambers and Alger Hiss, locked in a life-and-death struggle for the very survival of Western civilization. Chambers believed that his own testimony, with the resulting conviction of Alger Hiss, was not only a personal act of redemption but also a means by which the whole world might be saved. In deciding to testify against Alger Hiss, Chambers cast himself in the role of a prophet; he believed that he was driven by a supernatural power: "I do not know any way to explain why God's grace touches a man who seems unworthy of it. But neither do I know any other way to explain how a man like myself . . . could prevail so far against the powers of the world arrayed almost solidly against him, to destroy him and defeat his truth. In this sense, I am an involuntary witness to God's grace and to the fortifying power of faith."

Yet Whittaker Chambers never found the salvation he hoped for. His book reveals him to be a man tormented by the classic symptoms of paranoia, periodically convinced of his own righteousness and religion, then tortured by his fears, his agony, and finally his wish for an escape into death. One evening during the Hiss investigation, overcome by fears, he walked out into the darkness and hid himself in the solitude of his apple orchard. When his family realized that he was missing, they began to call, and when he did not respond they searched for him everywhere. But he would not answer. "With all the longing of my love for you, I wanted to answer. But if I answered, I must come back to the living world. I could not do that." Even when his wife and children became desperate, he would not reply.

Finally his son walked out toward the orchard, and Chambers confronted him. "He stepped outside in the dark, calling, 'Papa! Papa!' Then, frantically, on the verge of tears: 'Papa!' I walked over to him. I felt that I was making the most terrible surrender I should have to make on earth. 'Papa,' he cried and threw his arms around me, 'don't ever go away.' 'No,' I said, 'no, I won't ever go away.' Both of us knew that the words 'go away' stood for something else, and that I had given him my promise not to kill myself. Later on, as you will see, I was tempted, in my wretchedness, to break that promise."

Chambers closes his letter with a mystical passage that shows him leading his children, their hands in his, out into the pine woods that surrounded their farm. Having set the mood, he then changes the scene, placing himself and his children on the hill just outside biblical Jerusalem: "I am leading you, not through cool pine woods, but up and up a narrow defile between bare and steep rocks from which in shadow things uncoil and slither away. It will be dark. But in the end, if I have led you aright, you will make out three crosses, from two of which hang thieves. I will have brought you to Golgotha—the place of skulls—this is the meaning of the journey. Before you understand, I may not be there, my hands may have slipped from yours. It will not matter. For when you understand what you see, you will no longer be children. You will know that life is pain, that each of us hangs always upon the cross of himself. And when you know that this is true of every man, woman, and child on earth, you will be wise."

Once Richard Nixon resolved to believe Chambers and to pursue Alger Hiss to the finish, he worked furiously. He contacted Bert Andrews of the *New York Herald Tribune,* William P. Rogers, Charles Kersten, and John Foster Dulles, poring over the testimony and persuading them, too, that Chambers was telling the truth. By the time Hiss appeared for additional questioning in executive session, Nixon had what he thought was convincing proof. He pursued Hiss aggressively, firing question after question, pressing every detail of his past, hunting for the clues that would tie him conclusively to Chambers, laying traps, hoping that Hiss would stumble. Not surprisingly, Hiss grew increasingly hostile. "Hiss dropped all previous pretensions of injured innocence. He was on the defensive— edgy, delaying, belligerent, fighting every inch of the way," wrote Nixon. "With a look of cold hatred in his eyes, he fought like a caged animal as we tried to get him to make a positive identification for the record."

Between the public hearings Nixon worked with committee investigators, hunting down all traces of evidence that would assist in documenting the Hiss-Chambers liaison. Nixon acted as chief investigator, prosecuting attorney, judge, and jury, as he sought to dramatize his belief that communists could be found in the highest levels of government. "From the day of the private confrontation on August 17 to the public confrontation on August 25, I put in longer hours and worked harder than I had at any time in my life. I tried to anticipate how Hiss might try to explain the mass of contradictions in his story, and I sought to plug up each and every loophole with documentary proof. As the day for the hearing approached, I stepped up my activity until I was spending as much as eighteen to twenty hours a day at my office. I deliberately refused to take time off. . . ."

The committee hearings themselves had the aura of a grand inquisition. Klieg lights and television cameras, the press, and the spectators; it was the first time a major congressional hearing had been televised. As the excitement grew, Nixon was increasingly convinced that he was involved in an historic event. . . . "This case involved far more than the personal fortunes of Hiss, Chambers, myself, or the members of our Committee. It involved the security of the whole nation and the cause of free men everywhere."

When one reads these lines more than twenty years after the fact, it is difficult to believe that all this electricity could have been generated over an investigation to determine whether a single State Department employee had, ten years earlier, belonged to the Communist Party. At this stage of the investigation there was no hint that Hiss had committed a crime, that he was guilty of any wrongdoing, that he had done anything more than belong to a radical "study group" at a time when communism was widely considered to be a worthy social experiment. Yet overnight Hiss had become the object of nationwide publicity. When the notorious "pumpkin papers" were disclosed, offering possible proof that Hiss was guilty of espionage, the case took on apocalyptic significance.

Chambers had temporarily hidden five rolls of microfilm in a pumpkin on his farm, hence the "pumpkin papers." The microfilm, together with sixty-five typed copies of government documents and some office memoranda in Hiss's handwriting were offered as proof that Hiss had been part, not of a political study group, but of an underground communist cell. Chambers testified that Hiss regularly supplied him with classified documents which he in turn gave to Soviet agents. Ironically, these disclosures were made by Chambers in his own defense against a libel suit initiated by Hiss. Had he not taken that court action, Hiss would not have been convicted of a crime; he would not even have been officially accused of espionage.

Richard Nixon was cruising toward the Canal Zone aboard a pleasure ship with his wife when he was informed by radiogram of the pumpkin papers. Immediately he made arrangements to have a Coast Guard seaplane fly him back to Miami, then to Washington. Even before he had examined the new evidence, he told an AP reporter, "The hearing is by far the most important the Committee on Un-American Activities has conducted because of the nature of the evidence and the importance of the people involved. It will prove to the American people once and for all that when you have a Communist, you have an espionage agent." Nixon did not wait upon the deliberations of the courtroom to announce, or rather proclaim, that Hiss was guilty and that the entire Truman administration was to be condemned for its negligence. In fact, it took two lengthy trials to convict Alger Hiss of perjury. (He could not be tried for espionage because the statute of limitations provided for a three-year limit on that crime.) The first trial ended in a hung jury with an eight to four vote for conviction; the second in conviction and a five-year prison sentence.

Although there has been considerable debate as to the merits of the grand jury trial that resulted in Hiss's conviction (and considerable doubt that he was in fact guilty of espionage), for our purpose the more relevant consequences of the trial were the overwhelming effects upon Nixon himself and the nation as a whole. The dramatic events leading to the downfall of Hiss served to substantiate the still more fantastic fears of communist infiltration and a world communist conspiracy. The paranoid prophecies of Whittaker Chambers now became the prevailing opinions of millions of Americans. A nationwide anticommunist terror was fueled by the emotional powerhouse of a revival religion. The interplay of patriotism and piety, always a dynamic element in America, now reached unprecedented intensity.

In his summation at the first trial, the government prosecutor Thomas Murphy appealed to his jury by calling Alger Hiss "another Benedict Arnold, another Judas Iscariot." He added wryly that both of these traitors had been like Hiss himself, men of good reputation. Apparently Murphy had little difficulty in equating an act of treason with an act of sacrilege. In its excess, his comment illustrates the mood touched off by Hiss's trial. Whittaker Chambers gives us a glimpse of Nixon's own attitude at the time:

> Throughout the most trying phases of the case, Nixon and his family, and sometimes his parents, were at our farm, encouraging me and comforting my family. My children have caught him lovingly in a nickname. To them, he is always "Nixie," the kind and the good, about whom they will tolerate no nonsense. His somewhat martial Quakerism sometimes amused and always heartened me. I have a vivid picture of him, in the blackest hour of the Hiss case, standing by the barn and saying in his quietly savage way (he is the kindest of men): "If the American people understood the real character of Alger Hiss, they would burn him in oil."

Campaigning for the vice presidency in 1952, Nixon would again use his most violent imagery. Speaking in Bangor, Maine he promised to make "Communist subversion and corruption the theme of every speech from now until the election. . . . If the record itself smears, let it smear. If the dry rot of corruption and communism, which has eaten deep into our body politic during the past seven years, can only be chopped out with a hatchet—then let's call for a hatchet." Rhetoric of this kind has characterized much of Nixon's political career. Most commentators have picked up the strand of violence in his politics and have seen him as "the hatchet man," one who would engage in the sharpest political contests, always taking the low road of political combat while men like Eisenhower would soar to the heights.

But Nixon is only partly a fighter, and to appreciate the complexity of his character we will do well to note the contrasts in Whittaker Chambers' comment. The quotation that stuck was that if the American people understood Alger Hiss, they would "burn him in oil." But Nixon made that comment, Chambers tells us, "in his quietly savage way (he is the kindest of men)." And the other image Chambers used was not remembered—that of "Nixie, the kind and the good," playing with the Chambers children, comforting and supporting the entire family in their time of crisis. As we trace Nixon's career as Vice President, we find that the two dimensions of his character play off against each other—the aggressive, hostile, crusading impulses and the idealistic, humane, even gentle instincts. It is the contrast and complexity of Nixon's character that make him so enigmatic and ultimately so fascinating. And it is precisely this interplay between opposite poles in his personality that so many commentators have missed. As we review the events of the 1950s, it is illuminating to see the very disparate roles that Nixon played, particularly that of champion of the young.

Richard Nixon's second contest, the 1950 race for the Senate against Helen Gahagan Douglas, was also characterized by arguments, slogans, and symbols highly charged with meaning of the moment, now the yellowed remnants of another era. As Earl Mazo begins his chapter on the Senate campaign of 1950, "Nothing in the litany of reprehensible conduct charged against Nixon the campaigner has been cited more often than the tactics by which he defeated Congresswoman Helen Gahagan Douglas for Senator." In fact, a review of that bitter contest reveals the unflinching use of similarly shady tactics by all sides involved.

It was indeed a many-sided affair, beginning in the Democratic primaries, where six candidates jockeyed for position. At the outset the leading Democratic contenders were Mrs. Douglas and Representative Sheridan Downey. Mrs. Douglas accused her opponent of selling out to the oil lobbies in Washington; he returned her fire by linking her with "extremists" of the Left. The exchange was short but intense; almost immediately Downey, who had been reluctant to enter the campaign because of ill health, announced that he could not carry on. He would be unwilling to wage "a personal and militant campaign against [Mrs. Douglas's] vicious and unethical propaganda."

But Downey's use of the extremist issue was at once taken up by the remaining contenders, including Manchester Boddy, editor and publisher of the *Los Angeles Daily News,* who then became her chief rival. He opened his campaign with a bristling offensive: "There is indisputable evidence of a state-wide conspiracy on the part of this small subversive clique of red-hots to capture, through stealth and cunning, the nerve centers of our Democratic party— and by so doing to capture the vote of real Democratic citizens." He later added the specific allegation that Mrs. Douglas had revealed her communist leanings by voting with New York Representative Vito Marcantonio against "an appropriation to enable Congress to uncover treasonable communistic activities."

Though Mrs. Douglas survived these attacks in the primary, Richard Nixon refined the strategy and made more effective use of identical arguments in his own offensive. Borrowing slogans from the Senate race of his friend George Smathers of Florida and coordinating his anitcommunist themes with matching slogans, symbols, and cue words, he called Mrs. Douglas the "Pink Lady" —soft on communism—who would delight in the continuing success of the Red conspiracy. These hyperbolic, even slanderous innuendoes were buttressed by an adroitly composed "fact sheet" filled with dates and names and research data: the Douglas-Marcantonio voting record. This was a masterwork of the Chotiner method; the facts were all carefully arranged to fit the predetermined conclusion: Mrs. Douglas was an ally of the most notorious communist in government. "While it should not be expected that a member of the House of Representatives should always vote in opposition to Marcantonio, it is significant to note, not only the greater number of times which Mrs. Douglas voted in agreement with him, but also the issues on which almost without exception they always saw eye-to-eye, to wit: Un-American Activities and Internal Security." What the fact sheet did establish was that Mrs. Douglas had voted 85 percent of the time either with the majority of her own party or with the majority of the House. In only two instances did she vote against these majorities and with Marcantonio on matters of "internal security"—once when she opposed the Mundt-Nixon Communist control bill of 1948 (which was finally defeated in the Senate) and again when she voted to sustain President Truman's veto of the McCarran internal security bill of 1950. If the evidence of this document was not persuasive, the color did press the point: the frail statistics were printed on flaming pink.

Not to be outdone, the Douglas organization published a rejoinder to the successful pink sheet. The Democrats put out a "yellow paper" revealing Nixon's own alliance with Marcantonio in several important Congressional debates. Mrs. Douglas's followers also brought into current usage the notorious nickname for Nixon, taking their cue from an editorial in the *Independent Review:* they began to refer to him regularly as Tricky Dick.

Unlike the congressional campaign of 1946, this Senate race did not climax in a simple dramatic moment such as the first debate with Voorhis. It was characterized by the relentless and grinding pace of Nixon, who matched the excesses of his rhetoric by extremes of physical and mental exertion. Picture him rushing up and down the coast of California in a rented station wagon, with Pat in the rear seat, an aide at the wheel, and perhaps an adviser to help him along the way. On the rear deck was a record player and sound system which would issue appropriate music to attract the crowds at shopping centers, street corners, and local party headquarters. As soon as one rally was finished, they packed their gear, literature, and buttons in the back of the car and headed off for the next pit-stop. They pressed on from early morning until late at night, shaking hands with every warm body they could corral. As soon as they pulled to a halt, Nixon would emerge smiling to shake the hands of party workers, greet old acquaintances, and climb the tailgate of his station wagon to deliver his basic speech—a score of times each day: one thousand speeches in a period of sixteen weeks.

Frank Nixon's unsatisfied hunger for success was continued in his son, transformed from the aimless wanderings of a vagabond laborer and small-town storekeeper into the more focused crusades of national politics. Richard would translate the puritan ethic of his father into the rigor, the discipline, the unremitting hardships and sacrifice of the campaign trail. If the Chotiner tactics revealed a shallow appreciation of ethics in public debate, Nixon himself pursued his political objectives with religious zeal. It was by losing himself in the cause of his party's politics that Richard Nixon was to find himself. Yet he so thoroughly identified his ego with his public career that a challenge to his campaign ethics would be taken as an ultimate challenge to his own character. So in 1952, when the newspapers came out with their stories of A SECRET NIXON FUND, he would answer with a full-blown defense of his record and resounding (if maudlin) testimony that, in fact, his was an honorable profession.

★ V ★

Crisis of Conscience:
The Fund Scandal, 1952

In the frantic final hours of the 1950 campaign, Richard Nixon's organizers announced a telephone marathon. When party headquarters called, those of the public who answered with the response, "Vote for Nixon," were offered:

PRIZES GALORE!!! Electric clocks, Silex coffeemakers with heating units—General Electric automatic toasters—silver salt and pepper shakers, sugar and creamer sets, candy and butter dishes, etc., etc. WIN WITH NIXON!

When all the prizes had been given out and the votes were counted, Nixon found himself the victor by a margin of 680,000 votes. If there were any doubts about the substance of the campaign or the style of the Republican candidate, they vanished in the euphoria of triumph. If the "pink papers" had toyed with the facts, if "prizes galore" appeared crude, if accusations had been inflated, all were forgotten by proud party stalwarts. Herbert Brownell, Jr., who was later to become Eisenhower's chief strategist, praised the Nixon-Chotiner blitz as a "brilliant campaign." Earl Mazo captures the spirit in which Nixon was received into the higher circles of his party: "Freshman Senator Nixon quickly became his party's most sought-after speaker and soon blossomed into a Republican meld of Paul Revere and Billy Sunday. Across the land he trumpeted

Republican gospel and warned the countryside to stop Democratic hordes or face disaster. The Republican party had to win the next election, or die, he declared." Recalling his record in convicting Alger Hiss, he recommended a thorough "housecleaning" of communists and subversives from government and a "mighty ideological offensive" designed "to prove to peoples everywhere that the hope of the world" could be found in the American experiment in democracy.

Here was the young, dynamic party hopeful who would make a perfect foil for General Eisenhower's "Great Crusade" against the "crooks and cronies" in Washington. On the very day the first stories of the Nixon fund appeared in the papers, Eisenhower, campaigning in Iowa, promised: "When we are through, the experts in shady and shoddy government operations will be on their way back to the shadowy haunts in the subcellars of American politics from which they came." Meanwhile Nixon was preaching: "What corruption means to us all is that every time we pick up our paper, every day, we read about a scandal. . . . this administration is going to go down in history as a scandal-a-day administration because you read about another bribe, you read about another tax-fix, you read about another gangster getting favors from the government . . . and are sick and tired of it."

In a style characteristic of that crusading campaign, the vice-presidential candidate would end his whistle-stop speeches by calling out to the crowd: "Who can clean up the mess in Washington?" As expected, the partisan crowd would shout back in unison, "Ike can!" Once at Tulare, California the train started to pull out before Nixon could finish his speech—impulsively he called out, "Come along and join our crusade." And many of them did, running alongside as the train gathered speed and disappeared down the track toward victory.

The crisis that interrupted this carefully orchestrated secular revival had its beginnings at the Republican National Convention in July 1952. Nixon had taken Eisenhower's side in a series of intricate maneuvers with the California delegation, which was pledged to vote for Governor Earl Warren as a favorite son. Some of the delegates felt that Nixon had betrayed the governor's position by polling California Republicans in an attempt to demonstrate an overwhelming plurality for Eisenhower. Two of the more embittered delegates let out the rumor that Nixon, now the Republican candidate for Vice President, was being "kept" by a group of millionaires who paid him a secret salary. Washington columnist Peter Edson picked up this story and confronted Nixon with the charge after their appearance on "Meet the Press" on September 14. Nixon referred him to Dana Smith, originator and manager of the fund, to establish its authenticity as an innocuous method of financing Nixon's off-year political activity. Meanwhile other reporters, hearing more flamboyant accounts of it, also began calling Smith. Soon the news was full of stories, some adhering to Smith's flat explanations, others mixing in typical campaign fantasy. As the rumors took root in the public awareness, many began to believe that Nixon was involved in some sort of illegal operation, perhaps involving a tax dodge, bribery, or graft. Democratic National Chairman Stephen Mitchell issued a statement calling upon Eisenhower to demand that Nixon withdraw from the race. The "Nixon fund" had become the focal issue of the campaign.

At this point Nixon still shrugged off the incident, later writing that he thought it was "part of political warfare . . . that because the attack was entirely partisan, it would not stand on its merits. I thought it would eventually run its course and be forgotten, provided I continued to play it down."

But he had underestimated the high drama the story would occasion. Seizing the opportunity to reveal that the Great Crusade was, after all, the invention of ordinary mortals, opponents of Republican ambitions spread the fund scandal as rapidly as they could. A public always fascinated by the downfall of hapless politicians, clamored for even more scintillating "news." Democratic party organizers sent squads of followers to shout out embarrassing questions all along Nixon's campaign tour. As he was finishing his speech in Marysville, California, a car pulled to a stop alongside the crowd and a group of men leaped out, one of them running toward the train, yelling, "Tell us about the $16,000!"

"Instinctively," wrote Nixon, "I knew I had to counterattack. You cannot win a battle in any arena of life merely by defending yourself. I pointed my finger at the man who called out, directing the crowd's attention to him, and then I let him have it."

"You folks know the work I did investigating communists in the United States. Ever since I have done that work, the communists and left-wingers have been fighting me with every possible smear. When I received the nomination for the vice presidency I was warned that if I continued to attack the communists in this government, they would continue to smear me. And believe me, you can expect that they will continue to do so. They started it yesterday. They have tried to say that I had taken $16,000 for my personal use." Nixon was rather vague, as he stood with his finger pointing at the man who had asked about the $16,000, whether *he* was one of the communists who would press the attack upon him. He simply bypassed the direct question, fired a rebuttal at his "communist" opponents, and moved to the offensive. He attacked government officials who "put their wives on the payroll and take fat legal fees on the side, charging the American taxpayer with . . . expenses . . . in excess of amounts which were allowed under the law." It was the Chotiner tactic of deflating the opposition before their campaign can get off the ground. But this time it was too late.

Later that day Nixon learned that the *New York Herald Tribune* planned to come out with an editorial demanding his resignation. He knew that, as the leading Republican paper in the nation, with direct ties to top Eisenhower aides, the *Tribune* writers "would not have taken this position editorially unless it also represented the thinking of people around Eisenhower. And, as I thought about it, it occurred to me that this might well be the view of Eisenhower himself."

From this point until his final television rebuttal, Nixon found himself wrestling with a self-doubt and disillusionment that would shake his sense of vocation to its foundations. As word came that Eisenhower's own associates, and perhaps the General himself, were considering his replacement, Nixon's mood alternated from fury to despair. Isolated in his compartment with his top advisers, he struggled for control and managed to check his emotions. One of his cardinal rules, repeated liturgically in *Six Crises,* is that success often hinges on "the ability to keep coldly objective when emotions are running high." A situation may justify indignation, even fury, but the savvy politician will keep his cool. In this case, Nixon converted his ire into a chilly moralism. . . . "What none of us could understand was how any of those around Eisenhower could in fairness reach a judgment before they knew the facts. I knew I had done nothing wrong and had nothing to hide."

Later Nixon revealed his feelings to Pat, expressing the "fatigue and depression" that had begun to overcome his anger. He told her, "If the judgment of more objective people around Eisenhower is that my resignation would help him to win, maybe I ought to resign." But the campaign train continued the next morning, cutting its way through Oregon. "The train seemed like a prison with its inexorable schedule. The crowds grew even larger. . . . the hecklers were more aggressive. I fought back harder."

In Eugene, Oregon a sign was held up by a member of the crowd: NO MINK COATS FOR NIXON, JUST COLD CASH. This comparison to a secretary in the Truman administration who had accepted the gift of a $9,000 mink coat brought Nixon to the attack again: "That's absolutely right. There are no mink coats for the Nixons. I am proud to say my wife, Pat, wears a good Republican cloth coat." Slowly, Nixon was hoarding a supply of images and phrases that would dramatize his innnocence; he would save them for his final vindication on TV. The "Checkers speech" would be his most impassioned self-portrait, his best effort to establish before the entire nation that Richard Nixon was an honest man—(one of those old-fashioned lawyers, a lawyer who can't be bought).

Meanwhile, Dana Smith had released his figures on the fund. There were twenty-six donors who had contributed a total of $18,235, most of which had been spent over a two-year period for Christmas cards, travel, postage, and other campaign expenses. The bill for Christmas cards alone came to $4,237.54 for a single year. Imagine Nixon's sense of injustice in this situation: his reputation, his entire career was now at stake over such ordinary expenditures as Christmas cards and postage. By contrast, he believed that the Truman administration was infected with corruption and communist infiltration at the highest level. There is little evidence to suggest that Nixon was presenting his defense with anything but candor. His writing on the incident, years after the fact, betrays a depth of involvement and a consistency of character that go far beyond the requirements of a face-saving apology. He describes his preparation for the speech as a major crisis of conscience: "I had to make the decision to fight the battle or to run away. Ahead of me were still three days of almost superhuman effort: preparing for the battle and then the battle itself, a half-hour broadcast in which the slightest mistake might spell disaster for me, my family, and my party. But as I had learned in the Hiss case, the period of indecision, of necessary soul-searching was the hardest. Now the emotions, the drive, the intense desire to act and speak decisively which I had kept bottled up inside myself could be released and directed to the single target of winning a victory."

More skeptical observers concluded that Richard Nixon was simply acting the part of offended innocence. When movie producer Darryl Zanuck told him after the speech that it was "the most tremendous performance I've ever seen," many took the comment literally. Yet a reading of Nixon's detailed analysis of the hours prior to the speech, reveals his own sense that this was a test of soul which would permanently decide his fate.

Difficult as it was for Nixon to understand the sudden rush of public indignation against him, Eisenhower's indecision and the open betrayal by his own Republican allies on Eisenhower's staff were far more devastating. Communications between Nixon's headquarters and the Eisenhower train grew increasingly strained. Despite an earlier agreement that Nixon should be given an opportunity to vindicate himself before the nation, many Eisenhower advisers urged the President to insist that Nixon use this thirty minutes to announce his resignation. In a final conversation between the candidates, Nixon attempted to secure a firm commitment that once the public defense had been made, Eisenhower would decide. But the General would only say, "I am hoping that no announcement would be necessary at all, but maybe after the program we could tell what ought to be done."

" 'General,' I answered, 'I just want you to know that I don't want you to give any consideration to my personal feelings. I know how difficult this problem is for you.' "

Here was the lieutenant offering up his life to the trusted commanding officer. But *was* Eisenhower to be so faithfully obeyed? Richard Nixon knew that all the facts concerning his fund were available to Eisenhower. If there were any moral grounds for putting him off the ticket, the General could have decided the ethics of the case *before* the television speech. Or would the decision simply reflect a realist's calculation of the political odds? "We will have to wait three or four days after the television show to see what the effect of the program is," demurred the General. Three or four days to weigh the morality of the fund—or to count the public reaction? Could the Great Crusade afford the stained image of Richard Nixon, even if the facts justified his claims? "The great trouble here is the indecision," said Nixon, his will stiffening for a confrontation with Eisenhower. "I will get off the ticket if you think my staying on it would be harmful. . . . But there comes a time in matters like this when you've got to fish or cut bait."

Nixon's desire for an immediate decision from Eisenhower was an entirely normal reaction to a situation of such extreme anxiety. Yet he characteristically takes indecisiveness as a sign of moral weakness. Faced by elements of doubt or ambiguity, he regularly looks for the clear-cut, definitive solution. Here, again, the major strands of his personality come into play. Decisiveness is a quality that complements his combative instincts as well as his need to be caught up in a righteous cause. As Nixon struggles for his own resolve in the midst of the fund crisis, he sees himself compelled to wage holy war against his opposition.

After the telephone conversation with Eisenhower, Nixon felt that "a new tension was now building up . . . I had been deserted by so many I had thought were friends but who had panicked in battle when the first shots were fired." Nixon's sense of betrayal, his sense of urgency and desperation, continued to mount. "I knew I had to go for broke. This broadcast must not be just good. It had to be a smash hit—one that really moved people, one that was designed not simply to explain the complicated and dull facts about the fund to people, but one that would inspire them to enthusiastic, positive support. . . . I had no choice but to use every possible weapon to assure the success of the broadcast."

As Nixon put the finishing touches on his speech, he also struggled for composure. He tried to assure himself that this was not, after all, a scrappy and selfish fight in his own political interest. Suppressing his own personal anxiety and fears of defeat, he put himself at the disposal of the General—"with personal considerations subordinated, I could concentrate on the issue which was far more important than my own political career. That was the election of Eisenhower."

But Nixon's studied dispassion, along with his rationale, were to be shattered by a phone call minutes before air time from Thomas Dewey. "There has just been a meeting of all of Eisenhower's top advisers. They have asked me to tell you that it is their opinion that at the conclusion of the broadcast tonight you should submit your resignation to Eisenhower."

Nixon described his reaction to this call as one of shock. He was speechless for a few moments—so long, in fact, that Dewey thought they had been cut off. "What does Eisenhower want me to do?" Nixon asked limply. As Dewey repeated the decision that had been reached, Nixon looked at his watch. There was less than half an hour to make final preparations for his trip to the television studio. As he calculated the time it would take to review his notes, to shave and change his shirt, his mood shifted again from disappointment to rage. "My nerves were frayed to a fine edge by this time, and I exploded. 'Just tell him that I haven't the slightest idea as to what I am going to do, and if they want to find out, they'd better listen to the broadcast. And tell them I know something about politics too!' " He had found out that membership in the Eisenhower crusade depended not on strength of character, but on ability to help win the election. As a detriment to the ticket, he would be jettisoned by an overwhelming vote of those who had promised a new morality in government.

What seems surprising in Nixon's account of this "betrayal" is that he was morally offended, apparently, by the perfectly transparent behavior of men who had acted in their own self-interest. His crisis appears to be complicated by a confusion in his own mind between standards of personal relations and those of power politics. His outrage implies that he actually saw Eisenhower's associates as "friends" and brothers in a righteous crusade. When their actions appeared increasingly self-serving, his fundamental perceptions were challenged. And his own mental effort to assume an attitude of "selflessness" became an agony when the demand of the moment was seen to be a calculated act of self-preservation.

Faced by Dewey's phone call and the raw necessity of arguing his case before the television audience, he moved, perhaps by instinct, to make the final preparations. As the second hand on the studio clock counted off the final moments and the director brought down his hand, signaling Nixon to go, "I began to speak."

My fellow Americans, I come before you tonight as a candidate for the vice presidency and as a man whose honesty and integrity has been questioned.

"As I spoke, all the tension suddenly went out of me. I felt in complete control of myself and of my material. I was calm and confident." As Richard Nixon listened to his own words, he could once again identify with the Republican cause. And as he lost himself in the comforting assumptions of his own rhetoric, he found those "resources of physical, mental, and emotional power he never realized he had. . . . I knew what I wanted to say, and I said it from the heart."

I am sure that you have read the charge, and you have heard it, that I, Senator Nixon, took $18,000 from a group of my supporters. Now, was that wrong? . . . . It isn't a question of whether it was legal or illegal. That isn't enough. The question is, was it morally wrong?

Not surprisingly, Nixon's conclusion was that since the money was not used for his personal use, the morality of the fund was above suspicion. This constituted his entire argument to vindicate the act of collecting money for his own political ends. The remainder of his thirty-minute talk represents a subtle interweaving of personal and political themes largely unrelated to the question of whether it was morally wrong. (As to whether the fund was legal, he read from the opinion of an independent auditing firm to the effect that "Senator Nixon did not violate any federal or state law.")

He introduced the body of his speech by moving to the offensive —"incidentally, this is unprecedented in the history of American politics—I am going at this time to give to this television and radio audience a complete financial history, everything I've earned, everything I've spent, everything I owe." If *his* ethics had been challenged by a public long accustomed to the ploys of power politics, he would answer the attack by raising up a wholly new standard of conduct. What he introduces as "unprecedented in the history of politics" he then holds out as a principle to be adhered to by the other candidates. "I would suggest that under the circumstances both Mr. Sparkman and Mr. Stevenson should come before the American people, as I have, and make a complete financial statement as to their financial history. And if they don't, it will be an admission that they have something to hide."

Nixon's financial statement was more than an accountant's summation of his net worth. It represented a subtle mix of statistics and personal maxims. After listing his property (a 1950 Oldsmobile car; $3,000 equity in his California house; $4,000 in life insurance; $21,000 in his Washington home) and his debts ($30,000 in mortgages; $5,000 in loans; $500 in life insurance), he added, "Well, that's about it." (Here was Nixon speaking in his popular idiom, the informal folksy style he uses to identify with his constituency in middle America.) "That's what we have. And that's what we owe. It isn't very much. But Pat and I have the satisfaction that every dime that we have got is honestly ours. I should say this, that Pat doesn't have a mink coat. But she does have a respectable Republican cloth coat, and I always tell her she would look good in anything."

Nixon has never argued that his speech was not planned in advance for maximum impact. The informal tone was planned, as were each of the cues in this masterful presentation of the individualist ethic. "Every dime . . . is honestly ours." Read: ours by the long, hard sweat of our brow, not inherited money (like Steven-

95

son's), not stolen money or funny money earned in shady speculation on Wall Street, but honest money, our money, money that is
more than a measure of our wealth, money that itself symbolizes
our fortitude and character. So the cloth coat, and the dog, Checkers, and "our little girl Tricia," the pieces fit together perfectly.
This is an honest family which takes seriously its modest pleasures.
Was the dog a political gift? "You know the kids, like all kids, love
the dog, and I just want to say this, right now, regardless of what
they say about it, we're going to keep it." The love of this family,
their love even for a dog, would not be compromised by an aggressive and cynical foe.

"Mr. Mitchell, the Chairman of the Democratic National Committee, made the statement that if a man couldn't afford to be in
the United States Senate, he shouldn't run for the Senate. And I
just want to make my position clear. I don't agree with Mr. Mitchell
when he says that only a rich man should serve the government."
At this point Nixon began to identify the foe who would challenge
the sanctity of his family, "I believe that it's fine that a man like
Governor Stevenson, who inherited a fortune from his father, can
run for President. But I also feel that it is essential in this country
of ours that a man of modest means can also run for President,
because, you know—remember Abraham Lincoln, remember what
he said—God must have loved the common people, he made so
many of them."

As Nixon had set it up, it was himself, his own family, the Republican party, and all people of honest and respectable means,
together with Abraham Lincoln and Almighty God, against the
powerful leaders of the Democratic Party, the politicians of inherited wealth, and all others who would wittingly or unwittingly
sell out the United States of America.

In a speech designed to vindicate himself against a political
smear, Nixon put forward several fuzzy arguments of his own.
Referring to the Korean war, he said, "Those in the State Depart-

96

ment who made the mistakes which caused the war . . . should be kicked out . . . just as fast as we can get them out of there." The Democratic administration had caused the war, he argued, as they had caused the corruption in the federal government. So, reasoned Nixon, "I am going to campaign up and down America until we drive the crooks and the communists and those that defend them out of Washington." His critique was not directed against particular programs of the Democratic Party. Nor did he attempt to explain how Truman's policies had intensified the decadence of Washington bureaucrats or the lust for power among the North Korean high command. The Checkers speech was not, in this sense, a political speech at all. From beginning to end it was a moralistic statement, designed to persuade his audience that the Nixon-Eisenhower crusade would purge the nation of its sins, almost on the strength of moral example alone: "And remember, folks, Eisenhower is a great man. Folks, he is a great man, and a vote for Eisenhower is a vote for what is good for America." The Checkers speech was successful precisely because of its moral tone, a tone perfectly responsive to the lowest common denominator of popular morality —a high-minded corn.

Nixon had measured the mood of the nation with precision. Telegrams, letters, cards, and petitions poured in upon the Eisenhower train, into Republican Party headquarters in Washington and in every state, into the television and radio stations that carried the broadcast. Three hundred thousand messages were sent to party headquarters in Washington alone, their contents practically unanimous: "Keep Nixon on the ticket."

Yet Eisenhower's equivocation and Nixon's self-doubt persisted. Publicly Eisenhower was full of praise: "I happen to be one of those people who, when I get into a fight, would rather have a courageous and honest man by my side than a whole boxcar of pussyfooters. I have seen brave men in tough situations. I have never seen anyone come through in better fashion than Senator

97

Nixon did tonight." But he added in a telegram to Nixon that before he would "complete the formulation of a decision, I feel the need of talking to you and would be most appreciative if you could fly to see me at once." By way of explaining this further delay, he told his audience in Cleveland, Ohio, "I am not ducking any responsibility. I am not going to be swayed by my idea of what will get the most votes . . . I am going to say: Do I myself believe this man is the kind of man America would like to have for its Vice President?"

Eisenhower's ruminations typified the obscure ethics of his crusade, particularly his relationship to Nixon. His campaign called upon the most lofty ideals of morality and self-sacrifice, yet his rhetoric could not disguise the realities of power which would ultimately decide the outcome of his mission. In one sentence he would not be "swayed" by popular opinion; in the next it is "whether this man is the kind of a man America would like to have for its Vice President."

When Nixon learned of Eisenhower's insistence upon a personal confrontation at his convenience and prior to making his decision, he fell back into his stormy mood: "For the first time [it was the *third* time] in almost a week of tremendous tension, I really blew my stack. 'What more can he possibly want from me?'. . . . I announced to everyone in the room that if the broadcast had not satisfied the General, there was nothing more I could or would do. I would simply resign." Petulant and wounded, Nixon called his secretary and dictated a telegram of resignation to the Republican National Committee.

Murray Chotiner intercepted the message and immediately attempted to negotiate a reconciliation between Nixon and Eisenhower. He knew that the overwhelming popularity of the Checkers speech would secure Nixon his place on the ticket, but he hoped to save his friend the humiliation of "going to Eisenhower like a little boy to be taken to the woodshed, properly punished, and then restored to a place of dignity." If Nixon followed Eisenhower's suggestion that he fly immediately to Wheeling, West Virginia for a further consultation, it would demean his candidate's image. Chotiner spoke at length with Arthur Summerfield at Eisenhower's headquarters, insisting upon a pledge that if Nixon flew to Wheeling, he would come only to receive Eisenhower's favorable commitment. Summerfield was finally able to assure Chotiner that Nixon would be kept on the ticket. But Nixon still felt that an immediate trip to Wheeling was unacceptable. A call from another member of Eisenhower's staff, Bert Andrews, who had worked closely with Nixon during the Hiss investigation, finally convinced him that his refusal to answer Eisenhower's call might evoke an unfavorable public reaction. At last the two parties were nearing a compromise—Nixon would make his scheduled trip to Missoula the following day and then fly to Wheeling. Despite the victory of his speech, he was still feeling the tortuous interplay between his own ego, the necessities of his career, and the interests of General Eisenhower. His best efforts notwithstanding, he found that his victory was not final and his vindication far less than permanent.

As soon as his plane landed at the Wheeling airport, Eisenhower rushed on board, arms outstretched, to welcome Nixon back to the fold. Later, aboard the General's campaign train, the two discussed the exaggerated reports about the fund and additional rumors that had begun circulating about alleged misconduct on Nixon's part. Said Nixon: "This is just like a war, General. Our opponents are losing. They mounted a massive attack against me and have taken a hard beating. It will take them a little time to regroup, but when they start fighting back, they will be desperate, and they will throw everything at us, including the kitchen sink."

Six Crises is studded with expressions of Nixon's anxiety about hostile criticism. He appears to see a world full of enemies who may at any moment violate his privacy, assault his honor, and defame his reputation. As he wrote after the Checkers speech, "Why do I feel so deeply? Why do I feel that in spite of the smears, the misunderstandings, the necessity for a man to come up here and bare his soul, as I have—why is it necessary for me to continue this fight?" To bare his soul? That was not, overtly at least, the purpose of his television speech. The requirement of the moment was simply a cogent presentation of facts concerning the fund. He had included more intimate revelations about his wife, his children, and the family dog by way of attack.

Note his reasons for mentioning his wife's cloth coat as stated in *Six Crises*. "My remark in Eugene, Oregon, about Pat's cloth coat came to mind, and I marked it down as a good reminder of the mink coat scandals which were plaguing the Truman Administration." "Thinking back to Franklin Roosevelt's devastating remark in the 1944 campaign—'and now they are attacking poor Fala'—I decided to mention my own dog Checkers. Using the same ploy as FDR would irritate my opponents and delight my friends, I thought." Nixon was prepared to use (as he says) "every possible weapon" to advance his cause. Yet while he uses the most transparent devices of rhetoric to discredit his opposition, he portrays himself as motivated by absolutely innocent objectives. "Why then should an honest man enter public life and submit himself and his family to such risks?" (He does not say that power is his object, or fame, or even the interests of the Republican Party.) "The answer, of course, is that if men with good reputations do not take such risks, they leave the field of public service to the second-raters and chiselers who have no reputation to worry about." The warfare of politics may be amoral, but the war itself may be justified if "good" men do the fighting. Nixon repeatedly paints his political struggles as a contest between good and evil, between men of integrity and those obsessed by lust for power. While he seems genuinely concerned that his own conduct be above reproach, he somehow implies that the ethics of his opposition are suspect, simply because they oppose him.

Nixon's perennial problem, one might think, is a certain confusion of principle, self-image, and the realities of power politics. He attempts to operate simultaneously in accord with the lofty principles of a crusade and the shrewd tactics of warfare. Faced by contradiction between these two modes of behavior, one feels his tendency is to bolt erratically from his posture as a moralist to that of a fighter. As outside pressure mounts, the confusion intensifies. No doubt this problem in large part reflects the internal conflict between the prevailing trends in his own character, but it also reveals the larger dilemma of American society.

The American culture is a composite of conflicting ideals, among which the most visible contradictions are those within the political process. Chief among these is the discrepancy between the public demand for integrity in its elected officials and the practical requirements of waging a successful campaign. Though the basis of democratic politics is the free competition of men, issues, and ideals, in practice the system is compromised by the ancient devices of ambitious men and the more recent inventions of advertising and market research, image-making and computer technology, all of which together involve multi-million-dollar campaign expenditures. When Nixon denied that contributions of several thousand dollars to his "secret fund" were either immoral or illegal, he was correct, given prevailing standards of propriety. But the more important question raised by this example and others is whether we have made our politicians overdependent upon the special interest groups and skills which are increasingly necessary to finance and run a national campaign.

Richard Nixon's struggle to prove his integrity during the fund crisis offers a preview of the more general crises of credibility and of the political system itself. As it becomes more obvious that politics is a process tainted not only by ancient vices but now by the new inventions of technology, it is increasingly difficult for the public to believe that significant issues or ideals come into play at all.

In 1952 Nixon and a large majority of the public assumed that, while the ethics of an individual politician could be questioned, the system was on the whole to be trusted. The malaise of the seventies is rooted in the suspicion that the worst is true of the politician simply because he is part of the system.

Throughout his career, Nixon has been acutely sensitive to the public's need to believe in the integrity of its leaders. In fact, his success has been due in large part to his mastery of the moralistic style in his campaigns while at the same time commanding the machinery of his party. As the two major parties continue to lose their hold over the voting public, and as the public becomes more skeptical of a simple appeal to conscience, Nixon's method may become less and less effective.

The public needs to believe in the integrity of its leaders, now perhaps more than ever before. But if this belief is to be real, it must include an awareness of the factors that actually count in an election, even the unsavory ones. The nation now hungers for leaders who can demonstrate, by their policies as well as their polemics, that politics is an honorable profession.

★ VI ★

The Young Vice President

When Richard Nixon took his oath of office on January 21, 1953 he became the second youngest Vice President in the nation's history. Looking back upon the Eisenhower years, with the memory of John Kennedy still so powerful, it is difficult to believe that Nixon was fast becoming the hero of youth culture. Yet the energetic and idealistic Republican from California did capture the imagination of two generations of college and high-school students. In fact, public opinion polls would indicate that, even in 1960, he was the choice of a now surprising majority of students in the head-to-head contest with Jack Kennedy.

As Vice President, he was invited to speak at colleges and youth conferences across the country. He particularly enjoyed speaking at church conferences, where he would captivate his audience with stories of the Hiss case and his campaign for clean government, a strong defense, and a powerful presentation of the American way to the nations of the undeveloped world. In January, 1954 he was designated to lead the national observance of Youth Sunday, and rose to the pulpit of the Westmoreland Congregational Church in Washington to tell the youth of the nation that Americans could counteract communist propaganda only if they "show by their deeds that they believe in the dignity and equality of all men. . . . By our actions, both when we go to the East and when its people come here, we must show that we believe in the people of Asia as equals and respect their religion and culture." Nixon was primed with optimism about the destiny of this country and did not hesitate to blend his hopes with his messianic expectations. He saw only one obstacle to the realization of the nation's most profound ideals, and that was international communism. "There is no hate in the hearts of the young people of the world except where they have been touched by communism," he said. Here was a novel interpretation of the Christian doctrine of original sin. Only the communists were touched by hate, he argued; the rest of humanity could therefore be won over to the American way.

Speaking to a thousand delegates at the Christian Endeavor World Convention, he said in July 1954, "The struggle in which the world is engaged today is . . . a struggle for the souls of men. . . . And unless we realize that we are going to lose it." If the chief evil in the world was Soviet communism, so the chief problem at home was the threat of communist infiltration. During the 1952 campaign he had used the Hiss conviction as his entrée into the question of domestic security. "We can assume because of the cover-up of this administration in the Hiss case that the communists, the fellow travelers, have not been cleaned out of the executive branch of the government."

By 1954, the Eisenhower administration had its chance to purge Washington of the communists and fellow travelers. In fact, the purge was aimed not only at communists but at anyone whose character or politics was suspect. The witch-hunt was euphemistically titled "security clearance" and by November, 1954 Nixon could proclaim that "96 per cent of the 6,926 communists, fellow travelers, sex perverts, people with criminal records, dope addicts, drunks, and other security risks removed under the Eisenhower security program were hired by the Truman administration." In reality, subsequent tallies showed that close to a majority of those who were swept out of the government offices had actually been hired during the first months of Eisenhower's rule. Nevertheless, Nixon proclaimed his conviction that the Great Crusade was moving forward on schedule; Eisenhower, he said in 1956, had proven himself to be "a man whom every American can proudly hold up to his children as one who has faith in God, faith in America, and one who has restored dignity and respect to the highest office in the land."

Nixon not only preached his doctrines at home, he also took them abroad. In his first trip to Latin America in 1955 he stopped in Guatemala City to honor Archbishop Mariano Rossell y Arellano as "one of the greatest bulwarks against communism and totalitarian ideas." In Mexico, he visited the basilica of Our Lady of Guadalupe, the most revered shrine in the country. He was greeted by a crowd of more than two thousand in the basilica square and was welcomed by Archbishop Luis Maria Martinez. A small girl walked up to the Vice President and gave him a bouquet of flowers, which he placed at the feet of the shrine. He then spoke of the common faith, of Mexico and the United States; he asserted that the two countries would be held together by "a common dedication to the principle that man does not live by bread alone. . . . These common principles of belief in liberty and in God will continue to bind our two countries."

Back in the United States Nixon appeared as keynote speaker at the National Conference on Spiritual Foundations. He shared the dais with Lewis E. Strauss of the Atomic Energy Commission and Admiral Arthur W. Radford, Chairman of the Joint Chiefs of Staff. The Religious News Service reported the common theme of their speeches: "America's national security depends on a deep and abiding religious faith." Nixon asserted that it is the duty of organized religion to build the "spiritual foundations upon which alone world peace can be erected." During this period the Vice President's remarks often echoed the opinions of his chief speech writer. From 1953 until the campaign of 1960, Father John Cronin ghosted his major deliveries.

In 1956 Nixon took off on an evangelistic tour of the deep South, appearing with Billy Graham at three church meetings in a single day. The pair addressed Presbyterian, Baptist, and Methodist assemblies in South Carolina. This clearly was the decade for revival. In 1953 the prayer breakfast movement was initiated; in 1954 the phrase "under God" was added to the pledge of allegiance; in 1955 "In God We Trust" was made mandatory on all U.S. currency; in 1956 the same phrase was adopted as the national motto by a vote of the House and Senate—and there was neither debate nor a single dissenting vote in Congress. During the same period, the statistics on church membership and benevolences showed that Americans were flocking to their sanctuaries in unprecedented numbers *and* providing the funds for new buildings, programs, and endowments.

In assessing Nixon's continuing attraction for the generation of Americans who were adolescents and young adults in the 1950s, it is important to remember the close relation between the revival of religion and the renewed sense of national mission. During this period Nixon appealed at once to religious and nationalistic feelings; his style as a politician and a campaigner indicates a conscious attempt to ride the wave of revival. Though his resurrection in 1968 has most often been explained as a function of his hold upon the machinery of the Republican Party, one should not underestimate the reserves of positive feeling for him, particularly among those who remember the youthful and idealistic champion of the American cause in the Cold War. Nixon does not possess the charisma of Billy Graham, but he shares the evangelist's sensitivity for the importance of a popular religion. This sensitivity has been a continuing element in Nixon's politics, a factor that should not be overlooked by those who seek to understand his conduct of the presidency.

In 1957 Nixon told a group of his associates that he would soon participate in "one of the most courageous spiritual ventures in our generation." He was speaking of the evangelistic crusade that Billy Graham was soon to open at Madison Square Garden in New York City. More than any other single event, this New York Crusade typifies the revival of the 1950s. Both the theology Graham preached and the tactics he used to "penetrate the heart of the world's largest city," reveal much of the character of the religion that prevailed in the postwar years.

The Billy Graham Evangelistic Association operates its crusades with the methods and techniques of a presidential campaign. Preparations for the New York Crusade were typical. In May of 1956, over a year before it was to begin, a central office was opened on Forty-sixth Street just off Broadway. A Graham staff executive and secretary set up operations and at once organized the Crusade Executive Committee. According to pattern, the committee chairman was a prominent businessman, in this case, Roger Hull, then executive vice president of Mutual of New York. Other members included ministers from prestige churches and businessmen of an evangelical orientation.

Additional committees were set up to supervise each component of planning, operations, and follow-up. The metropolitan area was divided into seven regions, with organizations in each area. Local churches were solicited for volunteer help, for funds, for their official endorsement. Ministers and laymen were contacted months in advance to help with publicity, transportation, recruitment. Volunteers were solicited to stuff envelopes and man the telephones. Teams of counselors were trained to meet with converts on a one-to-one basis. Long before the crusade began, the metropolitan region was saturated with radio, television, newspaper, and billboard advertising. Advance men met with church and civic organizations to stimulate their interest; youth workers met with high-school and college students to enlist their support. Complimentary tickets were sent to prominent entertainers, show business personalities, politicians, retired generals, and anyone who might enhance the crusade

107

by appearing in the reserved seat sections. Especially important guests were invited to sit with Billy Graham on the speakers' platform. A choir of four thousand was pulled together out of volunteers from individual congregations.

The advertising budget for the New York Crusade exceeded a quarter of a million dollars. Another $400,000 was spent for television coverage of the Saturday night meetings, $360,000 for the rental of Madison Square Garden, and $105,000 for office expenses. The total expenditures exceeded two and a half million dollars. Curtis Mitchell, one of several authorized historians, typifies the success motif peculiar to the crusade organizers. "On the evening of September 1, 1957, Dr. Billy Graham faced the final and largest audience of his New York Crusade at an outdoor rally in Times Square. An estimated 125,000 people jammed Broadway from curb to curb and overflowed into a dozen side streets. . . . [The] New York Crusade broke all records for organized evangelistic crusades. It ran longer. It attracted more people. It resulted in more converts. It cost more money, almost $2,500,000. Extraordinary figures document the story. . . ."

But Billy Graham does not credit his advance men, his market research experts, his advertising executives, or his television, radio, and public relations specialists with his success. He pointed out the source of his power to Vice President Richard Nixon on July 21, 1957 as they walked side by side toward the speakers' platform, located on second base at Yankee Stadium. A crowd of more than 100,000 jammed the grandstands and filled the entire outfield to standing-room capacity. It was the largest crowd ever assembled at the stadium, and Nixon, not missing the opportunity to praise his friend, said: "Billy, you are to be congratulated on this tremendous audience." But the evangelist shot back, "I didn't fill this place, God did it." A large measure of Graham's power as a speaker stems from his absolute conviction that beyond all the advertising and marketing techniques, God is directly responsible for the success of his crusades. "They said Yankee Stadium wouldn't be filled. But it is. God has done this, and all the honor, credit and glory must go to Him. You can destroy my ministry by praising me for this. The Bible says God will not share His glory with another."

Billy Graham's belief notwithstanding, his crusades represent a most sophisticated use of the tools and technology of persuasion. Though he promises a salvation that depends solely on the relation between the individual and his God, the conversion experience is carefully orchestrated and controlled by his professional staff. As Graham learned from the revivalists of the nineteenth century, his success depends upon his ability to recreate his revivals in city after city, producing the same experiences and the same conversions with mechanical efficiency.

There is an affinity in this respect between the religion of Billy Graham and that of Richard Nixon. For while they both proclaim a dependence upon God, they rely upon their own discipline, planning, and control. Their convictions aside, they both act as though success depended upon ordinary techniques of mass persuasion. Propelled by the certainty that their cause is right, they are free to manipulate opinion without regard for the fundamental question as to the truthfulness of their message.

It was fitting that the Vice President should appear with the evangelist at his most triumphant moment, for as they stood together before the crowd at Yankee Stadium it was very clear that they were the two most representative figures in the revival of the 1950s. Nixon was given a standing ovation when he came forward to the podium and said: "I bring you a message from one who is a very good friend of Billy Graham and one who would have been here if his duties had allowed him, the greetings and best wishes of President Eisenhower."

The fact is, Eisenhower's duties regularly prevented him from attending Graham's crusades. Members of the White House staff had advised him that it would be politically dangerous to endorse "any

109

religious promoter," especially any organization or leader "that smacked of evangelism and proselytizing." Despite the widely held opinion that Eisenhower uniquely symbolizes the religiosity of this period, it was Nixon who aggressively pursued his contacts with the church. The image of a Nixon who instinctively played hatchet man for a more pious, fatherly Eisenhower does not accurately reflect Nixon's active and consistent support of Graham, his extensive contacts in the Roman Catholic community, his frequent public statements about religion, and—most important—his complete identification with the anticommunist revival. In this respect, his association with Billy Graham is especially significant.

The bunting at Billy Graham's crusades is invariably red, white, and blue. At Madison Square Garden, the auditorium was draped with bunting and a constellation of giant American flags was hung from the ceiling—flags so huge that they dominated the upper reaches of the Garden. At Times Square Graham said: "Let us tell the world tonight that our trust is not in our stockpile of atom bombs but in Almighty God. Let us make this a time of rededication—not only to God, but to the principles and freedom that our forefathers gave us."

Like Whittaker Chambers, Billy Graham believes that the struggle between the United States and Russia is an all-out cosmic war between good and evil. "America is the key nation of the world. We were created for a spiritual mission among the nations. . . . America is truly the last bulwark of Christian civilization. If America fails, Western culture will disintegrate." And by contrast: "Communism is a fanatical religion that has declared war upon the Christian God. . . . a great sinister anti-Christian movement . . . masterminded by Satan. . . . The false doctrine . . . lies across our world like a colossus. . . . Only as millions of Americans turn to Jesus Christ . . . can the nation be spared the onslaught of a demon-possessed communism."

When Billy Graham suggests that America will be saved as millions are converted to Christianity, this is not to say that the means of their salvation will be otherworldly. He believes that a life of hard work, discipline, and devotion to the church, together with a national commitment to the arms race and the cold war will be the specific agents of redemption. During the 1957 crusade, he spoke to an audience of businessmen on Wall Street and told them: "You ask, how can I contribute anything to America and to world peace? I'm just one individual. Well, I want to tell you this. You are America, and you can give yourself to God. You can do this by repenting of sin, receiving Jesus Christ, and then going back into the office to live for Him." What should the Wall Street brokers and bankers do when they return to their desks? In his book, *Peace with God,* Graham suggested: "Christ's way of life does not require that a man renounce any legitimate interests or ambitions . . . [rather] the Scripture exhorts us to carry on business as usual. . . ."

Like Richard Nixon, Graham was raised in a strict Protestant home where regular church attendance and unbending rules of conduct were enforced with a leather belt. And like Nixon he recommends a life of rigor and discipline, and practices what he preaches to the letter. During the New York Crusade he drove himself through his crowded schedule, from news conferences to luncheon meetings, to midday street-corner rallies, and then every night to the crusade itself. He pushed himself so forcefully that during the first six weeks of the crusade he lost twenty pounds. As with Nixon, his doctors implored him to rest.

One of Graham's more peculiar beliefs is that Jesus Christ perfectly illustrates the puritan formulas for success. His hard work, his discipline, his self-control gave him a strength and power without parallel in the history of the world. As Graham told his New York audience on Youth Night in 1957, "Our young people are becoming soft and flabby. Walking has gone out of style. . . . Youngsters are bored with so much idle time. They need to work. J. Edgar Hoover has stressed that young people should be busy do-

111

ing worthwhile things." By way of example, "Jesus Christ was the strongest man who ever lived. His muscles were perfectly coordinated. He was perfect." And the second-strongest man in the world was Samson, "He split the jaws of the lion with his hands." Graham uses these illustrations to prove his final point: "A Christian grows when he leads a disciplined life. Your bodies, minds and tongues should be disciplined. Practice self-control. The Holy Spirit will give you the strength to become Christian soldiers."

When Graham uses the symbolism of warfare, he takes himself literally. His enemies are the satanic powers of darkness, the fallen angels and shock troops of the Devil. Immediately prior to the opening of his New York Crusade, he told his associates: "This may be our last Crusade. The opposition from every quarter is terrific, and it will mount! Satan will use everything at his command to defeat the Crusade in New York. It may mean that I will be crucified—but I'm going!"

Though his southern Presbyterian and Baptist training forbids him to speak his mind directly on politics, there are enough signals in his sermons so that his position is perfectly clear to the attentive listener. In the 1950s there was no doubt that Graham's theological conclusions about communism resulted in rather special opinions on foreign and domestic policy. "The Bible teaches us that we are engaged in a gigantic spiritual warfare, and when God begins to move in a country, as He is now moving mightily in America, Satan also begins to move. . . ." But against the Devil and his legions, Graham saw armies of Christian soldiers engaged—businessmen, the young converts of his crusades, and certain Congressmen. "I thank God for men who in the face of public denouncement and ridicule go loyally on in their work of exposing the pinks, the lavenders, and the reds who have sought refuge beneath the wings of the American eagle, and from that vantage point try in every subtle, under-cover way to bring comfort, aid, and help to the greatest enemy we have ever known, communism."

During his vice presidency Richard Nixon appeared regularly with Graham at the crusades. The pair played golf together and became warm friends. Born in the same decade, converted to the same religion, they rose to national prominence on the same outpouring of chauvinism. They periodically trade compliments and flattering appraisals of each other's talents. Nixon once wrote that his friend has "the qualities that would have made Graham an able President of the United States. . . . As a background to these qualities Graham has his sense of history. I could tell in my conversations with him that he was a great student of history, and, consequently, he was able to evaluate current events with rare perspective and insight. This is one of the reasons his predictions on political trends usually prove strikingly accurate."

Like his friends Whittaker Chambers and Billy Graham, Nixon also saw the confrontation with communism as essentially a holy war. Though his imagery was not often as flamboyant as theirs, the structure of his thought followed similar patterns. As late as 1962 he wrote in *Six Crises:* "History tells us we are on the right side. Despite the temporary successes of dictators, it is the ultimate destiny of men to be free. Man needs God, and communism is atheistic. Man wants to be free, and communism enslaves him. Man cherishes his individual dignity, and communism collectivizes him." History, human nature, free enterprise, the United States, and God are arrayed against Karl Marx and his doomed philosophy. In one short paragraph Nixon has solved the riddle of the universe; his anticommunist doctrines provide the foundation for a personal ethic—for a view of time, history, and the future—for an economic and political system, a domestic and foreign policy.

The fundamental weakness in this system of thought was that it ignored, in its very simplicity, all that would not square with its orderly assumptions. If Nixon and Charles Kersten had read Fulton Sheen's book with greater care, they might not have stumbled into the excesses of the McCarthy era and the extremes of cold-war di-

113

plomacy. Their superficial reading of Sheen had exposed them to his opinion that "the future battle will be between the church and communism. Communism itself admits that it has only one enemy and that is the Catholic Church." But Sheen did not set up the American way as the diametric opposite of communism. In fact, the major thrust of his book was to point out the similar assumptions of both systems of thought. Sheen had argued that the very excesses of communism were the logical result of a nineteenth-century liberalism that emphasized the perfectibility of man and of human institutions. These root assumptions of "pragmatic liberalism" had been used by Marx to justify the utopian promises of his *Communist Manifesto*. In the hands of Lenin and Stalin, the same assumptions were used to justify the Red terror, labor camps, secret police, violence, and mass murder.

Yet in raising up the American way of life as the answer to a Red peril, the anticommunists also borrowed from doctrines of the nineteenth century. Concentrating upon the evils of Soviet Russia, they designed an American utopia that equally exaggerated the possibilities of human nature and the institutions of free enterprise. Having discovered the ultimate evil in the Red conspiracy, they assumed that the United States was the source of ultimate good. All mankind would be saved by a simple imitation of American mores and institutions. At precisely this point, however, men like Graham and Nixon exceeded the limits of nineteenth-century optimism by crossing the bounds of reason and returning to a primitive mythology.

Speaking in Philadelphia in 1952, Richard Nixon said, "We are on the side of freedom, of truth, of justice against godless totalitarianism, slavery, and oppression. All we need is leadership—courageous, strong, decent, firm American leadership. . . ." If the excesses of Nixon's faith in America had been limited to his rhetoric, and his confidence in the religion and mythology of Billy Graham confined to the podium, our discussion of his root beliefs might end here. But his beliefs have affected his behavior; they have shaped his policies first as Vice President and now as the nation's chief executive. Though the revival of the 1950s has cooled, the assumptions that Nixon articulated in the McCarthy era are still very much a part of his thinking and that of his administration.

In this regard, it is instructive to note the role Nixon played in the downfall of the most spectacular anticommunist of them all, Senator Joseph McCarthy. After the conviction of Alger Hiss, Nixon and McCarthy became the two most prominent anticommunists in the Senate. For a while they seemed to compete with each other for the headlines, escalating their charges against the Truman administration, inventing an entire lexicon of code words for their "crusade." Supporting Nixon in his demand that Dean Acheson resign as Secretary of State, McCarthy said, "He must go. We cannot fight international atheistic communism with men who are either traitors or who are hip-deep in their own failures." He then called the Democrats "the Administration Commiecrat Party of Betrayal." Campaigning in 1952, Nixon attacked Stevenson, referring to him as "Adlai, the appeaser . . . who got a Ph.D. from Dean Acheson's College of Cowardly Communist Containment." Soft on communism, commies, the Reds, the pinks, the lavenders, fellow travelers, front groups, propaganda, thought-control, un-American activity, dupe, brainwash, subversive, cold war—the special vocabulary of the 1950s would not be outdone in American politics until 1968, with Abbie Hoffman and the Yippies. The New Left borrowed the same tricks to denounce "Amerika the Pig Nation and the Pig Leader Nixon." What now so maddens the American majority, when articulated by the Left, was acclaimed in the fifties by the anticommunist right as entirely appropriate to political discourse. In that day the popular pests were the "rats."

After Eisenhower's election, the Republican Party found McCarthy's unremitting investigations—now of Republican appointments—both untimely and unwise. After an intricate series of attempts to reconcile the crusading Senator, Nixon was chosen to put him down. In a speech designed to tame McCarthy, Nixon maneuvered around his name. "Men who have in the past done effective work exposing communism in this country have, by reckless talk and questionable methods, made themselves the issue rather than the cause they believe in so deeply." Nixon's criticism was of McCarthy's methods; his *beliefs* were still beyond question, and perhaps even his rhetoric. "I agree," said the Vice President, "that the communists are a bunch of rats. But just remember this, when you go out to shoot rats, you have to shoot straight because when you shoot wildly . . . you make it easier on the rats." Nixon split away from McCarthy when the latter leveled his anticommunist blasts against the Eisenhower administration. He still felt a kinship with McCarthy's intentions, but shied away from his tactics because he viewed them as "so inept at times that he [McCarthy] eventually did our cause more harm than good."

The incident that finally touched off Eisenhower's action against McCarthy was an article written by J. B. Matthews, whom McCarthy had appointed as his director of investigation. Matthews had written that "the largest single group supporting the communist apparatus in the United States today is composed of Protestant clergymen." Members of the White House staff who were anxious to silence McCarthy arranged to have the National Conference of Christians and Jews send a telegram of protest to the President; they hoped to escalate the public outcry so that Eisenhower would be forced to condemn the Republican Senator. It happened, however, that McCarthy had already decided to fire Matthews. If his decision was announced before Eisenhower spoke out, the opportunity to discredit him would be lost. William Rogers (then Deputy Attorney General) received word that McCarthy was headed from his own office to the Senate floor. He feared that he was about to announce Matthew's resignation. To delay him, he called Nixon to see whether he could intercept. Just as Nixon put down the receiver, McCarthy wandered into his office. Nixon dutifully engaged him in a lengthy discussion of his plans for an investigation of the CIA. The maneuver was perfectly timed. While McCarthy was in the Vice President's office, the White House staff finished mimeographing Eisenhower's statement and rushed it to the press corps. As McCarthy left Nixon, he commented: "Gotta rush now— I want to be sure I get the news of dumping Matthews to Fulton Lewis in time for him to break it on his broadcast." As it worked out, Eisenhower's statement was reported almost an hour before Lewis went on the air.

Eisenhower's rebuke marked the beginning of McCarthy's rapid decline. In December of 1954 he was censured by the Senate; stripped of his power and reputation, he deteriorated rapidly, becoming a broken and bumbling drunk. In 1957 he died.

Despite McCarthy's fall the Senate, like Nixon, did not repudiate either his beliefs or the unethical and arrogant conduct of his investigations. He was censured for his refusal to appear before a Senate committee which was probing his own finances and for several insulting remarks he had made at another hearing. While he was effectively purged from the circle of power, the more fundamental assumptions of his technique were not widely questioned. And though McCarthy died, his cause survived, particularly in the person of Richard Nixon.

★ VII ★

The Anti-Communist
Crusade Continued

If Joe McCarthy had set back the anticommunist crusade, Vice President Nixon supplied a series of symbolic victories in the closing years of the fifties, by confronting communist mobs in Lima, Peru and Caracas, Venezuela, and finally by facing down Nikita Khrushchev during their "kitchen debate" in Moscow. These events enhanced the Vice President's reputation, and not only among his more rabid followers on the right. A majority of Americans thrilled to the image of Richard Nixon risking death in the streets of Venezuela and then taking on the leader of world communism in Moscow itself. In the weeks following his trip to Russia, the Gallup poll showed a dramatic rise in Nixon's popularity. Having trailed Kennedy regularly in earlier tests, he now equalled and even surpassed the Massachusetts Senator. In November 1959, it was Nixon 53 percent to Kennedy's 47.

In themselves, Nixon's foreign travels were of small import. His primary mission in Latin America was to express support for Argentina's new President, Arturo Frondizi. Ironically, Nixon had so loaded his schedule and was so anxious to have an impact upon the people of Buenos Aires that on the day of Frondizi's inaugural he was delayed as he mingled with the crowds and missed the swearing-in ceremony. The significance of the Moscow trip was undercut by Eisenhower's announcement, made while Nixon was

118

still abroad, that Khrushchev would visit the United States. Eisenhower said flatly that Nixon was "not a part of the diplomatic processes and machinery of this government." In fact, Nixon was not even informed of the negotiations with Khrushchev until the eve of his flight to Moscow.

Despite their minimal impact upon foreign affairs, Nixon's *account* of the two trips in *Six Crises* does bring his character into sharper focus. The contours of his personality stand out in contrast to the environment of Latin America and Soviet Russia.

Nixon captions his chapter on the Latin American trip with another maxim: "The classic crisis is one involving physical danger. What is essential in such situations is not so much 'bravery' in the face of danger as the ability to think 'selflessly'—to blank out any thought of personal fear by concentrating completely on how to meet the danger." Note that the central subject of Nixon's narrative is, from the beginning, himself. His trip waxes significant for him as one more in a series of tests of his character: the "lessons" he learns are largely personal—how to face a crisis, control his temper, react to a mob. His list of policy recommendations at the end of the chapter seem perfunctory at best. They stem from the conclusion that his experience in Caracas and Lima should stand "as a warning that we could no longer get by with fancy words and little action in dealing with the problems of our neighbors to the south." One wonders how many career diplomats were urging anything else at the time. Yet Nixon dutifully records his platitudes as though they were revelations. "American government personnel abroad must do a more effective job of reaching the opinion makers of Latin America." "There must be a new program for economic progress for the hemisphere." "Above all, there must be a better recognition in the United States at all levels that it isn't how much aid we provide, but how we provide it that counts." When Nixon expressed these opinions in public shortly after his return to the United States, Secretary of State Dulles commented lifelessly,

"I do not believe there is anything basically different that we can do."

But Nixon portrays his trip as though it were a seminal event in his own life as well as a critical moment in the cold war. From the outset he scheduled himself aggressively, attempting to contact as many people and cover as many countries as humanly possible. Typically he would make four formal speeches every day and visit with leaders of government, industry, labor, the press, and the church. "I had convinced the career men in the State Department that I should use such visits not only to talk to government leaders but also to meet the opinion makers and people of all walks of life." He would get up at five or six in the morning for breakfast and consultation with his staff. His appointments began at nine. There were rounds of breakfasts, lunches, afternoon teas, barbecues, formal dinners, dances; trips to factories, monuments, national shrines; confidential talks with public officials, diplomats; and always the unscheduled dash into the crowds for handshaking and a quick exchange, through an interpreter, with "the people." Then back to his limousine to speed off to the next appointment. Throughout the trip Nixon was supplied with ball-point pens inscribed with his name along with autographed cards which he could hand out generously wherever he went. His aides collected lists of names and addresses of people who would receive a personalized letter from the office of the Vice President. William Costello catches the spirit of Nixon's itinerant diplomacy.

Relying for guidance on the folkways of a small-town Quaker background, Nixon set out to find the grass roots of the world. He adopted uncritically the premise that by an energetic show of friendliness he could be accepted anywhere as a working symbol of the brotherhood of man. . . . With the characteristic egocentricity of the Western man, and with a somewhat missionary fervor he persisted despite all protests in practicing his private brand of egalitarianism . . . In his own picture of himself he was the iconoclast, the innovator, projecting a new and necessarily better set of values.

Still, Nixon was not unaware that the Latin Americans might find his effervescence unconvincing. He knew that there were serious causes for anti-American sentiment in Peru. A recession in the United States was at the time dampening the already precarious Peruvian economy. The price of copper, Peru's chief mineral export, had plummeted from 46 to 25 cents. Prices of lead and zinc were also declining, and even more serious repercussions would have been felt if the U.S. Congress had passed the more stringent import quotas then under debate. This country's policy of artificially supporting the domestic price of cotton, then dumping our "surplus" into the world market was particularly damaging to Peru. In this context, handing out a few ball-point pens could easily be interpreted as a cynical attempt to avoid the dark actualities of imperialism. Communists were not alone in their resentment of the U.S. colossus.

Following his most basic instinct, Nixon would "answer" the anti-American sentiment by moving to the offense, Chotiner-style. He attacked the communists for their "persistent and shamefully false propaganda"; he tried to outflank criticism of U.S. foreign policy by fingering communism as an even more serious threat. If the communists staged their demonstrations along the way, he would single-handedly face down the crowds, condemning their anger, their immaturity, their cowardice.

The first confrontation took place at San Marcos University in Lima, where a crowd of two thousand prevented him from making a scheduled speech. Knowing in advance that the demonstration would take place, Nixon could have cancelled his engagement. Warnings of planned violence reached him as he deliberated whether to go ahead according to schedule. He sat stoically in the

121

American Embassy with his top advisers, "discussing how to cope with a potential mob riot" the next day, while in the adjoining great hall a gala reception was being held for the elite of Lima. "We could hear the laughter and the tinkle of champagne glasses as we sat discussing the deadly serious question of what we should do the next day." Nixon's cynicism toward the Latin American aristocracy matches his hatred of the communist mob. See them wining, see them dining, he seems to say—when will they ever learn?

As it turned out, all of Nixon's advisers recommended that he cancel his appearance at San Marcos. But they warned that if he did fail to appear, the communists could claim a propaganda victory: "The communists will boast throughout Peru and all Latin America for weeks and months that the students of one of the oldest and greatest universities in the Western Hemisphere so disliked the United States that they refused to allow the Vice President of the United States to visit their campus and that he was afraid to go there because of the reception they had planned for him." In this long sentence, the one word that caught Nixon's attention was "afraid." He would not be bullied; the stakes were too high. "It would not be simply a case of Nixon being bluffed out by a group of students, but of the United States itself putting its tail between its legs and running away from a bunch of communist thugs." This sentence typifies Nixon's account of his Latin American crisis. On the one hand he personifies the conflict by concentrating on his own feelings and anxieties; on the other, he vests the situation with historic significance. Eisenhower had once faced a similar crisis, Nixon tells us: "He had . . . gone through hours and days of mental and physical tension before making the final decision for the time and place of the embarkation for the Normandy landing." And of himself, " I gave little thought to the possibility of personal injury to myself not because I was 'being brave' but because such considerations were not important in view of the issues. . . ." Yet while we are led at once into the private realm of his feelings and sense of participation in vast abstractions, he leaves the reader without serious analysis of the social and political factors that fed anti-American sentiment in Latin America.

At the last minute the Vice President decided to go to San Marcos. The demonstrators had been driven into an emotional frenzy, Nixon reports, making an unruly and dangerous mob. But: "I got out of the car and walked directly toward the crowd. There were more than two thousand of them against three of us; yet those in front backed away." Then, speaking in his Voice of America idiom: "I would like to talk to you. If you have complaints against the United States, tell me what they are, and I shall try to answer them. This is the free way, the democratic way to discuss the differences we have." But the crowd was not swayed; the cynical "communist operatives" urged them on, and the stones began to fly. Nixon ordered a strategic retreat: "As we got into the car, the rocks were flying around us, but I could not resist the temptation to get in one other good lick. I stood up . . . I shouted . . . 'You are cowards, you are afraid of the truth! You are the worst kind of cowards.' I felt the excitement of battle as I spoke but I had full control of my temper as I lashed out at the mob." *He* wasn't frenzied or wild; his was a calculated anger. "I was hopeful that people all over Latin America would see the lesson of what had happened—the Communists had had to stoop to violence to prevent a free discussion of ideas." He was apparently willing to risk his life to win his own "propaganda victory," provoking an already angry crowd in order to demonstrate his lesson on international communism.

As he returned presently to his hotel, he was confronted by another mob. "Just as I reached the hotel door, I came face to face with a man I later learned was one of the most notorious communist agitators in Lima. I saw before me a weird-looking character whose bulging eyes seemed to merge with his mouth and nose in one distorted blob. He let fly a wad of spit which caught me full in the face. . . . I felt an almost uncontrollable urge to tear the face

123

in front of me to pieces." Nixon depicts the communists in such ugly and distorted form that the reader almost forgets that there are genuine reasons for the fury of the mob—unemployment, economic recession, hunger—all aggravated by the import-export quotas of the United States Congress. Nixon draws us into his personal crisis —"I went through in that instant a terrible test of temper control." Neatly avoiding any discussion of the issues raised by the demonstrators, or any efforts to explore the important dilemmas of American foreign policy, he perversely uses the incident as further confirmation that the American way is superior.

As soon as he reached the safety of his room, one of his aides approached him.

"Sir, could I say something personal?. . . . Sir, I have never been so proud to be an American as I was today. I am honored to be serving under you."

"In my fourteen years of public life," writes Nixon, "I had never been so moved as by this remark, coming as it did from a Purple Heart jet fighter pilot of the Korean war."

Later Nixon held a press conference and lectured his Peruvian audience on how to deal with the Red peril: "I tried to spell out the true nature of the communist conspiracy and the danger that even a few communist agitators present to a free institution. My most telling point was that at San Marcos University probably no more than 200 trained agitators had led a demonstration of 2,000 students which had brought disgrace upon the whole of Peru. . . . When one of them spit in my face, he was spitting on the good name of Peru, he was spitting on the reputation of San Marcos, one of Latin America's greatest universities, and he was spitting on the memory of San Martín and all the men who through the ages have fought and died for freedom of expression." Nixon had successfully transferred public attention from the problems of U.S.–Latin American relations to the act of a handful of communist demonstrators. And now he held up their action as characteristic

124

of communism itself: "The mob violence at San Marcos had unmasked the ugly face of communism as it really was."

That evening Nixon heard that two career diplomats in his party had questioned the impact of his behavior. Roy Rubottom, Assistant Secretary of State for Latin American Affairs, and Maurice Bernbaum, Director of South American Affairs, had expressed concern that the San Marcos confrontation might have embarrassed the Peruvian Government. When Nixon heard that, "I blew my stack." He ordered the two foreign service officers into his room immediately. When his assistant returned with the message that they were dressing for dinner, he ordered them to appear as they were. "A few minutes later the two men appeared before me, half dressed. I ripped into them." Nixon told them that "no loyal staff member" would question a decision of his superior. . . . "Then I proceeded to deliver a tough lecture on some of my attitudes toward foreign service people in general."

Nixon's behavior before the two foreign service officers illustrates one of his most revealing weaknesses. When he is pressured or fatigued he becomes increasingly moralistic, preaching at those around him with righteous indignation. Under pressure, his moral judgments are often simplistic, yet once he has taken a stand on principle he is extremely reluctant to admit that his perceptions may have been faulty. His account of his explosion was written thirteen years after the fact, yet he insists: "What I said in the heat of anger, I still believe to be basically true."

The Vice President's next confrontation took place in Venezuela. Before his arrival in Caracas he had been warned that there would be still more serious trouble. "The Central Intelligence Agency advises the Secret Service in Washington that information has been received relating to rumors of a plot to assassinate the VP in Venezuela." The message had come from the U.S. Chief of Secret Service, and there had been other reports of demonstrations, plots against his life, potential violence. Yet, wrote Nixon, "My decision to go to Caracas as scheduled was not an act of 'bravery.' . . . It was far more significant to me that the State Department considered Venezuela potentially the most important stop of the entire South American tour." He liturgically disavows his courage, then proceeds to describe exactly how brave he was. When he places his "bravery" in quotations, he unconsciously discloses a fundamental confusion in his own self-image. As Nixon describes his behavior, he unflinchingly devotes himself to the purposes of his country, committing himself passionately to the anticommunist cause. Having so thoroughly identified himself with such a cosmic undertaking, his personal interests shrink to insignificance. Therefore he humbly backs down from the claim to "bravery."

Yet he is simultaneously preoccupied with the intricacies of his crisis. And if we judge his behavior in Latin America by his own standards, he clearly does fulfill every criterion for courage. (What he records in his own words is just the conclusion offered by his Purple Heart jet fighter pilot from Korea.)

The fact is, Nixon is caught in a bind familiar to any public figure who sets out to write an autobiography. He is torn between the desire to present a humble public face and still display his most outstanding accomplishments. He tries at once to sell himself and to preserve his credibility by speaking in an objective tone. What leaps to view in Nixon's writing is his awkward handling of this very delicate problem. His maneuvers are transparent, and the reader senses that he is *trying* very hard to have the proper impact. One continually wonders in reading Nixon—and in watching him over a period of years—whether this lack of grace betrays a central weakness in his character. Perhaps what *Six Crises* truly discloses is not so much his difficulty in knowing how to represent himself to the public as it is a more fundamental crisis of identity. And possibly the "real Nixon" is not to be found in some private sanctuary of his subconscious, but rather in the accidental markings of the public record. If this guess is correct, *Six Crises* may be one of the more re-vealing self-portraits drawn by a politician while still in power. By his awkward style, Nixon lays bare internal contradictions and com-plexities that most public figures keep to themselves. Though he intended his book to be a summing up of lessons he had learned from the most critical moments of his past, it actually demon-strates the continuing dialectic of his character.

In Venezuela, as in Peru, there were deep-rooted causes for anti-American feeling. The recently deposed dictator Perez Jimenez and his chief of secret police, Pedro Estrada, were living in luxurious sanctuary in Miami. A year before Nixon's visit President Eisen-hower had imposed a "voluntary" restriction on U.S. oil imports from Venezuela. The recession of 1957 was felt in Caracas, just as it had been felt in Lima. Given his advance warning and the latest Secret Service bulletins, Nixon was not surprised, when he emerged from his plane at the Caracas airport, to see a crowd of several hundred shouting demonstrators. "I was very surprised in one re-spect," said Nixon. "I expected placards, but I was surprised that they allowed the airport to be completely dominated by the Com-mies and their stooges."

Nixon describes the crowd and their noxious behavior in a tone of moral indignation. As they stood at attention near the terminal building, listening to the Venezuelan National Anthem, Nixon wrote: "I had my first experience as a target of spit in Lima. But this was a real baptism. Not just one but hundreds of people were there on the balcony spitting down on us as we stood listening to their national anthem. I saw Pat's red suit, which she had purchased especially for this trip, being splotched, and what made it worse was that some of the spit was dirty brown, coming from a tobacco-chew-ing crowd."

But Pat and Dick do not flinch: "We wanted to show them that we respected their national anthem even if they did not." Again he turns our attention to the details of the personal dilemma, capping his account with an entirely irrelevant indictment of the demonstrators for their supposed lack of respect for the national hymn.

The U.S. Vice President may have had a deep appreciation of the Venezuelan anthem, but his feeling for the Foreign Minister was somewhat less than cordial. When his host tried to wipe the tobacco stains from Nixon's shirt, he replied curtly, "Don't bother, I am going to burn these clothes as soon as I can get out of them." When the Foreign Minister tried to apologize for the behavior of the crowd, Nixon snapped: "If your government doesn't have the guts and good sense to control a mob like the one at the airport, there soon will be no freedom for anyone in Venezuela. . . . Don't you realize that the mob was communist led?. . . . Didn't they shout and spit during the playing of your own national anthem as well as mine?"

The Foreign Minister explained that the communists had helped overthrow Jimenez and that his government was attempting to work out a coalition with the left-wing elements in the country. Such an approach was incomprehensible to Nixon. "I sat back in silence and watched the cars of the mob buzz in and out of our motorcade like a swarm of angry bees. I realized that I had spoken to him rather brutally. But I felt that some shock treatment was necessary for one who was so naïve. . . ." Proof of the Foreign Minister's naïveté appeared soon thereafter in the form of a road block—three rows of buses, trucks, and automobiles had been parked across their lane of travel. As soon as they stopped, a crowd of several hundred descended upon the car, throwing rocks, smashing windows, wrestling with the Secret Service agents, and finally attempting to turn the car over. Nixon was particularly outraged in this instance by what he saw. "It made me almost physically ill to see the fanatical frenzy in the eyes of teenagers—boys and girls who were very little older than my twelve-year-old daughter, Tricia. My reaction was a feeling of absolute hatred for the tough communist agitators who were driving children to this irrational state."

Trapped in the center of the jeering crowd, seeing faces distorted in anger and clubs battering against his windows, fearful that his car would be turned over and burned, Nixon holds up this particular scene as a symbol of communism itself. "I felt as though I had come as close as anyone could get, and still remain alive, to a first-hand demonstration of the ruthlessness, fanaticism, and determination of the enemy we face in the world struggle." But Nixon did escape. His driver saw an opening in the road ahead and simply drove away. Then back to the American Embassy. Nixon instructed his aides to leave their battered car parked conspicuously outside. "Would the Venezuelans be embarrassed?" someone asked. "Leave it where it is," said Nixon. "It's time that they see some graphic evidence of what communism really is."

Reflecting upon his experiences in Latin America, Nixon later concluded that since the demonstrators "had used the same slogans, the same words, the same tactics in every country in South America I had visited . . . [this] was absolute proof that they were directed and controlled by a central communist conspiracy."

When Nixon went to Moscow in 1959, he challenged Khrushchev to justify the Soviet radio broadcasts that were inciting anti-American sentiment during his tour. Nixon raised the point while he and his wife were at lunch with the Khrushchevs, and pointedly drew the women into the debate, asking how the communists could have "approved the use of terrorism against Mrs. Nixon and me in Caracas?" The Soviet Premier affirmed his support of the demonstrators and tried to place their actions in a larger context. "He admitted that the sympathy of the people of the USSR was with the people who had been against me on my trip to South America, but their indignation was not directed against me and Mrs. Nixon personally—only against the 'imperialistic' policies of the United States." Rather than answering Khrushchev's reference to U.S. imperialism, the Vice President struck back. "I asked him what then, if he thought our policies were imperialistic, he would call his policy toward Hungary, Poland, and East Germany." Now Khrushchev evaded the attack by questioning the United States policy in Vietnam regarding the issue of free elections. Then Nixon deftly switched the focus to North Vietnam and the division in Germany. "In effect," wrote Nixon, "he was simply stating the proposition that he was for elections only when he was sure that the communists would win." Khrushchev, in turn, might have countered that U.S. policy seemed to favor free elections only where it was sure the communists would lose.

Khrushchev and Nixon were trading off charge and countercharge as though playing a word game in which victory goes to the most facile mind. In fact, Nixon himself described his relationship with Khrushchev in terms of an athletic contest. Writing about their "kitchen debate" at the American Exhibition in Sokolniki Park, Moscow, Nixon wrote: "I felt like a fighter wearing sixteen-ounce gloves and bound by Marquis of Queensberry rules, up against a bare-knuckle slugger who had gouged, kneed and kicked." Later Nixon switches his metaphor to that of a poker game. Again, "There is no doubt but that Khrushchev would have been a superb poker player; he plans ahead so that he can win the big pots. He likes to bluff, but he knows that if you bluff on small pots and fail consistently to produce the cards, you must expect your opponents to call your bluff on the big pots."

Having come to the capital of world communism, Nixon discovered in himself an affinity for Khrushchev. Though he criticizes the Soviet Premier for his rude manners and vulgarity, Nixon recognizes many of the qualities he most admires: "A picture of Khrushchev, the man, began to form in my mind. Intelligence, a quick-hitting sense of humor, always on the offensive—this was Khrushchev. A man who does his homework, prides himself on knowing as much about his opponent's position as he does his own, particularly effective in debate because of his resourcefulness, his ability to twist and turn, to change the subject when he is forced into a corner or an untenable position."

Unlike the demonstrators in Lima and Caracas, Nixon could not dismiss Khrushchev as a monster. He saw nothing in the Soviet Premier that did not square with his own ideals of leadership. Therefore, rather than faulting the Soviets for their imperfections, he inflates their virtues and challenges his readers to play the communist game and play it better.

Wherever Nixon went in Russia, he found that the communists were miniature Khrushchevs. "There was a steel-like quality, a cold determination, a tough amoral ruthlessness which somehow had been instilled into every one of them." Their goal, of course, Nixon deplores. "They would never be satisfied until they had achieved their ultimate objective of a world completely communist-controlled." Therefore, he argues, Americans must do even better. United States citizens must develop the same instincts for victory, the same unqualified devotion to their cause. "The question was one of determination, of will, of stamina, of willingness to risk all for victory. How did we stack up against the kind of fanatically dedicated men I had seen in the past ten days?" Nixon does not let his rhetorical question speak for itself. He goes on to urge upon the American public a total commitment. "We need all the weapons—military, economic, and ideological—to fight the most complex battle in world history."

Nixon's prescription for victory in this "greatest drama of human history" is precisely his own puritan code. He recommends that the nation transform itself into the selfless, dedicated, tireless fighter that he has been throughout his life. He closes his account of the trip to Russia with a paragraph of anticommunist theology: "History tells us we are on the right side. . . . Man needs God, and communism is atheistic. Man wants to be free, and communism enslaves him. . . ." Nixon argues, in sum, that the war against communism is a total war, a holy war in which the ultimate weapons will be "our spiritual and moral heritage." It is a war that must be fought relentlessly—"One thing I had learned through my years of conflict with communism, going clear back to the Hiss case, is that there is never a period when it is safe to let up in the battle with our communist opponents."

Given these sweeping declarations of war, uttered as they were by a man who has conceived his entire life in the metaphors of battle, it is curiously apt that Richard Nixon, the fighting Quaker, should find himself in 1969 this nation's Commander in Chief at precisely the moment when it became clear that the war could not be prosecuted to victory.

Yet there is a certain justice behind the irony. For when Nixon confronted Khrushchev more than a decade ago, he discovered that the leader of world communism followed the same puritan ethic he had so often recommended to the people of his own country. For Nixon in 1959, communism presented an unparalleled danger precisely because it called upon those same "spiritual resources" —the hard work, discipline, and devotion—that he believed to be the single most important element in the rise of the United States to a position of world power. When Nixon faced Khrushchev for the first time in Moscow, it was with a shock of recognition that he steeled himself for another decade of cold war.

Now, as President Nixon moves to normalize relations with Russia and China, as he reaches out in "a spirit of negotiation" to renew contacts within the communist world, he may again be impressed by the communist leadership. Though there have been dramatic changes in his policies toward the two countries, the communists have a persistent fascination for Richard Nixon, even an affinity which now may draw him into more meaningful negotiations as it once drew him into the throes of the cold war.

Nixon's continuing preoccupation with foreign affairs, his flair for drama and surprise, his desire to act among the great forces of history, may fortify his present feeling that the confrontation between East and West will be met most effectively by reconciliation (in which he plays a primary part) rather than by the endless hostility of a cold war. Within the complexities of his self-image there is room for the Man of Peace. Yet, as we shall see below, his pursuit of peace may have the same mythic proportions as his involvement in the cold war.

★ VIII ★

Martyrdom: Campaign 1960

Richard Nixon has often expressed his faith in the political process: "There is nothing wrong with this country that a good election cannot cure." When we consider his reactions to the malevolent forces that emerged during his first presidential campaign, we may begin to appreciate that his convictions are held with something of a zealot's fidelity even against the facts of his own experience. His account of his 1960 defeat is the most carefully written chapter in *Six Crises*. As it stands, it represents a short autobiography, a summary of his life experience, and for him a deeply personal account of what he calls "the longest, hardest, most intensive campaign in American history." It also tells us a great deal about the role of religion in American politics and Nixon's own faith in the political process.

From the beginning he realized that religion would play a direct part in the campaign; he also knew that this was one issue he could not discuss, even if it were to be the deciding factor. He had seen a memorandum circulated at the 1956 Democratic Convention by Kennedy's staff. Its conclusions, based on election statistics, were that a Catholic candidate on the national ticket "could assure a Democratic victory—not despite but rather because of his religion." The memorandum, which was later printed in the *U.S. News and World Report,* detailed the specific states and cities where a Catholic vote would strengthen the Democrat's hand.

Nixon knew that he could not openly take hold of this issue. He was tied, in part, by awareness of the taboo against discussion of religion. It is one of the profound ironies of American opinion that while the nation's "moral and spiritual heritage" is seen as vital to the very survival of the culture, nevertheless, religion, as such, is absolutely forbidden as a topic of partisan debate. Though belief in God is a *de facto* requirement of presidential candidates, the quality or content of a candidate's belief may not be mentioned. As Nixon wrote: "I, personally, would never raise the question and would not tolerate any use of the religious issue by anyone connected with my campaign, directly or indirectly. I did not believe it to be a legitimate issue. There were several questions as to Kennedy's qualifications for the presidency, but I never at any time considered his religion in this category." During the campaign Nixon qualified this position slightly, adding, "There is only one way I can visualize religion being a legitimate issue in an American political campaign. That would be if one of the candidates for the presidency had no religious belief." A week later he said that the only important criterion was whether a candidate held a "basic belief in God. . . . Since all the candidates recognize and cherish both in their personal and public lives the religious and moral principles which are the very foundation of our American ideals, there is no excuse for continued discussion of a so-called religious issue."

When we set this opinion over against his insistence that at specific moments in the past this nation's Presidents *have* been guided by their religion—that in fact this is the most important lesson to be drawn from American history—the mind boggles at the contradiction. The relevant question it would seem, however, is not whether all candidates agree on a "basic belief in God"; more critical is their sense of how first principles apply to the issues under debate. As we shall see, Nixon very clearly ties his policies on a range of issues to his own form of Quaker faith. Yet he knows that in certain contexts, the mere suggestion of a relationship between religion and government can be suicidal.

Norman Vincent Peale tried to discuss the "religious issue" on Nixon's behalf and found himself overwhelmed by public resentment. On September 7, 1960 he chaired a meeting of Protestant clergy and laity calling itself the National Conference of Citizens for Religious Freedom. A spokesman for this group reported that they had come together because they were "frankly concerned about the political aspects of Roman Catholicism" and hoped to provide "an intelligent approach to the religious issue on a high philosophical level." The level of Dr. Peale's philosophy is indicated by his comments on John Kennedy's candidacy: "It's a good thing to have this crisis forced upon us; it will bring us together, and we've got to stay together. . . . Our American culture is at stake. . . . I don't say it won't survive, but it won't be what it was." As the meeting closed, Dr. Peale commented upon "this wonderful spirit of brotherhood" which he saw reflected in his group (thirty-seven denominations were represented at the meeting).

Dr. Peale later described his colleagues as "more or less representative of the evangelical, conservative Protestants." Yet despite their obvious bias, the group expressed its hope that the religious issue would be discussed "only in a spirit of truth, tolerance, and fairness." More predictably, they concluded: "It is inconceivable that a Roman Catholic President would not be under extreme pressure by the hierarchy of his church to accede to its policies." Moreover, they argued, a Roman Catholic President would be prohibited from attending interfaith meetings and could not represent the wide range of opinions in a pluralistic society; he would "thus be gravely handicapped in offering to the American people and to the world an example of the religious liberty our people cherish."

Public reaction to this pronouncement was so intense that Dr. Peale recanted. He sent the Citizens for Religious Freedom a telegram regretting that he could "not participate in any further activities of the group." He offered his resignation to the officers of the Marble Collegiate Church and issued a statement to the effect: "The

136

people have a right to elect a Catholic, a Jew, a Protestant, or even someone of no religious affiliation as President, and he has a right to serve."

Five days after CRF had made its position public, Richard Nixon repudiated any attempt to raise the religious issue by anyone, especially members of his own staff. He told his "Meet the Press" audience that he had "issued orders to all of the people in my campaign not to discuss religion, not to raise it, not to allow anybody to participate in the campaign who does so on that ground, and as far as I am concerned, I will decline to discuss religion. . . ."

For his part John Kennedy was equally emphatic, equally certain that religion could have no legitimate bearing on the campaign. On September 12 in Texas, he addressed a meeting of the Greater Houston Ministerial Association and promised: "Whatever issue may come before me as President, if I should be elected—on birth control, divorce, censorship, gambling, or any other subject—I will make my decision in accordance with . . . what my conscience tells me to be in the national interest, and without regard to outside religious pressure or dictate. . . . I believe in an America where the separation of church and state is absolute. . . . I believe in a President whose views on religion are his own private affair. . . ."

Paradoxically, both Kennedy and Nixon had been forced by public demand to take positions as artificial as that of Dr. Peale and his associates. In fact, their insistence that religion should have absolutely no effect upon the campaign or their policies as President makes Peale's assumptions respectable by comparison. When John Kennedy said that he would make all his decisions in accord with what "my conscience tells me" and without regard to "religious pressure or dictate," he submerged the fundamental question as to whether his religion had any bearing upon "his conscience" at all. In order to appear unbiased, both Kennedy and Nixon were willing to say, in effect, that religion is an entirely irrelevant matter, having no significant influence upon their decisions. Given this blanket

137

denial that religion has any social import, one must ask what does contribute to the formation of a politician's conscience.

The taboo against a discussion of religion imposes a severe limitation upon American political discourse. Since so many of the decisions a President makes do have moral and theological implications, it is crucial that the public should be alert to this dimension of the decision-making process. Whether or not a President consciously follows the dictates of a particular church, his root assumptions, feelings, and beliefs obviously play a central role in his conduct of the office. If his root values are not the product of religious training, they still mirror his own background, environment, and culture. And it is precisely these guiding values and beliefs which are the proper subject of theological inquiry.

While the blackout on religious discussion means that an essential element of the political process is simply not open to examination, religion continues to play a decisive part in politics. The 1960 campaign offers a classic example of the irrationality and irony involved in the silence on religion. While the candidates reiterated their opinion that religion should have no influence upon the campaign—while their statements were being written and rewritten, released, and distributed to the media for prominent coverage—underground the "religious issue" was being blown up into what would become the most difficult and complex topic of the campaign. Although the public demanded silence from its leaders, a plethora of religious and quasi-religious groups were churning out pamphlets, fliers, books, sermons, and public pronouncements about the religious implications of the campaign. Collected later by the Fair Campaign Practices Committee, this literature indicates that the public consumed ton after ton of the most flamboyant and provocative material.

At the same time, the candidates were not unaware of the depth and power of the emotions involved. Both Nixon and Kennedy had ethnic specialists assigned to check the pulse of the country's racial and religious groups. By 1960 the art of market research had been polished to a degree where each candidate could count the religious vital statistics down to the precinct level. And as Richard Nixon's specialists looked at the map—and the strategy of the Kennedy campaign—they noticed that the public disavowal of the religious issue was not matched by the tactics employed. Nixon's experts told him that Kennedy's Houston speech "was recorded in video tape, and it was being played and replayed across the country—but, according to our reports, far more in northern cities, where it might be expected to appeal to Catholic voters, than in the south and midwest, where one would expect the heaviest anti-Catholic or simply non-Catholic population." Moreover, his advisers had accumulated a file of "scare" headlines from papers in all parts of the country which they felt had been generated intentionally by Kennedy associates to portray their candidate as the innocent victim of religious bigotry. In *Six Crises* Nixon included a selection of these headlines, printed in bold caps.

DEMOCRATS HIT BACK ON RELIGION (New York
  Times)
JACK'S BROTHER SAYS RELIGION TOP ISSUE
  (Columbia, S.C., *State*)
RELIGIOUS ISSUE STRESSED AT KENNEDY
  CONFERENCE (Nashville *Banner*)
JOHNSON BLASTS "HATERS" ATTACKS ON
  CATHOLICS (Washington *Post*)
MRS. FDR HITS RELIGIOUS BIAS IN TALK TO
  NEGROES (Baltimore *Sun*)
UAW PAMPHLET LIKENS KENNEDY FOES TO
  BIGOTS (Washington *Star*)

Nixon also provides his readers with a full page of quotations from prominent Democrats as proof that they were attempting to bend the religious issue in their candidate's favor. "So it went, at every possible juncture and on every possible occasion, Kennedy's key associates were pushing the religious issue, seeing to it that it stayed squarely in the center of the campaign, and even accusing me of deliberate religious bigotry. They were, in short, contributing all they could to make religion an issue while piously insisting that to do so was evidence of bigotry. And they were using it where it would do them the most good. It was, for Kennedy, a 'heads I win, tails you lose' proposition."

Few commentators have taken note of the emphasis which Nixon puts upon this point, or the feeling of helplessness he expresses in not being able to counter the Kennedy sacrilege. In his book Nixon substantiates his ecumenical credentials by listing the Roman Catholic members of his staff. "My aide, Don Hughes, my personal secretary, Rose Mary Woods, my receptionist, Betty McVey, three of my top secretaries . . . there were probably more Catholics on my payroll than there were in Jack Kennedy's office, right across the hall from us." Nixon also enumerates his good relations with "top members of the Catholic hierarchy in the United States" and reminds us of his favorable reputation in the Catholic community. Though his tone is unctuous, his point is justified by the record. As a Senator, as Vice President, and now as President, Richard Nixon has repeatedly demonstrated his warm feelings for Catholics, and at critical points in his career has found their cooperation of immeasurable value.

To carry the import of this close relationship across to the reader of *Six Crises,* he insists, "It was the Catholics on my own staff and among top officials of the Adminstration who were now most outraged at the tactics used by some Kennedy supporters." Nixon reports that many of these people urged him to denounce publicly what they called "reverse bigotry" in the Kennedy camp. "As they well pointed out, I was getting it from both ends: Republican Catholics were being urged to vote for Kennedy because he was of their religion; and Republican Protestants were being urged to vote for him to prove that they were not biased against Catholics!"

When Billy Graham told Nixon that he had written an article for *Life* magazine lavishly endorsing his candidacy, Nixon had to veto its publication. . . . "Even though he was basing his support on other than religious grounds, our opponents would seize on his endorsement as evidence of religious bigotry." What Nixon does not admit is that Graham's feeling for him *is* enhanced by a shared evangelical faith. They both believe that their own version of Christianity could purge the nation of its sins, and in this sense an endorsement by Graham would reflect a profound bias. Moreover, Nixon does not mention the actual exploitation of anti-Catholic sentiment by some of his allies. The literature amassed by the Fair Campaign Practices Committee documents an appeal to prejudice by disciples of Kennedy and Nixon alike. Nor was Nixon guided in his silence by the dictates of pure principle. As Dr. Peale's misfortune clearly established, there were votes to be lost by the mere suggestion of bigotry.

And still Nixon hedged on the Graham endorsement. He invited the evangelist to give an invocation at his rally in Columbia, South Carolina, where he knew the subtlety of such a gesture would not be lost on a strongly Protestant audience. In many sections of the country, particularly in the South and West, this widely advertised appearance represented an endorsement of Nixon by the unofficial head of the Protestant right. (In fact, Protestant Democrats defected to Nixon more heavily in the South, particularly in those areas where church attendance is most regular.)

As the campaign progressed, Nixon and his associates grew increasingly frustrated by the obligation to silence on the issue of religion. On November 2, at the Waldorf Hotel in New York City, Nixon met with his top advisers in a last-minute attempt to counter the Kennedy tactic. Despite Nixon's public insistence that he would not discuss religion under any circumstances, his associates were now unanimous that he should speak out. But he vetoed the suggestion, presenting himself as the champion of ecumenical understanding: "I reasoned that if I made a speech late in the campaign on the religious issue and then won the election, it would inevitably be charged that my victory was the result of my having deliberately injected the issue into the waning days of the campaign. The cause of religious tolerance, which had advanced slowly and painfully for so many years, would be substantially set back."

So, according to his own report, Nixon chose to lose the election rather than venture even a moderate statement of his convictions. After the election, when it became apparent that religion had hurt him severely, he placed the blame directly upon John Kennedy and his entourage for cynically appealing to the basest emotions of Protestant guilt and Catholic pride.

This sense of fighting a just cause against a cynical foe pervades Nixon's account of the entire campaign. In addition to the Machiavellian tactics of the opposition, he saw an element of fate in his 1968 defeat. He portrays himself as once more the innocent victim of malevolent forces which conspire to bring him low despite his own best efforts to the contrary.

On August 29, after a triumphant tour of the Deep South, Nixon was informed by his doctor that a minor injury to his knee had become infected. He was hospitalized immediately. Bedridden during the first critical weeks of the campaign, he philosophizes during his confinement. "I found, too, that illness has its compensations. Thousands of letters and get-well cards poured into my office and into the hospital. One, from a twelve-year-old girl in Baltimore, provided probably the best lesson of all: 'God sometimes makes us lie down,' she wrote, 'so that we will look up more.' "

As soon as he was released from the hospital he pressed his staff to speed up his schedule, ignoring the advice of doctors to ease back into pace. Baltimore, Indianapolis, Dallas, San Francisco, Portland, Vancouver, Boise, Peoria, St. Louis—he drove himself

without mercy. On the eve of his speech to the International Asso-
cation of Machinists in St. Louis, he struck a note of optimism:
"I looked back over the first three days of the week with considerable satisfaction. The crowds had consistently exceeded our expectations, and the campaign was rolling along with good momentum."
Nixon pictured it as having a powerful impact upon the people.
Kennedy, the press, and fate might conspire against him, but the
people were in his fold. Yet even as he finished his notes for the
Machinists' speech the next morning, his body was near collapse.
Beset by chills and a fever of 103°, he still would not cancel his
speech. He persuaded his doctor to reduce his temperature with
medication and he forced himself to face his audience: "I don't
know when I have ever felt so weak before walking out onto a
public platform, but I was determined to let no one know my condition. I then proceeded to make what some of the reporters have
called my best speech of the campaign."

It is one of Nixon's most rooted convictions that he is at his best
under pressure, in the midst of crisis, when his mind and body are
stretched to maximum output. He writes with pride of the break-
neck pace he maintained in 1960: "I wished I could have done even
more than I had done during those last two months of intensive
campaigning . . . a campaign which . . . had exceeded in intensity
any in American history up to that time." But these passages are
punctuated by a periodic awareness that he was pushing himself
too hard, that his body (and appearance) had suffered from self-
imposed fatigue. "I did not realize how bone-tired I really was until
I opened my eyes about noon on Sunday and found that I could
hardly pull myself out of bed to get on with the mass of preparatory
work that had to be done before we started out on our second
week's swing."

Similarly, when he confronted Kennedy at the first debate, "I
had never felt better mentally before any important appearance
than I did before the first debate. My knee still bothered me a bit,

but when I am keyed up, as I was on this occasion, I do not notice physical pain at all." Then, after the debate: "I stepped on the scales in the bathroom at the Pick-Congress and realized for the first time how much had been taken out of me, physically, by two weeks in a hospital bed followed immediately by two weeks of intensive campaigning. I weighed 160—ten pounds below normal. . . ."

Why does Richard Nixon feel at his best when his body suffers? He apparently draws deep satisfaction from the self-denial, discipline, and extreme exertion of the campaign as he loses himself in his cause. It is a peculiarity of the puritan psyche to feel satisfied by self-inflicted wounds; as we shall see, the mental and physical pain Nixon endures seem to increase his certainty that his cause is just. And it is precisely this moral certitude that steels him for defeat, strengthening his will for the continuing shocks of political combat. His moral conviction may well be the secret of his resilience, even after the repeated disasters of 1960 and 1962.

Yet it is difficult to accept his testimony that he "never felt better mentally before any important appearance than I did before the first debate" and at the same time recall the accounts of how he *looked* at that time. Here is Theodore White's description: "The Vice President, by contrast, was tense, almost frightened, at turns glowering and, occasionally, haggard-looking to the point of sickness. Probably no picture in American politics tells a better story of crisis and episode than that famous shot of the camera on the Vice President as he half slouched, his 'Lazy-Shave' powder faintly streaked with sweat, his eyes exaggerated hollows of blackness, his jaw, jowls, and face drooping with strain. It is impossible to look again at the still photographs of Nixon in his ordeal and to recollect the circumstances without utmost sympathy."

Nixon saw the debates, too, as one more element in the working out of his martyrdom. The rivals met for the first time on Monday, September 26 in Chicago. As usual, his schedule during the days and hours just prior to the TV appearance had been grueling. After five hours of cribbing on the issues, he rode from his hotel to the television studio: "I had crammed my head with the facts and figures in answer to more than a hundred questions which my staff suggested might be raised in the field of domestic affairs. . . . I felt that I was as thoroughly prepared for this appearance as I had ever been in my political life. . . ."

But then at the studio, he saw Kennedy: "This was the first time we had met each other since the Senate had adjourned. I had never seen him look more fit." Here is Nixon, the diligent and disciplined fighter, grinding through the campaign on his relentless will, set back by infection, fatigue, and flu, tensed up by a split-second schedule and his own belief in selfless devotion to a cause. And in walks John Fitzgerald Kennedy of Harvard and Hyannisport, tanned and smiling. Richard Nixon had listed Kennedy's assets as "high intelligence, great energy, and a particularly effective television personality." And one more. "He also had unlimited money." Now here he was: "I remarked on his deep tan, and he jokingly replied that he had gotten it from riding in open cars while touring sunny California." Nixon had driven himself to the point of physical collapse; Kennedy strode in joking about his suntan.

Nixon's arguments were replete with the facts and figures he had crammed into his head during a five-hour blitz; Kennedy raised the sleeping memory of Abraham Lincoln and Franklin Roosevelt to suggest that "this generation of Americans has a rendezvous with destiny."

Said Nixon in reply: "I subscribe completely to the spirit that Senator Kennedy has expressed tonight, the spirit that the United States should move ahead. Where, then, do we disagree? . . . Our disagreement is not about the goals for America but only about the means to reach those goals."

"I realized," wrote Nixon long after the debate, "that I had heard a very shrewd, carefully calculated appeal, with subtle emotional overtones that would have great impact on a television audi-

ence. And particularly it would impress unsophisticated voters."
The author of the Checkers speech had reason to be concerned
about Kennedy's eloquence. Though his account of the debate was
written a full two years after the event, Nixon's writing still mani-
fests the confusion of a man taken completely by surprise. He cannot decide between stubbornly holding to his own tactics or adopting
those of the enemy. Kennedy's charisma he denounces as immoral.
"Looking back, I suppose the politically expedient course would
have been for me to grant without argument that we had been
standing still for the past eight years and then promise, if I were
elected, to do everything he had promised, and more besides. But
I rejected this demagogic approach. . . ." That strategy would have
been both stupid and suicidal, as Nixon well knew. Yet he is so
accustomed to his own role as crusader, so ready to believe that
his opponent is lacking in the last traces of conscience, that he
depicts himself as having to weigh the comparative merits of the
sublime and the ridiculous. Reviewing the essential issues of the
debate, he writes, "In our closing statements, both Kennedy and I
returned to the basic positions we had taken at the outset, I to the
need for sound and stable progress with an emphasis on free choice
and private initiative, and Kennedy to a demand that we simply
"get moving." In short, Kennedy is all charisma and no substance.

Yet illogically Nixon also admits "the basic mistake I had made.
I had concentrated too much on substance and not enough on
appearance." He vows to concentrate in the next debates, not so
much on the content of his arguments as on his image. He will devour vanilla milkshakes, hire new technicians, use better make-up.
He resolves, in short, to boost his image in a similar appeal to the
"unsophisticated voters." While privately taking steps to counter
Kennedy's physical advantage, he publicly escalated his attack upon
the dishonesty of the Kennedy techniques. It was in the fourth
debate that Nixon saw the most blatant example of his opponent's
duplicity.

On October 20 Kennedy had advocated that the United States intervene in Cuba "to strengthen the non-Batista democratic anti-Castro forces in exile, and in Cuba itself, who offer eventual hope of overthrowing Castro." As Vice President, Nixon knew that Eisenhower had already initiated a program of arming and training Cuban exiles for an invasion of the island. Nixon also believed that Kennedy was aware of this operation—that he had been briefed on Cuba by CIA representatives as early as July. "Kennedy was now publicly advocating what was already the policy of the American Government—covertly—and Kennedy had been so informed. . . . I thought that Kennedy, with full knowledge of the facts, was jeopardizing the security of a United States foreign policy operation. And my rage was even greater because I could do nothing about it."

What Nixon decided to do was construct an elaborate argument against intervention, to insist, against his own beliefs, that the United States should not interfere with Cuba's internal affairs. "I must attack the Kennedy proposal to provide such aid as wrong and irresponsible because it would violate our treaty commitments." Nixon, in fact, constructed a powerful statement against the policy which he had privately advocated in the chambers of the National Security Council. "I think that Senator Kennedy's policies and recommendations for the handling of the Castro regime are probably the most dangerously irresponsible recommendations that he's made during the course of this campaign." He based his position on clearly binding treaties forbidding U.S. intervention in Latin American affairs and warned that an invasion of Cuba would lead to a confrontation with Russia. In fact, his real opinions were diametrically opposed to these manufactured arguments. After the Bay of Pigs invasion, President Kennedy called Nixon in for consultation on what he should do. In that conference Nixon neatly dismissed the treaty obligations, arguing boldly, "I would find a proper legal cover, and I would go in." As to the moral question, he would simply offer "a new definition of aggression."

147

This incident appears all the more significant because it under-scores the sense of righteous indignation that characterizes Nixon's account of the entire campaign. Again he is confronted by morally reprehensible conduct on Kennedy's part, again "my rage was greater because I could do nothing about it."

After the publication of *Six Crises* in 1962, President Kennedy's press secretary issued an official denial from the White House that the CIA briefing had included information about the Cuban opera-tion. In subsequent editions of his book, Nixon reiterates that he had checked his information initially and reconfirmed it after the White House statements. Yes, Kennedy was "fully briefed on our foreign problems." Beyond this, he concludes, "My book speaks for itself."

What the book illustrates is that the public could choose to be-lieve whomever it wished to believe. In the meantime Nixon con-tinued in the opinion that Kennedy had based his campaign upon issues which were fundamentally fraudulent; whether actual fabri-cation or lies were involved is a moot point. In Nixon's view Ken-nedy's strategy and message were immoral at the core, and Nixon saw himself as confined by principle and by circumstances beyond his control.

Nixon also claimed foul play in Kennedy's approach to civil rights. As most observers have noted, the Democrat captured the initiative by sending a telegram to Mrs. Martin Luther King, Jr. after her husband had been arrested in Atlanta for sitting-in at the Magnolia Room restaurant. That simple expression of concern—together with a telephone call from Bobby Kennedy to the judge who had sentenced him—seemed to be instrumental in gaining King a speedy release from prison. Harris Wofford, a Notre Dame law professor who directed the civil rights section of the Kennedy campaign, printed up a million pamphlets describing this incident. The pamphlets were distributed one Sunday morning outside churches in the black community of Chicago and elsewhere across the country. Said The Rev. Martin Luther King, Sr., "Because this man was willing to wipe the tears from my daughter's eyes, I've got a suitcase of votes, and I'm going to take them to Mr. Kennedy and dump them in his lap."

Nixon applied a lawyer's ethic to Robert Kennedy's action, criticizing him for discussing the case with the judge. John Kennedy's letter he dismissed as a typical "grandstand" ploy. Again Richard Nixon was indignant: "The ironic part of the whole incident is that well-informed Washington observers knew that I had been one of the most consistent and effective proponents of civil rights legislation in the Administration." He leaves us then with the impression that his own convictions on civil rights are unimpeachable and that Kennedy's popularity is based exclusively upon a deft public relations maneuver.

Nixon describes his last week before the election as one of mounting public enthusiasm, again suggesting that he still believed, despite the evidence, that the people were with him.

A cheering crowd of 30,000 crammed every inch of the space that had been roped off for our meeting [in Columbia, South Carolina]. . . . This tremendous turnout had shifted the tide in our direction [Houston, Texas]. . . . It was the same story the next day when record crowds cheered us along the way in Fort Worth; Cheyenne, Wyoming; Spokane, Washington; and Fresno, California. . . . We knew our campaign was going well in my home state when the next day not even a dose of California's "unusual weather"—in the form of drenching rains— dampened the size or the enthusiasm of turnouts in San Jose, Hayward, Oakland, and Van Nuys. . . . Some of the reporters traveling with us, who had been conceding California to Kennedy, began to hedge their predictions.

Nixon caps his narrative by reminding the reader of his ultimate purpose. "I returned to the theme of my acceptance speech at Chi-

149

cago. I did this deliberately, to complete the circle of three months' effort. I restated the one great and overriding issue of the campaign: How to keep peace without surrender of territory or principle, and how to preserve and extend freedom everywhere in the world. This, I said, was the supreme challenge to our national purpose and our leadership. And *the key was to be found in the moral and spiritual strength of a free people* [emphasis mine]. . . ." And then, as he had begun his campaign with a prayer, he closed with an invocation of divine assistance: "And my prayer and my hope . . . is very simply this: that the next President of this country . . . will be a worthy successor of Dwight D. Eisenhower and that he will be worthy of the high ideals and the great purpose of the American people."

Nixon's summarizing remarks occupy sixty pages in the last chapter of his book and constitute his most revealing self-portrait. As he withdraws from the campaign, his narrative shifts from the panorama of national politics to the personal reactions of his friends and family. In his conversations with his most intimate companions we find clues to his private feelings. On the flight to California, back home for election day, Nixon turns our attention toward his family: "I had planned to sleep on the flight from Chicago to Los Angeles. Tricia and Julie, who had joined Pat and me for the last day of campaigning, dropped off almost at once on bunks that we had made up for them. . . . My thoughts now turned primarily to those who had given so much of themselves for our cause." First, there was Pat. "She had been at my side in all the years of campaigning. She had never once lost her dignity or her poise in the face of even the greatest provocation. She had to go through the indignity of being spit on in Caracas [by a communist inspired mob] and splattered with rotten eggs in Mukegon, Michigan [by Democratic opponents at home]." Here, in parallel, is the image of his wife facing the cruel opposition of communist and Democrat alike, always acting with utmost dignity and grace. Then there were his "top campaign associates," his personal secretary, Rose Mary Woods, other secretaries, advisers, party workers, the "dedicated Volunteers for Nixon Lodge," "the gifted Voices for Nixon," and "the Nixonettes —1500 of these teen-agers had provided us with a guard of honor at our airport reception in Burbank."

From here on his personal reflections are spaced by reports of election returns. As the tally was added, Nixon reminds us, Kennedy's lead narrowed. It grew smaller with each hour; it was trimmed even more the next day. Weeks go by and still the question lingers: Who really won? At nine o'clock Eastern time on election night the major networks began predicting a Kennedy victory, but Nixon writes: "What was particularly significant was this: while Kennedy led in the popular vote as well as the electoral vote, his popular margin was not increasing."

Yet Nixon knew that Kennedy's lead in the electoral college would be nearly impossible to surmount, and therefore decided to prepare himself—and his children—for defeat: "Tricia greeted me with, 'Hi Daddy, how is the election coming?' For a fleeting moment I didn't have the heart to tell them what I had concluded from the trend of the returns. But then I knew I could no longer put off preparing them for the bad news that was to come. I replied, almost too bluntly, 'I'm afraid we have lost, honey.' Tricia, who had been smiling bravely up to this point began to cry uncontrollably. She said through her tears: 'I'm not crying because of myself but for you and Mommy. You have worked so hard and so long.' "

The consistency of Nixon's reactions—and those of his family— is telling. Everyone is noble in defeat, proud of their effort, their work, even their suffering. And yet always there is the suspicion— that an injustice has been done.

As Nixon prepared to go downstairs to his campaign headquarters to issue his first statement—not exactly a concession, but a gracious gesture toward his opponent—"Bob Finch rushed in to tell me that the popular vote margin was now less than a million— less than 900,000 in fact—and growing smaller. . . ." And then his statement: "My deep thanks to all of you who are here. . . . My congratulations to Senator Kennedy for his fine race in this campaign." (Just a few pages earlier he has described in detail his reasons for thinking the Kennedy strategy pernicious and cynical.)

After his public statement, "Kennedy's popular vote margin kept on shrinking: it was now only 800,000 out of 54 million votes recorded. . . . At four, Kennedy's popular vote margin was down to 600,000." Nixon went to bed with the thought that "someone might awaken me with a report that the miracle had come to pass—that we had turned the tide by winning California, Illinois, and Minnesota." But in the morning Julie woke him, asking for the news, and Nixon told her, barring a miracle: " 'Julie, I'm afraid we have lost.' She started to cry and the questions tumbled out through her tears! 'What are we going to do? Where are we going to live?' " Richard Nixon reassured his daughter that she could be confident "there would be no problems that we could not work out." But then she put forward the deeper, more difficult question, "Daddy, why did people vote against you because of religion?"

"What in the world gave you that idea?" asks the defeated candidate, now searching for an explanation for the injustice he, too, had found so difficult to tolerate. "I tried to explain it to her this way. 'Julie, people do not vote for one man or the other because they happen to be Jews or Catholics—or Protestants, as we are. They vote for a man because they believe in what he stands for. . . .' " He would have his daughter believe in the political process even as he believes, ultimately, that the system is just. But he hides from his children the opinion that had called forth his own indignation: that when people vote, often their choices have been decided by an appeal to ethnic pride, guilt, prejudice, or fear. Nixon conceals these malevolent realities from his daughter, reminding her of their Catholic friends, Father John Cronin, biographers Earl Mazo and Ralph de Toledano. "So, you see, Julie, it isn't a question of a man's religion when he decides to vote for you or against you. It is whether he believes in you and respects you as an individual."

But Julie, it would seem, had learned her lessons well. " 'I think I understand, Daddy. . . . Well, maybe we didn't win the election, but we won the hearts of the people.' I had seen many people in tears the night before as they heard the returns, but for the first time I was confronted with the same problem. I told Julie my hay fever was bothering me as I wiped my eyes with a handkerchief."

And it is not only Julie, Nixon confesses, who questions the justice of the political process. "I have seen many men become bitter after an election defeat when they saw friendships melt away; friendships they thought were personal turned out to be purely political." This is followed by several paragraphs describing the fickle behavior of his own political associates, and then: "Some of my younger and less experienced staff members were bitterly disillusioned by the sudden desertion of some of those we had thought were close and loyal friends, even as the unfavorable returns started coming in." But not Richard Nixon. The scars of 1952 would now serve him well. "Those who reach the top, particularly in the political world, have to develop a certain tough realism as far as friendships and loyalties are concerned." On the surface, then, a protective shell of realism, and beneath, a profound faith that in the final analysis good will prevail.

In the meanwhile, "Kennedy's popular margin had now been pared to less than 500,000." Yet the electoral college still hung decisively in Kennedy's favor—303 to 219. So the concession must finally be made: "I WANT TO REPEAT THROUGH THIS WIRE THE CONGRATULATIONS AND BEST WISHES I EXTENDED TO YOU ON TELEVISION LAST NIGHT. I KNOW THAT YOU WILL HAVE THE UNITED SUPPORT OF ALL AMERICANS AS YOU LEAD THE NATION IN THE CAUSE OF PEACE AND FREEDOM DURING THE NEXT FOUR YEARS."

It is the painful responsibility of a defeated candidate to insure that, in fact, the nation does support the victor, even when he feels that his defeat is not deserved. Nixon's obligation to this task would weigh heavily upon him in 1960, for the doubts would linger, fed by rumors of fraud at the polls. When he told his daughters of his scheduled meeting with Kennedy, they reacted fiercely: " 'How can you possibly talk to him after what he said about you in the campaign?' I replied, 'After all, he won the election, and this is the only proper thing for me to do under the circumstances.' " But Julie still protested: " 'He didn't win. Haven't you heard about all the cheating in Illinois and Texas?' " This time Nixon was *not* ready with a reply. "The popular vote margin had now been whittled down to 113,000. A change of half a vote per precinct, nationwide, would have shifted that margin to me. One enterprising statistically minded commentator even pointed out that if the votes for Alabama's six uncommitted electors were subtracted from Kennedy's total, I would have led in the popular vote count."

As to the charge of fraud, Nixon lists a full page of allegations, "each one sworn to and widely published." Yet, again, as in so many instances throughout the campaign, he cannot act. To challenge the results in a national election would lead to chaos and bitterness throughout the country. "If we could not continue to set a good example in this respect in the United States, I could see that there would be open season for shooting at the validity of free elections throughout the world." Again Nixon envisions himself as having made the heroic choice for the benefit of all mankind and against his own self-interest, thus benevolently sacrificing his last chance for the presidency. On January 13, 1961 Cardinal Cushing of Boston nominated Nixon "good will man of the year." He said: "During the recent campaign which tested and taxed all his powers, physical and mental, he never exploited the religious or any other issue that would tend to divide the American people." Nixon ends his account of the campaign in a rising and affirmative mood, quoting Sophocles: " 'One must wait until the evening to see how splendid the day has been.'. . . For me, the evening of my life has not yet come. But for the boy who, forty years ago, used to lie in bed in Yorba Linda, California, and dream of traveling to far-off places when he heard the train whistle in the night, I can say even now that the day has been splendid."

Having vented his outrage and poured forth his martyrdom, Richard Nixon resolved to forgive the system its errors and plunge back into the arena. For his nerves were tuned to the rigor of combat; he had "drunk too deeply of the stuff which really makes life exciting and worth living to be satisfied with the froth." He would put Tricia to bed with the promise that, in the end, the good would finally win. And she would smile at him and say, "You see—the people still like you."

Though the public remembers a sour Nixon whining to the press after his defeat in 1962, this other image of the man is far truer. Despite his antipathy for certain reporters, he has a deep inclination to affirm the political process and proclaims his faith wherever he goes. One has to remember that the "candid scenes" of the defeated candidate consoling his family were all written for public consumption. When he assures his daughter that, after all, the election was fair, he is playing the archetypical role of national leader: the role of father to a people anxious about their identity. Nixon takes to this responsibility with great conviction, for his self-image is so bound up in the vocation of politics that an attack upon the system is tantamount to an assault upon his own character. If some would question the integrity of the democratic process, Nixon offers himself as a shining example of faith in America.

Yet we are left with the gnawing suspicion that his faith has a fatal flaw. For his reassurances to his daughters and to the nation simply ignore the more troubling implications of his confrontation with Kennedy. Accepting his version of that contest at face value, we are left with little reason to affirm the political process (and Nixon does not even begin to discuss the ethics of his own campaign). As we look deeper into his career, we see still more clearly that his is a "faith" which persists despite the most extraordinary contradictions of reason and common sense.

★ IX ★

A Man of Peace

When Richard Nixon assumed the title and responsibilities of the presidency in January 1969, he realized that his first priority would be to convince the American people that he was, after all, a man of peace. As we have seen, he used his inaugural address to emphasize this concern, speaking in the cadences of a Franciscan prayer. The new President reached out for an appropriate biblical reference, saying, "The peace we seek—the peace we seek to win—is not victory over any other people, but peace that comes with healing in its wings; with compassion for those who have suffered; with understanding for those who have opposed us; with opportunity for all the peoples of this earth. . . ."

These might well be words from a sermon on brotherhood, but ironically the biblical passage which he adapted in his phrase "the peace that comes with healing in its wings" is from the book of Malachi, and the complete passage refers to a peace that results not from "negotiation" but rather from the final victory of the Lord over his enemies. "For behold, the day comes, burning like an oven, when all the arrogant and all evildoers will be stubble; the day that comes shall burn them up, says the Lord of hosts, so that it will leave them neither root nor branch." But upon the true believers, "the sun of righteousness shall rise, with healing in its wings. . . . And you shall tread down the wicked, for they will be ashes under the soles of your feet. . . ."

It was certainly unintentional that, in describing his commitment

157

to peace, Richard Nixon chose one of the most bloodthirsty and militaristic passages in the Bible. His words of peace were drawn from the traditions of the holy war. Yet as we examine his record with respect to the question of war and peace, it is difficult to believe, even after the withdrawal of U.S. ground troops from Vietnam, that Nixon's new image as peacemaker is consistent with his ruling convictions.

Nixon's attitudes toward the war in Indo-China first took form during the McCarthy era and then were honed down during the Korean war. In 1951 President Truman removed General Douglas MacArthur from his command as chief of the United Nations forces in Korea. At once Richard Nixon rallied to the General's defense and urged that MacArthur's policies be initiated. He submitted a resolution to Congress, demanding MacArthur's reinstatement and recommending escalation of the war. Arguing that the conflict could not be resolved through negotiations, he said: "the only way to end the war in Korea is to win it on the battlefield." Nixon supported MacArthur's policy of taking the air war to mainland China. In his view, Asia was a single unit; a communist advance in any country represented a threat to the entire area, even to the world. Any settlement in Korea short of a military victory would lay "the foundation for eventual communist domination of all Asia and in the end an inevitable world war. . . ."

From his first campaign in 1946 through the fall of 1967, for more than twenty years, there was never a hint of doubt from Richard Nixon. He knew that if the United States were to emerge victorious from "the greatest drama in human history," it must be willing to commit itself militarily against communism anywhere in the world. He argued that in a total war the United States could not split hairs, defending only those countries whose system of government it approved. Speaking after a visit to Greece in 1952, he said: "There was no more corrupt or unstable government in the world than the government of Greece. But we recognize that it was not a question of the Greek government or something better, but a question of the Greek government or something worse, and we gave the Greek government the assistance which enabled it to defeat the communists." Having made the prior decision on principle that communism represented the ultimate evil, it then became entirely logical to employ any means, and to support any government, however corrupt, if communism could be stopped.

The point to be noticed here is that Nixon is using a unique criterion with respect to an anticommunist war. He does not argue exclusively from traditional considerations of national security, but also from a moral judgment. Communism is not just a set of ideas which may be faulty, or a coalition of nations that threatens U.S. security. It is simply and savagely evil. And the corollary to this sweeping judgment is that since communism represents such a transcendent evil, ordinary moral restraints do not apply in the inevitable wars that will be fought against it.

Ten years before Lyndon Johnson decided to commit massive numbers of American troops to Vietnam, Nixon commented that he would be willing to send 500,000 if it were necessary to save South Vietnam from a communist take-over. When he mentioned his willingness to deploy ground combat troops to the American Society of Newspaper Editors in April 1954, the reactions to his suggestion were so intense that the White House had to deny that the Vice President was speaking on behalf of the Eisenhower administration. Throughout the early years of escalation in Vietnam, Nixon supported the war policy. In 1964, when major criticism of the war began to surface, Nixon wrote an article for the *Reader's Digest* entitled "Needed in Vietnam: The Will to Win." "What we must do is to instill in ourselves and our allies a determination to win this crucial war—to win it decisively. We must recognize that we are in a life-and-death struggle that has repercussions far beyond Vietnam, and that victory is essential to the survival of freedom. . . . A victory for us in South Vietnam will shatter the myths of com-

159

munist invincibility and of the inevitability of a Chinese take-over in Southeast Asia. It will restore all the prestige we have lost and more besides. . . . All that is needed, in short, is the will to win—and the courage to use our power—*now.*" To those who criticized the morality of the war, Nixon responded by reversing the question. "Has the United States the right—after pledging to support a small nation in its fight for freedom—to negotiate a settlement that would destroy that nation's freedom?" While some argued that Vietnam was not of vital interest to the security of the United States, Nixon reaffirmed his concept of the total war. "Communism isn't changing; it isn't sleeping; it isn't relaxing; it is, as always, plotting, scheming, working, fighting. . . . We must understand that the communist threat is worldwide. . . . I completely reject the idea that there are so-called peripheral areas . . . like Cuba and Vietnam—that are not important."

While the policies of search-and-destroy, saturation bombing, free-fire zones, defoliation, pacification, and resettlement of refugees were being shaped and pursued, Nixon faithfully supported Lyndon Johnson. In March 1966, Johnson called Nixon to the White House to express his appreciation for that support. In April 1967, Nixon went to Vietnam for discussions with Ambassador Henry Cabot Lodge. In a public statement made in Saigon, Nixon prophesied that the chief issue in the 1968 election "will not be how to negotiate defeat but how to bring more pressure to bear for victory."

Nixon could not have been more decisive; his commitment to victory, his call for courage, his resolution to continue the war were unflinching—until October 1967. The political reality of an electorate that did not respond to the call to victory had become overwhelming. At that time he set forth the principles later to be articulated as "the Nixon Doctrine." Though the ideas he presented were quite traditional, it was surprising to hear them from Richard Nixon. Arguing essentially from balance-of-power assumptions, he wrote: "To ensure that a U.S. response will be forthcoming, if needed, machinery must be created that is capable of meeting two conditions: (*a*) a collective effort by the nations of the region to contain the threat by themselves; and, if that effort fails, (*b*) a collective request to the United States for assistance." Nixon talked eloquently of fashioning "the sinews of a Pacific community"; what he had actually to face was the fact that his anticommunist crusade had come to an ignominious end in a paralysis of the American will.

Since the fall of 1967 Nixon has tried to design a new rationale for the war; he has tried to shape a new foreign policy around the lifeless skeleton of his cold-war theology. His speeches present an array of arguments, a dazzling variety of explanations, but at heart there are only the dried bones of his moribund crusade.

The fall of 1969 brought the first waves of demonstrators to Washington. They came by the tens and then hundreds of thousands to protest the war in Vietnam. They came to protest Mr. Nixon's war, for now as the President braced himself for his first full winter in the White House, it was clear that his plans for ending the war, plans that he had guarded so secretly during his presidential campaign, contained no magic formulas for peace. When he went before the nation on November 3, 1969, he would offer only a plea for patience and that ringing bifurcation: "The great question is: How can we win America's peace?"

Here was the nation's veteran cold warrior borrowing his phrases from the doves. "I respect your idealism. I share your concern for peace. I want peace as much as you do. There are powerful personal reasons I want to end this war. . . . I have chosen a plan for peace. I believe it will succeed." Yet for all his passion, his concern, his respect for the idealism of his critics, he could not bring himself to endorse that most terrible of all prospects: a precipitate withdrawal. That would be, he said, the expedient decision. "From a political standpoint, this would have been a popular and easy course to follow." But the President who had never in his life admitted the mere expediency of a major decision could not break his record for self-sacrifice at this juncture. "We became involved in the war while my predecessor was in office [sic]. I could blame the defeat, which would be the result of my action, on him—and come out as the peacemaker. Some put it to me quite bluntly: this was the only way to avoid allowing Johnson's war to become Nixon's war." No, Nixon would not take that demagogic approach; he would not shrink from the heroic decision to continue the fighting. "I had to think of the effect of my decision on the next generation, and on the future of peace and freedom in America, and in the world." Thus far, his apology is classic Nixonese. First he set up the false proposition of a "popular and easy" withdrawal, and then, with a stirring show of conviction, shot it down. "I had a greater obligation than to think only . . . of the next election." From this point on, his reasoning became more difficult to follow. He moved by indirection, scattering his arguments randomly, repeating the same point in different contexts, rephrasing a single assertion to make it look like two, spacing contradictory assumptions to disguise their incompatibility. It was a lengthy, rambling speech, but stripped to its essentials, he was offering two reasons for continuing the war.

First, he argued that the defense of Vietnam was of vital interest to the United States, even to the world. "In my opinion, for us to withdraw . . . would mean a collapse not only of South Vietnam but Southeast Asia. . . . Our defeat and humiliation in South Vietnam without question would promote recklessness in the councils of those great powers who have not yet abandoned their goals of world conquest. This would spark violence wherever our commitments help maintain the peace—in the Middle East, in Berlin, eventually even in the Western Hemisphere. Ultimately, this would cost more lives. It would not bring peace. It would bring more war." Nixon here pushed far beyond the limits of a paltry domino theory. No longer arguing simply that the fall of South Vietnam would facilitate infiltration of neighboring countries, he pictured instead communism leaping across national and regional boundaries, bolting over entire continents, touching off wars instantly and recklessly around the world. He would have his public believe that a communist take-over in Vietnam would be a catalyst shifting the balance of power dangerously to the left throughout the world.

Nixon's second reason for continuing the war rested upon an assessment of the American character. Since this nation had gone into Vietnam committing her honor, her pride, her reputation, and her unbroken string of victories to the South Vietnamese, a defeat would strike a mortal blow to the American ego. "For the United States this first defeat in our nation's history would result in a collapse of confidence in American leadership not only in Asia but throughout the world." And, "Far more dangerous, we would lose confidence in ourselves . . . inevitable remorse and divisive recrimination would scar our spirit as a people." Besides, argued Nixon, the majority were with him. "If a vocal minority, however fervent its cause, prevails over reason and the will of the majority, this nation has no future as a free society. . . . So tonight, to you, the great silent majority of my fellow Americans, I ask for your support."

Minutes earlier he had said that he could not take "the popular and easy course" of withdrawal; he would risk his election in choosing what was right despite popular opposition. Now, at the end of the same speech, he claimed the tacit support of the majority. Nixon wanted his martyrdom and his majority at a single sitting, and to achieve it he appealed to the one streak in the American ethos that had served him so handily in past crises: "Today we have become the strongest and richest nation in the world, and the wheel of destiny has turned so that any hope the world has for the survival of peace and freedom will be determined by whether the American people have the moral stamina and the courage to meet the challenge of free-world leadership." Here was the appeal to morality, the sure-fire key to American consensus, and Nixon pulled out all the stops: "I pledge to you tonight that I shall meet this responsibility with all of the strength and wisdom I can command, in accordance with your hopes, mindful of your concerns, sustained by your prayers."

Yet there was a missing link in the chain of Nixon's cold-war assumptions—and it was a critical omission. He had not called for the one thing that all his arguments would logically require: a military victory. If communism does move inevitably from country to country and continent to continent until it consumes the world; if you believe, as Nixon appears to, that no temporary setback will stop the relentless march; then surely there is only one course that can be followed in good conscience, which is to pursue the war to the finish. Anything short of a decisive victory on the field of battle will only make a larger more tragic war certain.

Yet as Nixon measured the will of his silent majority at the close of his first year in office, he saw that victory was a goal too costly, an ideal too high for a public gravely tired of war. Imagine the dilemma which Nixon faced. Here was a man who believed that human nature, history, common sense, morality, and truth dictated the successful completion of the war; yet after twenty years of trumpeting this message—after finally gaining the presidency, the position from which he could command such a policy—at the decisive hour of his lifetime he could not issue the single order his conscience told him was right: he could not urge the winning of the war.

He had, therefore, no recourse but to search out a substitute for victory. If he could not do what was right, neither would he settle for the wrong. He put his staff to work, and eventually they produced a plan that had practically all the virtues of victory. They called it Vietnamization. And if Vietnamization could not exactly win the war, it could *succeed*. On the evening of April 30, 1970, President Nixon addressed the nation.

To protect our men who are in Vietnam and to guarantee the continued success of our withdrawal and Vietnamization programs, I have concluded that the time has come for action. . . . In cooperation with the armed forces of South Vietnam, attacks are being launched this week to clean our major enemy sanctuaries on the Cambodian-Vietnam border. . . . Tonight, American and South Vietnamese units will attack the headquarters for the entire communist military operation in South Vietnam. . . . This is not an invasion of Cambodia. . . . We take this action not for the purpose of expanding the war into Cambodia, but for the purpose of ending the war in Vietnam and winning the peace we all desire.

He not only extended the fighting; he also escalated the morality of the war, offering a broader appeal to conscience. Vietnam, he said, was not primarily a military struggle; it was a moral challenge which must be met in order to save Western civilization from certain doom.

My fellow Americans, we live in an age of anarchy, both abroad and at home. We see mindless attacks on all the great institutions which have been created by free civilizations in the last 500 years. Even here in the United States great universities are being systematically destroyed. . . . If, when the chips are down, the world's most powerful nation, the United States of America, acts like a pitiful helpless giant, the forces of totalitarianism and anarchy will threaten free nations and institutions throughout the world. It is not our power but our will and character that is being tested tonight.

The invasion of Cambodia was thus sold to the American people as a means by which they could save the university and other troubled institutions of the Western world. In 1970 Nixon concluded that Vietnamization not only satisfied the dictates of conscience; it rendered this war the most perfectly moral in all history. "When men write the history of this nation, they will record that no people in the annals of time made greater sacrifices in a more selfless cause than the American people sacrificed for the right of eighteen million people in a far-away land to avoid the imposition of communist rule. . . ."

But Nixon's two reasons for a continued presence in Vietnam were incompatible. If it is in the vital interest of the United States to maintain the Thieu-Ky regime, then the fight is not selfless or sacrificial. This contradiction was covered, however, by the monotonous insistence that the policy would succeed. Nixon joined his three predecessors in affirming, despite mounting criticism and increasing evidence to the contrary, that this country's policies for Vietnam were, at last, successful. On June 3, one month after the action in Cambodia began, he concluded: "Based on General Abrams' report, I can now state that this has been the most successful operation of this long and very difficult war. . . . As of today I can report that all of our major military objectives have been achieved. . . . This operation has clearly demonstrated that our Vietnamization program is succeeding." His praise of the nation's sacrifices was matched in every one of his speeches by the litany of her success.

As he began his third year in office, Nixon issued a major summing up of his record in Vietnam. Included as part of his annual State of the World report to Congress, his message bore the optimistic title: "United States Foreign Policy for the 1970s: Building for Peace." Here again was the portrait of success in Vietnamization. "After two years of the mandate by the American electorate, we can look back with satisfaction on the great distance we have traveled." Nixon measured the "distance" of his journey toward peace in the steady withdrawal of American troops. As he had done so many times before, he tallied off the numbers: "Two years ago the authorized troop strength for Americans in Vietnam was 549,500. . . . On January 1, 1971, that authorized level was 344,000, and on May 1, 1971, there will be a new ceiling of 234,000. Troop levels have dropped at a steady rate. The process will continue." And then there was the weekly "body count." "Two

166

years ago American combat deaths . . . averaged 278 weekly. In 1969 . . . 180. In 1970 . . . 80; in the last six months . . . 51." The statistics supported his optimism; the war could hardly continue with such a massive reduction of troops. And yet, buried further on in his message were the figures that effectively cancelled out each and every reduction. In an effort to show that the South Vietnamese were "increasingly capable of providing security for their country," he announced that "there are now 1.1 million men bearing arms for the Government—200,000 more than in 1963." In addition he argued that the continued growth of local and irregular forces in the South had freed more units for direct combat against the NFL. Adding these figures, a simple arithmetic would demonstrate that during his first two years in office the number of men fighting on behalf of the Thieu-Ky regime had actually remained constant. For every U.S. soldier withdrawn from combat, the United States had provided equipment and support for an additional Vietnamese.

Nixon talked about winding down the war, but he was not cutting his losses in Vietnam. Included in every speech was an open-ended commitment to hold on until the prisoners are released—until the South Vietnamese have a reasonable chance for survival—until a mutual withdrawal or a mutual cease-fire can be arranged. By refusing to set a definite date for withdrawal, he saved himself the option of supporting, at any moment, an additional foray into Cambodia or Laos, an intensification of the air war, even a raid on North Vietnam itself. While these options were studiously protected, the massive effort to train and equip the South Vietnamese continued.

And still Nixon talked about peace. On March 10, 1971 he told C. L. Sulzberger of the *New York Times,* "I rate myself as a deeply committed pacifist, perhaps because of the Quaker heritage of my mother. But I must deal with how peace can be achieved and how it must be preserved. . . . The kind of relative peace I envision is not the dream of my Quaker youth. But it is realistic, and I am convinced we can bring it about." Nixon even permitted himself a visionary prophecy: "This war is ending. In fact, I seriously doubt if we will ever have another war. This is probably the very last one." As always, however, the assurances of his pacifist leanings were combined with a commitment to a massive military presence: "Our idea is to create a situation in which those lands to which we have obligations or in which we have interests, if they are ready to fight a fire, should be able to count on us. . . . We cannot foolishly fall behind in the arms competition. . . . Our responsibilities are not limited to this great continent, but include Europe, the Middle East, Southeast Asia, East Asia, many areas. . . ." For all his talk of self-help and self-defense, the Nixon Doctrine promised that American arms and American men would be used to preserve the balance of power wherever it was threatened. And still Nixon said: "I can assure you that my words are those of a devoted pacifist."

Beyond the literal contradiction involved in promoting himself at once a pacifist and a cold warrior, there is a deeper and more tragic paradox at the heart of his policy. The very idea of winning a just peace in Vietnam after so many years of the most terrible crimes (both the continuing mass violence of American bombings and the selective terror of the Vietcong)—the mere suggestion that we can extract a just peace from such a jungle of injustice is patently absurd. That peace alone could finally be achieved in a country in which bribery and murder have become routine would itself be a gift of grace. Whether it be the repressive peace of communism or the decadent peace of Thieu-Ky, the choice is still the least of three evils, and the greatest of the three is the war. That Nixon can achieve justice in Vietnam is a suggestion perverse in its impossibility. For as the American troops withdraw, the Vietnamese are left helpless between the terror of Hanoi and the depravity of Thieu-Ky. The people of Vietnam stand as symbols of the tragedy implicit in the continuing politics of cold war.

A world balance of power which is founded upon the threat of force cannot be preserved without the eventual use of that force. The Indo-China war is only the logical consequence of a global strategy in which the major powers maintain a massive nuclear presence to secure a relative peace. In an imperfect world, the corollary to a relative peace is limited war. An ethicist Paul Ramsay has often pointed out, a peace founded upon the policy of massive retaliation makes the world safe for guerrilla war.

Beyond Vietnam, the problems intrinsic to this nation's global strategy are staggering. While Administration apologies for a continued presence around the world sound increasingly optimistic, the attendant risks do not diminish. President Nixon believes that the United States has both the right and the responsibility to preserve order throughout the world. He is prepared to endorse not only localized wars, as in Vietnam, but a total nuclear war. His State of the World Message reaffirmed the U.S. commitment to provide a nuclear shield against a threat not only to U.S. security but to the security of any of her allies. Considering the sheer number of this nation's treaty obligations, it does not require clairvoyance to realize that the possibility of avoiding a future war is small indeed. Wholly missing from Nixon's public utterances is a recognition of the awful possibilities which his cold war policies entail. Any nation which sets itself up as watchman of the world order cannot escape the likelihood that its power will be employed.

And the realities of the seventies offer resounding evidence that Vietnam, far from being an exceptionally evil war, is only typical of the conflicts in which we may become involved. The devastating debate over the war crimes, the disillusionment about corruption in the Thieu-Ky regime, the demoralization of U.S. troops in Europe as well as Asia, all stem from the prior doubt as to our very presence in Vietnam. We are unlikely to find a convincingly righteous war anywhere. The ancient assumption that this country will take up arms only for selfless motives against an evil opponent does not match the reality of world conflict.

Henry Kissinger spoke in February of 1971 of the ambiguity which the Nixon administration has faced in deciding its policies for the Indo-China conflict. His remarks focus in on the dilemma ignored by the President throughout his career. "All the tough decisions, the sort of decisions that come to the President are very close. . . . You make your decision on the basis of maybe a 55–45 balance. . . . But once you've made the decision, you are committed to it—or you are stuck with it 100 percent." Asked whether he thought that the Nixon administration might have miscalculated by that critical 5 percent in its Vietnam policy, Kissinger answered: "Yes, we could be wrong. You wouldn't get a Harvard professor to say otherwise on national television. But we considered this as deeply and as thoughtfully and, given the anguish that the war has caused, I must say, as prayerfully as we possibly can."

The terrible divisions that have fragmented this country during the Vietnam war reflect a growing realization that political power—that is to say, force—cannot be employed without guilt. It is impossible to carry on counter-insurgency warfare—certainly nuclear warfare—without massive civilian casualties and devastating, perhaps even terminal effects, upon both sides. The questions raised by the tragedy in Indo-China strike to the heart. They are the fundamental moral, even theological questions. Is it possible to maintain that warfare is just, when the cost of war is precisely the survival of those people whom it was designed to protect?

What is missing in Nixon's politics and his religion is a consistent recognition of the tragic and the demonic. The closest he seems to come to a perception of evil is the evil he sees in communism. Yet however dangerous communism may be—however terrible its crimes—it cannot be held accountable for the human propensity to violence, a menace predating Karl Marx by a few thousand years. Self-interest, conflict of interest, and war typify man's international relations, and the United States is part of the human process. The

170

irrationality, the arrogance, and the narcosis of Soviet Russia are matched in kind, if not in degree, within this country.

The medieval myth of the Devil will not be revived in a secular age, but at least the Devil served as a symbol for those paradoxes of human behavior which Nixon's religion does not explain. Satan was feared as a wily and depraved creature of super-human power. He could pervert any ambition and corrupt any ideal, no matter how noble. By the most ingenious subterfuge he could even invade the mind of a monk at prayer, taking hold of his thoughts, altering his words, shifting his attention by the most subtle degree, so that entirely without his knowledge, he would worship Satan, thinking that he was the true God of Mother Church.

In its most creative form the fear of Satan could counter the temptation to self-righteousness and pride, for no matter how good the action, no matter how noble the thought, it might still be tainted by the Devil. Hence the final arbiter of truth was not the individual, but God. Only when the Devil was made into a device to generate fear did the myth become as limited in its significance as the church which sought to control it.

This nation is in need of a similar awareness of human fallibility. Largely absent from American mythology is an awareness that noble intentions can often lead to the most tragic results. A nation stubbornly convinced of its own righteousness can present as great a danger as a nation openly bent on war. Though Richard Nixon claims that his intentions are purely and exclusively a "just peace," the desire to achieve peace is wholly inadequate as a justification for war—this war or any future wars. As Saint Augustine put it sixteen hundred years before the era of counter-insurgency and nuclear deterrence:

Any man who has examined history and human nature will agree with me that there is no such thing as a human heart that does not crave for joy and peace. One has only to think of men who are bent

171

on war. What they want is to win; that is to say, their battles are but bridges to glory and peace. The whole point of victory is to bring opponents to their knees—this done, peace ensues. Peace, then, is the purpose of waging war; and this is true even of men who have a passion for the exercise of military prowess as rulers and commanders. What, then, men want in war is that it should end in peace. . . . And even when men are plotting to disturb the peace, it is merely to fashion a new peace nearer to the heart's desire; it is not because they dislike peace as such. It is not that they love peace less, but that they love their kind of peace more.

It is a fitting but awful coincidence that has Richard Nixon now declaring his desire for peace, proclaiming his nation's innocence, at precisely the hour when its policies are unmasked in all their folly. If the war has been a test of the nation's character, then that test really lies in the question whether some awareness of the self-interest and self-deception so active in our Vietnam policy can bring us to a more honest assessment of the ambiguities bound up with our power. If the country can accept its involvement in the very process that leads to war without being overcome in a paralysis of guilt, then Vietnam may have contributed to the maturity of this nation.

Nixon, however, does not appear to have noticed any ambiguity in our military presence in Vietnam or anywhere else. Speaking to the graduating class of the U.S. Military Academy in May 1971, he promised, "You can be proud of your country's power because that power is wholly committed to the service of peace. That power is—without exception—the instrument of principle, of high respect for the basic rights of men and nations. To those who speak of American might as something arrogant, something ominous, you need only ask one question: 'In the world today, a world which permits no vacuum of power, what other nation would you trust more with that power than America?' "

Nixon's rhetorical question excluded the single answer that would

172

do justice to the reality of political conflict. *No* nation can be "trusted" with power; every nation is driven by desires it only partly understands, only partly controls, only partly confesses. Theologians have expressed this reality in the doctrine of original sin. Though the dogma has been rejected out of hand by a culture anxious about its freedom, the realism of the doctrine must be recovered if the country is to avoid the twin perils of a blinding self-confidence or a demoralizing guilt.

Yet even in the face of genuine confusion over the validity of our presence in Indo-China and around the world, Nixon steadfastly holds to his simplistic defense of massive military expenditures and the sincerity of his "Quaker" search for peace. While the nation plunges deeper into self-doubt, Nixon's simple "faith in America" appears oppressively inadequate.

As we turn to his domestic policies, we see a similarly tragic flaw. Nixon would preach the virtues of America even as the nation's crises escalate. Instead of offering leadership, guiding the country toward a resolution of her fundamental ills, he continues to mask the problems behind generalizations, platitudes, even prayers. And most tragically of all, his forecasts of a "nightmare of recrimination" that would follow a withdrawal from Vietnam may prove to be a self-fulfilling prophecy if he, or his successor, fails to answer the doubts and face the Herculean questions posed by the war.

★ X ★

The Nixon Theology

For Richard Nixon, 1968 was the year of an amazing grace. Defeated in 1960, pronounced dead in '62—the nation believed his own obituary delivered to the press: "You won't have Nixon to kick around any more." Yet he would not stay down; soon he was back, fighting again for the presidency, riding on the years of loyalty to his party. When the Republicans nominated Goldwater in '64 and so many were chilled by the prospect, Nixon rallied for another national campaign, stomping the same cities and states that had turned against him in '60, talking, even warming again to the reporters, cementing old ties, renewing his contacts. He simply kept at it. The years ticked by and his habits propelled him.

He had found a hospitable base in the law firm of Mudge, Rose, Guthrie, Alexander and Mitchell. For the first time in his life he had money—more than $200,000 a year. And class. He moved into a Fifth Avenue address with New York Governor Nelson Rockefeller and William Randolph Hearst, Jr. He joined the proper clubs—Metropolitan, Links, Recess in the city, and in the country Blind Brook in Westchester, Baltusrol in New Jersey (though failing to check whether they were segregated). Tricia and Julie were enrolled in the Chapin School and went on to Eastern colleges—Finch and Smith. They were received into New York society at the International Debutante Ball.

But Nixon was not satisfied with these pleasures. In 1966 he toured thirty-five states for Republican candidates in seventy congressional districts. In 1967 he traveled to Europe, meeting Prime Minister Wilson in England, Foreign Minister Couve de Murville in France, Chancellor Kiesinger in West Germany, President Saragat of Italy, Secretary-General Ceausescu of Romania, Antonin Snejdarek in Czechoslovakia, and His Holiness Pope Paul VI in Rome. It was not the sight-seeing jaunt of the average American. Nixon, it was clear, had come alive. By 1967, the Gallup poll would rank him the number one choice among Republicans for the presidential nomination. On November 3 Lyndon Johnson, who was suffering his own difficulties with the press, presented Nixon with front-page headlines, attacking him during a presidential press conference. Nixon, he said, is a "chronic campaigner."

On January 31, 1968 Nixon addressed an open letter "To the Citizens of New Hampshire. . . . The Nation is in grave difficulties, around the world and here at home. The choices we face are larger than any differences among Republicans or among Democrats. . . . They are beyond politics. Peace and freedom in the world, and peace and progress here at home, will depend on the decisions of the next President of the United States. . . . I have decided, therefore, to enter the Republican Presidential primary in New Hampshire." It had begun. Nixon signaled the nation that he would again seek the presidency. The speech writers and strategists, the advance men and ethnic specialists, began their work. And in 1968 more than ever, the media experts would prevail: Haldeman, from J. Walter Thompson; Shakespeare from CBS, and Garment, Safire, Klein, and Traleaven. As we have already seen (p. 45), the speech writer Ray Price dictated a memorandum on strategy for the primaries, including these words: "Selection of a President has to be an act of faith. It becomes increasingly so as the business of government becomes ever more incomprehensible to the average voter. This faith isn't achieved by reason: it's achieved by charisma, by a *feeling* of trust. . . . The natural human use of reason is to support prejudice, not to arrive at opinions." Price argued that the Nixon organization, working as they were with a candidate of minimal charisma, should create an image that the voters could trust; they must project their man so that the voters would *feel*

NIXON'S THE ONE. VOTE LIKE YOUR WHOLE WORLD DEPENDED UPON IT.

The campaign would be effective, wrote Price, only "if we can get people to make the *emotional* leap, or what theologians call [the] 'leap of faith.' "

Nixon had consoled himself after the disaster of 1960 that he had endured "the last national election in which the religious issue will be raised at all." But now in 1968 his own ethnic specialists were pointing out the importance of projecting the subtle hues and suggestions of religion to the potential voter. From the South came the reminder: "Billy Graham is the second most revered man . . . among adult voters." Commenting on the Nixon television film *Great Nation,* Kevin Phillips, knowledgeable on voting blocs across the nation, wrote: "This is fine for national use, but viz. local emphasis, it strikes me as best suited to the South and the heartland. They will like the great nation self-help, fields of waving wheat stuff and the general thrust of Protestant ethnic imagery."

How Protestant is Richard Nixon's constituency? Garry Wills tallied the 1333 delegates at the Republican National Convention in Miami on August 5: "The group was laughably WASP—2 per cent Negro (vs. 11 per cent of the population), 2 per cent Jew (vs. 3 per cent of the population), 15 per cent Catholic (vs. 23 per cent of the population). Not only was the group 82 per cent Protestant (vs. 35 per cent of the population); the leading denomination was Episcopalian (16 per cent vs. 2 per cent of the population), and the lowest was Baptist (7 per cent vs. 13 per cent of the population)—giving a heavy preponderance to fashionable Protestantism." While Richard Nixon could not appeal directly to the religious instincts of the Republican delegates (the nation would

176

also be listening to this convention), still he could safely delineate the American dream so as to include all the benefits of his Protestant faith. Religion, it was clear, played a critical role in his own rise to the mountaintop.

Tonight I see the face of a child. . . . He hears a train go by. At night he dreams of faraway places where he'd like to go. It seems like an impossible dream. But he is helped on his journey through life. A father who had to go to work before he finished the sixth grade sacrificed everything he had so that his sons could go to college. A gentle Quaker mother with a passionate concern for peace quietly wept when he went to war, but she understood why he had to go. A great teacher, a remarkable football coach, an inspirational minister encouraged him on his way. A courageous wife and loyal children stood by him in victory and also in defeat. And in his chosen profession of politics, first there were scores, then hundreds, then thousands, and finally millions who worked for his success. And tonight he stands before you, nominated for President of the United States of America.

The hard work, the sacrifice, a gentle Quaker mother, an inspirational minister, a courageous wife, all pushed him along through sacrifice and suffering so that he could stand before the delegates of the Republican National Convention and proclaim himself the incarnation of the American dream. "You can see why I believe so deeply in the American dream: For most of us the American revolution has been won, the American dream has come true."

The campaign of 1960 may have been the last in which the "religious issue" was *raised,* but certainly not the last in which religion would be *used.* Nixon's Protestant past weighs so heavily upon him that it would show through regardless of the cynical calculations of his ethnic experts. He *believes* that faith has been instrumental in his success, and the speech writers do not have to urge Protestant imagery upon him. His advisers simply modulate the code words and symbols so that the received image has a positive impact upon the widest possible constituency. That "an inspirational minister

177

encouraged him on his way" may appeal to Protestants of every denomination, and it is just vague enough to avoid anti-Catholic or anti-Semitic connotations. But it would have been suicidal to admit, for example, that Billy Graham convinced him to run or that Norman Vincent Peale had encouraged him to lead the nation in a puritan revival. Even the suggestion of his mother's "passionate concern for peace" had to be softened with her tears as "she understood why he had to go" to war.

Beyond the convention, Nixon knew that he could not appeal exclusively either to Protestants or to Republicans. To gain his plurality he must draw heavily from independents and Democrats, and that meant Roman Catholics. In this regard, he was an ironic benefactor of John F. Kennedy. One of the major contributions of the Kennedy era was to enhance the ecumenical ethos and further blur the distinctions between Protestants and Catholics. Kennedy had so successfully transcended the particulars of his Catholic training that he had been received into the American majority. On the other hand, if Kennedy had boosted the hopes of his upwardly mobile Catholic brethren, Nixon might inspire them to shuck off their Democratic politics on their way toward affluence. Kevin Phillips, therefore, prevailed upon him to advocate a policy that Kennedy would not have dared. In the closing weeks of the '68 campaign Nixon announced his support of federal aid to Catholic schools.

While the ethnic specialists busied themselves sorting out the sensitivities of every state and region, Nixon launched into a campaign that would appeal to the country's most noble ideals, without actually mentioning how they would be realized. The Republican Party platform spoke forcefully of the soldiers in Vietnam. "Our pride in the nation's armed forces in Southeast Asia and elsewhere in the world is beyond expression. In all our history none have fought more bravely or more devotedly than our sons in this unwanted war in Vietnam. They deserve—and they and their loved ones have—our total support, our encouragement, and our prayers."

Reading this passage, one would never have guessed that the Republican candidate had refused even to discuss the merits or morality of the war. "Our pride in the nation's armed forces . . . is beyond expression." Yet, despite their valor and their devotion to the cause —"never has so much military and economic and diplomatic power been used so ineffectively." That was the sum of Nixon's contribution on the most critical issue of the campaign. The polls showed that he led Hubert Humphrey, and he would not jeopardize his lead by literally spelling out his position. He would simply appeal in the broadest possible terms to the deepest sentiments, and hide his specific plans and programs under the all-embracing shadow of his oratory. "A new voice is being heard across America. It is different from the old voices, the voices of hatred, the voices of dissension, the voices of riot and revolution. What is happening is that the Forgotten Americans, those who do not indulge in violence, those who did not break the law, people who pay their taxes and go to work, people who send their children to school, who go to their churches, people who are not haters, people who love this country . . ." Facing the possibility that all these people would turn away from hate and revolution and toward the church, the schools, and the Republican Party, Nixon prophesied not only a new coalition of silent Americans, but a New Age. "Forces now are converging that make possible for the first time the hope that many of man's deepest aspirations can at last be realized." Shortly after his term began, he articulated his personal faith in words that connected his vision for this country with his own religion:

More than a hundred years ago our greatest American philosopher, Ralph Waldo Emerson wrote: "I say the real and permanent grandeur of these United States must be their religion. Otherwise, there is no real and permanent grandeur."

As a life-long Quaker and church-going Christian, I deeply believe those Emersonian sentiments are truer today than in his own time. The principal challenge for us all is: Have we the moral drive and the

179

spiritual resources to take charge of our destiny once again, to regain the momentum and the international leadership that was ours after our victories in World War I? I believe we have.

Both as a believing Quaker and as America's 37th President, I am determined to prove that we have such God-given resources as individuals and as a people.

President Nixon had ample reason to believe in the importance of religion, for as he reviewed the record of his narrow victory over Hubert Humphrey he may well have perceived that the difference between defeat in 1960 and triumph in 1968 was primarily the fact that religion hurt him in his first bid for the presidency and helped him in the second.

In winning the presidency, Nixon felt his deepest convictions about the efficacy of faith and the ultimate destiny of this country resoundingly confirmed. Yet as he applied religion to the conduct of the nation's affairs he found his mandate not nearly so clear-cut. During his first two years in office, the influence of religion was most obvious in his fundamentalist application of the moral law. He waged a campaign against individual sins which he feared were threatening the very survival of Protestant culture. His response to the "drug problem" was typical. Having expressed his determination to stop the flow of marijuana into the United States, he instituted a rigorous search-and-destroy operation at the Mexican-American border. Though he personally appointed the thirteen members of the National Commission on Marijuana and Drug Abuse, he announced that he would not consider legalization of the drug if that happened to be the commission's recommendation. No evidence, no matter how persuasive, could reverse his prejudgment that marijuana is immoral.

To emphasize the religious dimension of his stand, he invited eighty of the nation's most influential religious leaders to an all-day conference at the White House. Calling drug abuse a "spiritual problem", he told the clerics, "If there's an answer to it, you have

it." In addition to his own comments Nixon had the denominational officials listen to reports from half a dozen government officials. In Nixon's view the immorality of marijuana was not open
to question; hence the laws against it could not be repealed. Before
the commission began its hearings, its staff director confessed that
he "could write the report right now."

In similar vein, Nixon categorically dismissed the report issued
by the Commission on Obscenity and Pornography on September
30, 1970. Chief among its recommendations was the suggestion
"that federal, state, and local legislation prohibiting the sale, exhibition or distribution of sexual materials to consenting adults
should be repealed." Nonsense, concluded Nixon—that proposal
was "morally bankrupt." "So long as I am in the White House there
will be no relaxation of the national effort to control and eliminate
smut from our national life. . . . Pornography can corrupt a society
and a civilization. If an attitude of permissiveness were to be
adopted regarding pornography this would contribute to an atmosphere condoning anarchy in every other field."

The President saw symptoms of decadence not only in prestigious
federal commissions, but in the affluence and laxity of the population as a whole. Speaking to a group of 130 newspaper and broadcast editors in Kansas City in July 1971, Nixon said that when he
is in Washington and looks at the pseudo-classical architecture of
U.S. public buildings, "I think of seeing them in Greece and Rome,
and I think of what happened to . . . [the] great civilizations of the
past. As they became wealthy, as they lost their will to live, to improve, they became subject to the decadence that destroys the civilization. The United States is reaching that period."

The symptoms of decadence are most evident among the nation's youth, Nixon frequently implies. In an interview with Barbara
Walters on NBC's "Today Show," he asserted that the "fundamental cause" of unrest and protest is not the war, poverty, or
prejudice, but "a sense of insecurity that comes from the old values

being torn away." Attributing the ferment to the weakened influence of religion and the family, he echoed the fundamentalist opinion that the vitality of a culture may be insured by strict adherence to a specific moral code. During his commencement address at General Beadle State College in Madison, South Dakota, he addressed the challenge represented in "youth culture": "We live in a deeply troubled and profoundly unsettled time. Drugs, crime, campus revolts, racial discord, draft resistance—on every hand we find old standards violated, old values discarded, old precepts ignored. A vocal minority of the young are opting out of the process by which a civilization maintains its continuity: the passing on of values from one generation to the next."

Ironically, Nixon's ideal campus moralist, the Rev. Theodore Hesburgh of Notre Dame, had earned the President's praise by handing down guidelines for campus disorders so strict that they were virtually unenforceable. In essence, he would have given student demonstrators a twenty-minute warning. If they did not "cease and desist" at that moment, they would be instantly expelled without a disciplinary hearing. Hesburgh invoked his guidelines unilaterally without consulting the student-faculty committee responsible for discipline. The student senate, quite fairly, censured him for ignoring the established democratic procedures for arbitrating campus conflict. Set in this context, Nixon's own advice to the students of Beadle State has a hollow ring: "The values we cherish are sustained by a fabric of mutual self-restraint, woven of ordinary civil decency, respect for the rights of others, respect for the laws of the community, and respect for the democratic process of orderly change."

Further proof of the unreality of Nixon's legalism is his attitude toward work. Here his fundamentalism is reinforced by childhood trauma. Extolling the virtue of work at the Republican Governors Conference in April 1971, Nixon said, "Scrubbing floors or emptying bedpans—my mother used to do that—is not enjoyable work, but a lot of people do it, and there is as much dignity in that as there is in any other work to be done in this country—including my own." Only in the most abstract and theoretical sense can the chores of a scrubwoman be compared with the responsibilities of the President—especially if one is forced to take on menial labor as a result of unfavorable employment opportunities or other factors outside the individual's control. A closer look at Hannah Nixon's dilemma reveals the ambiguity behind that tidy phrase, "the dignity of work." When Nixon's brother, Harold, was afflicted with tuberculosis, the family doctor urged that they send him to "an excellent county tuberculosis sanitarium at Olive View in the foothills above Los Angeles." Rather than accept the free treatment offered at this public facility close to home, Hannah Nixon took her son to Arizona to a private sanitarium. Frank Nixon borrowed money and Hannah scrubbed floors, staying away from her home, her husband, and her sons for two full years. As Nixon described it to British journalist Peregrine Worsthorne: "Both my mother and father were almost fierce in their adherence to what is now deprecatingly referred to as puritan ethics. Not only were they deeply religious, but they carried their principles over into their lives in other respects and particularly in an insistence that to 'accept help from the government' no matter how difficult our own circumstances were, was simply wrong from a moral standpoint." In order to protect her intense pride, Hannah disrupted the family unit, depriving four sons of her attention during two critical years in their childhood. There was dignity in Hannah Nixon's work, but she defended her principle at the peril of her family.

To endure suffering in an act of moral courage is very different from being victimized. And it is precisely the latter possibility that Nixon leaves open when he applies his puritan ethic to welfare reform by including a work requirement in legislation for a minimum income. As he explained his convictions to the U.S. Chamber of Commerce: "Because I believe in human dignity—I am against a guaranteed annual wage. . . . When you make it possible for able-bodied men and women to get welfare, you make it impossible for those people to get ahead in life. If we were to underwrite everybody's income, we would be undermining everybody's character." While there may be social risks involved in current programs for a guaranteed annual wage, one must also count the effects which chronic unemployment, automation, and cyclical recessions have upon breadwinners who are marginally employable. A government does not build character when it allows its citizens to cower under the relentless anxiety of an uncertain income. It is far from clear that forcing a welfare mother to leave her home to work, usually at the most unfullfilling labor, will benefit either her character or the well-being of her children. The inconsistency of Nixon's opinion is doubly apparent in the context of his opposition to the federal funding of day-care centers that would provide an adequate environment for children of those same working mothers.

Nixon believes that the puritan ethic is not only the bulwark of the American character, but even the key to continued economic growth. In his Labor Day message of September 7, 1971, he asserted that it was precisely its "work ethic" that "made it possible for this country to lead the world."

Nixon consistently ties his political judgments to morality and to his Quaker upbringing. In the memorandum to Peregrine Worsthorne cited earlier he wrote, "Not only at home but in church and school we had drilled into us the idea that we should if at all possible take care of ourselves and not expect others to take care of us." Nixon turns his individualism into a political theorem, arguing that the individual is served best when the federal government serves him least. This, of course, is the major tenet of the American right. It is a theory which may be defended on several grounds: not only the Protestant individualism which Nixon articulates, but also the more secular fear of the dangers inherent in centralized

184

power. It is characteristic of Nixon to choose the moral and religious argument over the political.

Similarly, his statement on abortion, issued April 3, 1971, employs the categories of theology. Reversing an Army decision to liberalize its policy on abortions at military hospitals, Nixon ordered each military base to follow the laws of the state in which it was located. Despite the inequity and inconsistencies the policy would entail, Nixon defended his action: "From personal and religious beliefs I consider abortion an unacceptable form of population control. Further, unrestricted abortion policies, or abortion on demand, I cannot square with my personal belief in the sanctity of human life—including the life of the yet unborn." As public reaction following the statement indicated, the "sanctity of human life"can be cited in various ways. Those who argue for liberalization or repeal of abortion laws affirm the sanctity of the mother's life by respecting her right to decide the proper means of family planning. Dr. Richard Frank, president of the American Association of Planned Parenthood Physicians, has written: "In a pluralistic society, the religious and moral beliefs of those who regard abortion as preferable to compulsory child-bearing deserve the same respect as the beliefs of those to whom abortion is unacceptable. We reaffirm our policy which states that 'it is the right of every woman to decide whether and when to bear a child.' "

Even more revealing of the Nixon theology was the second half of his abortion statement. He went beyond his critique of the liberal position to affirm: "Ours is a nation with a Judeo-Christian heritage. It is also a nation with serious social problems—problems of malnutrition, of broken homes, of poverty and of delinquency. But none of these problems justifies such a solution. A good and generous people . . . will open its hearts and homes to the unwanted children of its own, as it has for the unwanted millions of other lands." This sweeping generosity ignored the political fact of an electorate hostile to the very welfare programs designed to assist the nation's unwanted and illegitimate children. And worse, the open-ended promise of a continuing generosity to "the unwanted millions of other lands" grossly overlooks our nation's actual position in regard to the illegitimate children of American servicemen in Vietnam, not to mention the tens of thousands of children made homeless by the war.

The chief problem with the fundamentalist application of moral principle to politics is that laws and acts based simply on a moral norm often have results directly opposed to their intent. To outlaw abortion may not only force the welfare mother to resort to the illegal and often fatal abortion mill; it may also exacerbate the conditions of overpopulation in the very areas where illegitimacy and child abuse are already most intense. A simplistic prohibition against pornography may contribute to the black market in illicit literature, fostering the intrigue involved in the purchase of books and magazines which on their own merits would be dismissed with the condescending humor they deserve. Again, the vindictive laws against marijuana may have the negative effect of promoting the underground "drug culture." The magic and mystery generally attributed to the drug would be greatly dissipated if its users did not receive the added satisfaction of a rebellion against society. Finally, the mere inclusion of a work requirement in a federal program will not strike at the varied economic and psychological factors that make for chronic unemployment—not to mention underachievement.

In each of these issues there is a profound lack of consensus as to their causes and significance, whether of drug abuse and promiscuity, overpopulation and poverty, or unemployment and underachievement. In no case will either the political conflict or the moral dilemmas be resolved by simple insistence that certain behavior is immoral and ought to be prohibited. A crusade against sin, no matter how impassioned, does not strike at the root of the nation's problems. And Nixon knows it. Despite the moralistic stand he has taken on these issues his central assumptions are liberal and pragmatic. Here, too, he is guided by theological presuppositions rooted in his Protestant past. His individualism posits not only an inherent dignity but even a divine quality reflecting man's supernatural beginnings: "My Quaker upbringing and my religious experience in the Society of Friends strengthen me today as they have in the past. My Christian creed includes the noble insight of Quaker Founder George Fox: 'There is that of God in every man'; and therefore every man the world around—regardless of his race or religion or color or culture—merits my respect.''

Though his record has been tarnished recently by the debts he has had to pay to the southern strategy, nevertheless Nixon's are the universalist instincts that made him an early advocate of civil rights. During his congressional career he voted for the anti–poll tax bill and the Fair Employment Practices Act. As Vice President, he handed down a key ruling that expedited the Senate passage of the 1957 civil rights act. Eisenhower appointed Nixon as chairman of the Committee on Government Contracts, which he had created with the goal of "improving and making more effective the non-discrimination provisions of government contracts." While he has never been identified as a champion of civil rights, his have been the sins of omission. Unlike Lyndon Johnson, for example, he was never a segregationist. Likewise in foreign affairs, he has been a strong advocate of economic assistance to underdeveloped countries, voting for foreign aid appropriations even against the majority in Congress. His support of the SALT talks on disarmament and the visits to China and Russia are both consistent with his universalist beliefs. He has repeatedly linked his interest in foreign affairs to Quakerism. As Vice President, even at the most intense period of the cold war, he described himself as an internationalist, commenting: "I'm not necessarily a respecter of the status quo in foreign affairs. I am a chance taker in foreign affairs; I would take chances for peace—the Quakers have a passion for peace, you know."

Though Nixon believes that the family of man is one, it is in the United States that he finds evidence of the deepest human ability: "The American dream has been one of extraordinary power," wrote Nixon, "precisely because it is related to the innermost striving of man's spirit. It was Ralph Waldo Emerson who said, 'I sing the infinitude of the private man.' To release those energies and develop these infinite potentials is the continuing challenge of America." But whatever he means by "infinite potential," Nixon appears not to allow for a tragic flaw in human nature. His prophecies are all glowing (bar the accident of a nuclear holocaust). For this country, the promises are utopian.

Americans have an unparalleled basis for confidence, Nixon told the U.S. Chamber of Commerce in March 1971. "In dealing with the future of this country, if you want to be a realist, you have to be an optimist. Two centuries of struggle have earned us a right that is not in our Constitution, but a right that permeates our national life: the right to be confident in our own ability to shape the future— the future of America—and even to affect the future of the world." By way of characterizing that future, Nixon listed his favorite goals: full employment, prosperity without inflation, a full generation of peace, freedom, equality for all. But even in this speech he could not help turning "right" into a duty. Americans not only have reason to be confident, they *ought* to be confident, because if they are not, the nation may fall apart—its institutions, economy, and government notwithstanding. He was playing his confidence game in earnest. For this is the very heart of his theology: the key to his politics and his personal life is precisely the faith that Americans can improve. He believes in progress; he has fought for it all his life. "No people has ever been so close to the achievement of a just and abundant society, or so possessed of the will to achieve it."

So near—yet so far. "Sometimes when I see those columns, I think of seeing them in Greece and in Rome, and I think of what happened to . . . [the] great civilizations of the past. . . . The United States is reaching that period." This wildly conflicting diagnosis reflects the habits of a moralist. Nixon balances the promises of what can be accomplished if his values are adopted against the threat of disaster if his exhortations go unheeded. When we view his speeches in this context, many of the inconsistencies become entirely comprehensible. He does not attempt a rational analysis of the American scene, but rather presents a utopian hope balanced by an apocalyptic threat. Since he became President, however, his prophecies are overwhelmingly utopian and exhortative. As he describes the future, he adroitly avoids the suggestion that the country may not be able to realize all these hopes. He promises full employment *and* an end to inflation; military superiority around the world *and* an altering of domestic priorities, a crusade against pollution *and* continued economic growth, the maintenance of order *and* the pursuit of justice, alliances with corrupt dictatorship *and* the respect of democratic peoples. The United States has the ability to become not only rich and powerful, but also generous and compassionate.

On January 23, 1971 Nixon stood before the joint session of Congress to deliver his State of the Union Message. "What this Congress can be remembered for is opening the way to a New American Revolution—a peaceful revolution in which power was turned back to the people." He went as far left as he could to promise power to the people; then as far right as he could to parallel the spirit of '76. "This can be a revolution as profound, as far-reaching, as exciting, as the first revolution almost 200 years ago." But while his rhetoric could span the centuries, he foresaw greater difficulty in accomplishing the deed. "I realize that what I am asking is that not only the executive branch in Washington but that even this Congress will have to change by giving up some of its

189

power. . . . Giving up power is hard. But . . . the truly revered leaders in world history are those who gave power to the people, not those who took it away."

Like the leaders of the Revolution? The Americans had violently wrested their power from the British. What leaders are revered for giving their power away? Nixon had no examples to give, but still believed that if Congress passed his recommendations, "just five years from now America will enter its third century as a young nation new in spirit, with all the vigor and the freshness with which it began its first century." With all its innocence and naïveté? He was appealing to one of the oldest American instincts, the hunger for revival, for a redemption that would sweep clean the state of frustration and compromise—a new birth.

His proposals, by contrast, were scaled to the dimensions of the possible. "I propose that the Congress make a $16 billion investment in renewing state and local government—$5 billion of this will be new and unrestricted funds. . . ." Nixon would set aside $5 billion for the cities and states—less than a quarter the cost of this country's first expedition to the moon—yet he called an act of this magnitude a New Revolution. His proposals for welfare reform, revenue sharing, reorganization of the federal bureaucracy, and so on may well have merited more objective treatment than they received from a Democratic Congress. What interests us here is the concept of power he used to sell his idea of decentralizing the state. "I have faith in people," he began. "I trust the people. Let us give the people of America a chance, a bigger voice in deciding for themselves those questions that so greatly affect their lives. . . . If we put more power in more places, we can make government more creative in more places." His argument was, as he said, founded on faith. He had no evidence to suggest that decentralized power is less corrupt or inefficient. "I have faith in the people." Abbie Hoffman, Hubert Humphrey, and Barry Goldwater have faith in people, too, but the generalities of their several faiths would lead in diverging

190

directions. The idea that fundamental inequities in the American system could be corrected simply by an act of Congress giving its power away—such a proposal presupposes a community far simpler and less problematic than the one Richard Nixon inhabits.

The operative ideas in Nixon's New Revolution are middle American liberal. He has accepted the assumptions of Keynsian economics, the policies of deficit financing, national health insurance, a minimum income, wage and price controls, and made them his own. The most substantial criticisms coming from his Democratic rivals have been that his commitment was not deep enough, his funding inadequate, his techniques irrelevant. When Nixon proposed a national program in ecology, Muskie said he should do more. When the President advocated a national health insurance, Kennedy recommended that it be organized under different auspices. When Nixon announced his trip to China, Bill Buckley wrote an article for the *New York Times Magazine* saying that he had realized for years that Nixon had sold out to the welfare state, but to open his arms to Red China betrayed a weakening of his last claim to conservative loyalties. The idea of Nixon calling the truce in the holy war against communism—that was the end!

The most accurate description of Nixon's politics was offered by Garry Wills, who called him the "last liberal." Sharing the liberal belief in progress, Nixon typically ignores the tragic flaws in the American character, the American political system, and his own policies for the realization of the American dream. When he preaches "faith in America," he rests that faith upon the proposition that in the final analysis there is no limit to what man can achieve if he will only make use of his intelligence, his technology, and his ideals. Nixon overlooks the tragedy of the human condition even when he turns to the most serious problems of American society. For example, the cities: "Let us not . . . pose a false choice between meeting our responsibilities abroad and meeting the needs of our cities at home. We shall meet both, or we shall meet neither."

191

Nixon made this statement at a time when the deterioration of the cities and their helplessness was so great that many despaired of saving them, even with a major overhaul of the national economy.

Nixon's optimism was shared neither by conservatives, who thought the federal government should not come to the rescue of cities; nor by liberals, who feared that the government would not help; nor by the radicals, who accused the government of making things worse. Faced by critics who pressed him for justification of his optimism, Nixon seems always to retreat to his creed: "I am determined to prove that we have such God-given resources." "Only societies that believe in themselves can rise to their challenges." Societies that believe in *themselves*. That surely is a curious twist from a man who claims the Judeo-Christian God as his strength. As Nixon's theology ignores the tragic elements in human nature, it also avoids the transcendent elements in the divine. On July 26, 1971 he wished "godspeed" to the Apollo 15 astronauts, issuing a statement which said in part,

Apollo 15 is safely on its way to the moon, and man is on his way to another step across the threshold of the heavens. Man has always viewed the heavens with humility. But he has viewed them as well with curiosity and with courage, and these defy natural law, drawing man beyond his fears, into his dreams and on to his destiny. The flight of Apollo 15 is the most ambitious exploration yet undertaken in space. Even as it reflects man's restless quest for his own future, so it also re-enacts another of the "deeper rituals of his bones"—not only the compulsion of the human spirit to know where we are going, but the primal need in man's blood to know from what we have come.

That Nixon takes the moonshot as a fitting symbol of man's destiny—the expression of his "primal need" and future hope— suggests his conviction that man's destiny is not, as Shakespeare put it, in the stars. For Nixon it appears to lie, quite literally, in the adventure of human technology. That is, he sees salvation in the relentless striving of the American spirit, a striving which, like Billy

192

Graham's revival or the war on poverty, has no end because the truth is in the process itself. Nixon's is a revival religion which posits the need for salvation and then spends decade after decade planning and programing for revival. His politics assumes the possibility of progress and then spins out program after program, while never actually confronting the root causes of social injustice. And as he ignores the tragic factor in politics, so is he also insensitive to the element of mystery in religion. That he should choose to emcee his own services at the White House perfectly reveals the tenor of his faith. He sees no contradiction in the act of organizing and controlling his own worship, just as he controls his emotions, plans his political strategy, and follows his rules and social norms to the letter. The lack of humor and spontaneity in his style suggests a deeper poverty of spirit. For Nixon, even God is part of the norm, part of the universe of his ideas. "Let me make one thing perfectly clear . . . America's faith in God . . . is her fundamental unifying strength." The geography of his soul centers in this land of dreaming innocence, and his horizons are one-dimensional. (The moonshot was no departure from the American norm; it was only the latest example of the unremitting search for a new frontier. We *had* to be first on the moon—first, biggest, and best. It is, after all, our destiny.)

Nixon systematically appropriates the vocabulary of the church —faith, trust, hope, belief, spirit—and applies these words not to a transcendent God but to his own nation, and worse, to his personal vision of what that nation should be. Lacking awareness of the self-interest that corrupts even the best intentions and the most pragmatic policies, he allows himself a free hand to range around the world, applying American power in the firm belief that he is being counseled by the "best angels" of his own nature; lacking a transcendent God, he seems to make patriotism his religion, the American dream his deity. Far from returning to the "spiritual sources" that made this nation great, he accomplishes a macabre reversal of those traditions, selling the mirror image as the original.

★ XI ★

The Death of God

On October 15, 1971, President Nixon again graced with his presence a meeting involving the nation's most popular evangelist; he appeared as keynote speaker on Billy Graham Day in Charlotte, North Carolina. Once more he lavished praise on the evangelist and repeated his favorite saws: "It is the character of a nation that determines whether it survives. It is the spiritual and moral strength of its people that determine whether it . . . meets the great challenge of leadership." He had used the same words many times before; in fact, it is remarkable that there is so little variety in his continuing analysis of the national religion. He uses identical phrases in his Proclamations of Prayer, in his speeches at the presidential Prayer Breakfasts, in his messages and communications to religious groups; he uses them with a slight softening in his major speeches, partisan campaigns, and in support of congressional legislation.

On Billy Graham Day he delivered his message in slow, deliberate cadences, as if he were struggling to give fresh expression to his most cherished sentiments. He circled and paused as he approached his conclusion, as if to wait upon the guidance of an inner voice—yet he could only find the tired clichés of speeches written years before.

I want all of you to know that as I stand here today. . . . I have great faith. I have faith in [America] not because we are the strongest nation in the world, which we are, and not because we are the richest nation in the world, which we are; but because there is still, in the heartland of this country, and the heartland of America is in every State of America, there is still a strong religious faith, a morality, a spiritual quality which makes the American people not just a rich people, or a strong people, but makes the American people a people with that faith which enables them to meet the challenge of greatness.

One gains the impression in reviewing all Nixon has said and done that, while he incessantly harks back to his religion, he does not find in it a source of personal insight or social vision. He constantly talks about shaping the future, but there is little in his prophecies that would fire the social imagination, and slight evidence that his programs flow from a compelling vision of the future. He forecasts a richer, safer, cleaner world, but he does not seem to imagine or desire fundamental changes in the quality of life. Apparently his hopes would be fulfilled if all the world could share the affluence of one of this country's better suburbs. And in his view these are goals which do not require fundamental changes in this nation's politics, economics, culture, or religion. The essential ingredients are hard work, the competitive spirit, pride in the system, moral and spiritual "strength," faith in America.

As we have seen, his own character and his image of the country are spiced with elements of the puritan ethic and a Protestant piety. As he preaches his gospel these fundamentals are not open to question; he holds them with the tenacity of an evangelist. Yet his ideals are remarkably vague—they float like shadows on the distant horizons of his thought, shaping his decisions and policies by inference and intuition alone. While his religion *is* a deeply personal matter, it rises to the surface irregularly and inconsistently—it is difficult to predict when he will call upon the liberal and humanitarian influences of his mother, or bear down upon the narrow moralisms that were first implanted by his father and later reinforced by the evangelism of Billy Graham.

It is perhaps fortunate that Nixon does not attempt to tie his religion more rationally to his politics. For though it does not provide him with a consistent analysis of American society, neither does it bind him to a narrow ideology. Because his idealism is so inconsistent and so vague, he is free to experiment with a wide range of tactics in making his American dream come true.

His proposals for welfare reform, for rescuing the environment, for a national health insurance and restructuring the federal bureaucracy, his experimentation with wage and price controls, his trips to China and Russia, have demonstrated that there is an amazing latitude to his pragmatism. His initiatives have revealed a surprising openness to experiment, a willingness to alter his own priorities and even reverse himself when faced by arguments of expedience. He seems to sail into the wind of public opinion, tacking with each change, maintaining his lead over the opposition by matching his own moves to theirs.

While Vietnamization smothers the emotions of the doves, his program for welfare reform and revenue sharing defuses the outrage of urban minorities; while his southern nominees to the Supreme Court counter the threat to his right, the new economic policies check his critics to the left. He leads, not so much by consensus as by surprise. Within the perimeter of his liberal assumptions he is free to consider programs that seem wildly contradictory to anyone guided by a systematic analysis of American society. His flexibility is his greatest asset. Yet it is frustrating to many of the less favored elements in the population, for Nixon comes across as arbitrary, even capricious, as he leans here to the left, there to the right. Beyond the question as to where his "real" commitment lies, there is the gnawing inconsistency in his application of principle to practice.

In one breath he argues that the government should enforce the puritan code in its laws against pornography and drugs, and in the next favors freedom of choice and local control in race relations. Insisting on strict enforcement of the law against dissenters, he urges lenience toward a convicted war criminal. Willing to risk high rates of unemployment in his fight against inflation, he continues to extol the importance and dignity of work. Insisting that the American spirit thrives on individual initiative and sacrifice, he fosters economic policies that favor the giant corporations and monopolies which are most secure in their collective power. It is this inconsistency, coated with a tone of moral conviction, that provokes outrage in Nixon's enemies, and the failure to project a coherent moral vision continues to explain his reputation for duplicity.

In part, this trait is a function of the very system through which Nixon has come to the top. In attempting to prove that the American dream is real, that by hard work, sacrifice, and faith in America even a boy from Whittier, California can be elected President, Nixon has become its victim as well as its champion.

One must imagine the terrible strain that two decades of political combat have imposed upon his psyche. For more than twenty years he has faced the terrible necessity of winning a majority at the polls. Constantly engaged in the process of juggling faction against faction, jockeying for position against rivals in his own party, piecing together the necessary coalition of hostile minorities, weighing his promises against the urgencies of the moment, Nixon has survived his tortuous pilgrimage to the presidency under the constant reminder that a single careless phrase or minor miscalculation might cost him his career. His memory is filled with the names of fallen candidates who, despite their work, sacrifice, and convictions were put out of the race: Voorhis and Douglas, Stassen and Taft, Adlai Stevenson and Robert Kennedy, Romney and Rockefeller. Nixon's own narrow escape from the fund crisis, his bitter outburst before the press in 1962, his thin plurality in 1968, all are unnerving reminders that a political career is built on the most uncertain foundations.

In the presidency Nixon is regularly presented with the latest

197

readings of the polls, the instant reaction to every decision and speech. His advisers continually focus on the press as the source of anti-Nixon sentiment; but the public may turn against a President for reasons far more mysterious than a hostile press. Nixon writes in *Six Crisis* of the scars that have hardened him to the shocks of political life; he says that he protects himself against the trauma of betrayal and defeat with "a certain tough realism as far as friendship and loyalties are concerned." Yet the psychological mechanisms required of the politician are more complex than those he describes in his book. An element almost of schizophrenia is required of those who seek public office (not to mention the routine deceptions that figure in the credibility gap).

The candidate must live in two worlds at once: there is a deep division between his private and his public lives. Though he must privately fight for survival, he must appear to be primarily concerned with "the issues" and selflessly devoted to public service. While the public demands dialogue and debate, it responds to image and appearance. While commentators insist that the politician consider the long view, that he explore the root causes of our woes, voters grow impatient when instant solutions are not forthcoming and quickly turn to the new face and the fresh image. It is not surprising that men like Nixon, who have lived out the split personality that politics requires, ultimately believe in their own deceptions. The contradictions between the image and the image-maker, the man and the machine seem so internalized in Nixon that it is impossible to disentangle the realities of the private and the public man.

He is certainly no less sincere and his tactics no more immoral than those of most politicians. But his long years of political combat have affected his moral judgment. He does not project a consistent vision because the contradictions of the system have made a telling incursion into his conscience. His split personality is apparent in every public utterance, even his most candid statements of belief.

On Billy Graham Day Nixon intended to make a simple affirmation of faith. He began to say: "I have faith in [America] . . . because there is still, in the heartland of this country, a strong religious faith." But he realized that as President and as politician he could not identify exclusively with the "heartland of America" —that is to say, the suburban and rural sections of the South, Midwest, and West. So the simple statement of faith became an awkward political maneuver as he pronounced it: ". . . there is still, in the heartland of this country, and the heartland is in every State of America, there is still a strong religious faith." His intention was straightforward and sincere, but as he spoke his sentiments were refracted and diffused so that his words revealed the contradictions of his own psyche rather than the simple piety he had hoped to convey.

The tragedy of Richard Nixon is that while his religion is important to him, while he does call upon those "spiritual resources" that have propelled him to his place of power, nevertheless it is not equal to the terrible responsibilities and complexities of the presidential office. Consequently, when he "speaks from the heart," his sentiments are often irrelevant to the problem at hand.

On September 10, 1971 he appeared before Congress to defend Phase I of his new economic policies. The issues raised by his new programs were intricate and complex. Few in his audience had a comprehensive view of the variables involved in the management of wage-price controls, the import surcharge, or the underlying complexities of the international monetary crisis. Therefore it was quite understandable—given the necessity to sell his programs— that the President chose to package Phase I in an appeal to conscience: "All of these programs—all of the new economic programs—that I have described today will mean nothing, however, unless the American spirit is strong and healthy—the spirit of our people across this land. . . . A strong and healthy spirit means a willingness to sacrifice. . . . A strong and healthy spirit means a willingness to work. Hard work is what made America great. . . ." But this sermon on the virtues of hard work blithely ignored the actual issues raised by the new program. Certainly there are profound ethical implications to actions as serious and far-reaching as the wage-price freeze; but the belief that hard work has been important in the economic development of this country is hardly the first point that would come to mind. Aside from the debate over the President's handling of the economy, we are here concerned with his management of the country's morality.

There is danger in constant use of the moral argument as an instrument of policy, for the public can become as hardened to the incessant call to conscience as it can to any other tool of persuasion—perhaps more so in a time when its traditional values are already suffering from shocks of change and doubt. When morality is invoked simply as a device of rhetoric to rally support behind programs that have no direct relationship to the principles used in the appeal, this weakens its legitimate role in decision-making. We can sympathize with the President's desire to rouse the nation's conscience, but he can only dull it when he bends his ethics to his own political purposes.

At the same time, it is obvious that Nixon is not alone in using the moral authority of his office for amoral ends. Most politicians face a similar pressure and cave in to the temptation. Constantly involved in the process of image-making, in the nurturing of a constituency, in the defense of a power base and the raising of funds, few politicians are able to protect their integrity, and fewer still are capable of separating moral imperatives from the necessities of their own careers.

In addition to the general pressures of his vocation, the President has the particularly burdensome duties of his own office.

Standing atop the largest bureaucracy in the world, his time and energy are packaged and consumed with ruthless efficiency. He seldom has the opportunity, even if he has the inclination, to ponder issues of penultimate importance. Though the public looks to the President as perhaps the highest moral authority in the land, the range of options open to him is severely limited. He appears to the public eye as a single individual, free in his position of power to bend the very forces of history. Yet he is to a large degree frozen-in by public expectations, by tradition, by the machinery of government, and by his own political debts, leaving him a relatively narrow range of options. His freedom is further curtailed by his own staff, who act as a steadying influence, screening the flow of information and ideas directed toward him. H. R. Haldeman thus described to Allan Drury his theory in hiring members of the President's staff:

We have tried to keep a spread of opinion on the staff, so that no one is to the left of the President at his most liberal or to the right of the President at his most conservative. . . . Ehrlichman, Kissinger and I do our best to make sure that all points of view are placed before the President. We do act as a screen, because there is a real danger of some advocate of an idea, rushing into the President or some other decision maker, if the person is allowed to do so, and actually managing to convince them in a burst of emotion or argument. We try to make sure that all arguments are presented clearly and fairly across the board.

Ignoring, for the moment, the contradiction involved in trying to present all arguments fairly after having limited the staff to men no more liberal and no more conservative than the President, there is still a tremendous inertia at the highest reaches of power.

Committed to winning and maintaining the support of a majority, hedged in by a system of checks and balances, protected by his advisers from "extreme" ideas of either left or right, it is questionable whether any President could use his office to advance a

201

set of values or a world view that was not prefabricated in a centrist mold.

Moreover, the sheer weight of the demands upon his time prevent the President from regularly engaging in such in-depth reflection as would allow him to develop new conceptions and arrive at a fresh overview of the nation and its problems. Nixon spoke of this dilemma to some women correspondents in March 1971: "We are all talking, yapping. . . . We are on TV. We are making speeches and we aren't thinking enough about it. That is why there are so few great speeches. That is why there are so few great thinkers." Though he was generalizing about the pressures of public office, Nixon was clearly expressing his own experience. Every public figure should have two days a week "to read, to think, in a philosophical vein, about the enormous problems that he has to deal with. I do more of that than many of my predecessors," he added, "only because I discipline my time in such a way. But I wish there were more time for that." On several occasions, Nixon has expressed his desire to pursue a more intellectual life. While Agnew has scoffed at pseudo intellectuals, Nixon has called himself an egghead, has expressed a desire to teach at a major university and to write, in his words, "two or three books a year."

Those who have seen the President's personal library do not find evidence that would confirm these intellectual pretensions. Commentator Mark Harris sums up his own perusal of Nixon's bookshelves in *Mark the Glove Boy:*

All were upon the shelves. There were many new books—books of travel, books of information, memoirs of prominent men in the news, and some novels (perhaps detective stories), but few I had heard of, and none I had read. The books offered the general impression of a practical man not given to symbolic routes toward illumination. There was no poetry there, and, to my surprise, no philosophy, though Mr. Nixon had mentioned in *Six Crises* the companionship of philosophy; no books of doubt or indirection. The works of Eisenhower were there, but not Jefferson. It wasn't a library I'd want to be shipwrecked with; it carried no suggestion that the man who owned the house owned a vision of the end. Here were facts, maps, data, things you could verify without argument, so that your answer might be Yes or No or 21,365 but never Maybe or God Only Knows or, worst of all, I Don't Know. It was the library of a man training for a quiz show, and I knew now what he meant by "boning" and "homework," those words he had used with such regularity in *Six Crises,* numbers and names on the tip of your tongue, to give you the sound of decisiveness. . . .

But if its dreariness depressed me, its honesty cheered me. Mr. Nixon could have chosen to stock his library with good books he wouldn't read, upon the advice of an informed person hired, like an interior decorator or a ghost-writer, to express acceptable emotions. It was better this way: better a short vision than deceit. For me, it was a discovery I was pleased to make, and to carry to the end: it was not that Mr. Nixon was deceitful; it was only that he knew no better: these were his limits.

Likewise, there is no record that Nixon has read widely in ethics or theology. For a man who proclaims the importance of religion in his own decision-making, this omission is remarkable. Since he is so insistent in arguing the morality of his Indo-China policy, so certain of the connection between his new economic policies and the puritan ethic, one would hope to find in him some knowledge of the just-war theory, or Protestant teaching in social ethics. Yet he seems to have bypassed the intellectual roots and rational analysis that might either support or challenge his position on these issues. Instead, he relies on the more popular advice of a Billy Graham. He spends his leisure time, not with men of commanding vision, but with those whose talents are more practical, more mundane, like Bebe Rebozo.

Despite the folk wisdom which endows the President with tremendous power, he is, like ordinary mortals, largely the product of external forces. Conditioned by his environment, shackled by social and political factors outside his control, his ability to shape the

203

quality of life in this nation is of surprisingly humble proportions. With the single exception of his war-making powers (an exception of massive consequences in an atomic age), the President may be described as a technician.

Yet more than anyone else in government he is expected to articulate the hope that government is responsive to the people, that its actions are guided by coherent values—in short, that it is an agent of moral authority. While all these assertions are valid to a degree, there is a great tendency to exaggerate the power of government and of the presidency. As we have seen, both Nixon and his critics are tempted to inflate his responsibilities and powers to mythic proportions.

One of the most urgent requirements of the moment is that we demythologize the political process, particularly presidential politics. The persistence of the credibility gap and the more serious alienation of the counter-cultures, both argue for a more realistic discussion of the limits and contradictions of power. The alienation now prevalent among so many of the nation's minority groups, including much of the middle class itself, betrays a general recognition of the discontinuity between rhetoric and reality, between promise and fulfillment. While politicians continue to offer up their utopian fantasies, the media bring home the increasing urgencies that daily threaten a worldwide population. While our Presidents have traditionally performed the pastoral function of sanctifying the nation's ruling values and institutions, they have neglected the prophetic function. Richard Nixon is glaringly inadequate in his ability to identify with the pain and ills of the people, preferring to blanket the nation's worst sores with a pious affirmation of faith. Given the present feeling that the system has come unhinged, the President who does not respond to those feelings is guilty of the most fundamental kind of repression. Nixon's is not a repression by force, but a deliberate distortion of reality in order to create an illusion of national well-being.

He has been able to boost his standing in the polls by a series of startling and dramatic announcements, orchestrated for maximum impact. The Cambodia invasion, the visit to Red China, the new economic policy, the trip to Soviet Russia, all give the appearance of change without actually altering national priorities or readjusting the structures of power. Yet he continues to project his promise of a New Revolution and to present his programs as though they were of cosmic significance.

If there is a contradiction between political promise and reality, the first requirement from our elected officials is for candor. The President should demonstrate a sensitivity to the pain of the people, as well as their pride. He should show an awareness of the system's worst injustices, should project an understanding of the nation's subcultures and minorities. If the President and lesser politicians are not more straightforward about the faults of the system, then the critique must come from voices outside government.

The single institution best equipped to discuss the dangers, even the demonic temptations, of politics is the church. The Judeo-Christian tradition contains the intellectual and theological resources for a realistic analysis of the political process. Unfortunately the church, like the state, is also a victim of the prevailing mix of patriotism and piety. It is the conviction of this writer that, while the religious community often fails to offer a prophetic witness, the Judeo-Christian tradition does provide the appropriate resources for a loyal opposition. And it seems particularly fitting that the insights of religion should be used to undercut the misues of religion—and morality—by secular politicians. There is much in the religion of the West that speaks against the myths of a nationalistic faith.

A sense of the sublime makes more obvious the superficiality of political rhetoric. A sense of the transcendent exposes the pretensions and the inflated promises of those who hold power. A concern

205

for the eternal underscores the folly of shortsighted, patchwork solutions. A knowledge of the divine makes more apparent the fraility and fallibility of human institutions. Yet even in the perception that institutions of state are vulnerable constructs of human engineering, there should develop a renewed sense of responsibility to those institutions. If the courts and Congress, the executive and even the military-industrial complex are seen for what they are, that is to say, mere human institutions capable of mismanagement and manipulation, then it becomes a uniquely human responsibility to reform and control those institutions.

While we need, on the one hand, a more realistic assessment of the realities of power, we also need a renewed sense of politics as a vocation. Without uncritically adopting a utopian ideal, there are changes that can be made, changes which have profound moral implications. It is not within the scope of this book to discuss in depth the interrelations of morality and public policy, politics and religion. But I will mention a few areas where ethical and theological factors are involved, where theological reflection and courageous action are urgently needed.

Perhaps the most important single question now facing this country is whether and to what degree we should maintain our military capability, including both conventional forces and a massive nuclear stockpile. Whether this nation has the right or the responsibility to maintain its arsenal is a subject all too seldom debated. Though the popular justification for our power is that it is purely defensive, it is clear that we also seek to protect our strategic interests and prestige. Can we continue to justify our willingness to protect these interests under the shield of a massive nuclear umbrella? Beyond the debate over the morality of the Vietnam war, there is the more serious question as to whether there is any justification for the targeting of our nuclear warheads directly at civilian populations. Though the atrocities of Vietnam have been shocking, we live every day under the promise that this

206

government stands ready to deliver instant death to tens, perhaps hundreds of millions of Soviet and Chinese civilians. It is an outrageous illustration of our moral insensitivity that there is so little public discussion of such an overwhelming question, certainly theological in its dimensions.

Concerning domestic policy, there is likewise an almost total absence of intelligent moral analysis of the implications behind the current catchword of "national priorities." When the government decides to assume responsibility for health care and income maintenance, it reaches into the lives of millions of persons and alters the burdens of responsibility for the individual. When the government decides to decentralize its power or share its revenues, again it alters the range of responsibilities which must be assumed by individuals. Even when it decides to do nothing, its decision represents a statement about the values of this society; and when government acts, it expresses the collective conscience of the people. In this sense, all its actions are open to moral and theological analysis. Such an analysis is urgently needed at a time when morality and religion are used so routinely, and often so erroneously, as an instrument of partisan interests.

Religion may legitimately serve the body politic by its satire of the pretensions of power and by its sense of responsibility for the works of man. But it cannot provide these perspectives if it merely echoes conventional wisdom. It cannot contribute to the culture if it merely repeats the liberal pragmatism of the majority. If patriotism and piety are inseparable attitudes, as they seem to be for President Nixon, then religion can only be a bastion of established ideas. If the symbols of religion are used chiefly to sanctify the status quo, as Nixon uses them, then religion cannot perform its prophetic function.

For prophecy implies a freedom to stand apart from existing institutions and expose their failings. It also inspires an identification with the oppressed and the alien. This is not to say that religion

207

compels a retreat from the world—quite the contrary. It often expresses itself in a disciplined devotion to the affairs of state, not because the state is an object of devotion, but because it is the primary instrument of social justice.

In addition to its priestly and prophetic functions, religion can contribute to society as an agent of social change. It can provide a powerful impulse to move a people toward the fulfillment of the universal dream of justice. Clearly religion has been a factor in the recent movement for civil rights and peace. In both these instances, ideals rooted in the Judeo-Christian tradition have generated specific legislation and policy decisions. The relationship between religion and social change becomes more confused, however, where there is not such a clear relationship between principle and practice. Though American politicians consistently appeal to the conscience, calling upon the twin emotions of patriotism and piety, there are a number of factors that count against this traditional approach. The widespread awareness of persistent poverty, over-population, and pollution dictate against facile claims of American righteousness. Equally important, the increasing pluralism of American society—and the vitality of the counter-cultures—suggest that political leaders will face mounting difficulty in the attempt to call upon a universally acknowledged set of values or beliefs. The candidate who would appeal to the conscience of a more diverse electorate must wed his morality to reason and he must speak with candor. He must present a reasoned argument, rather than a sweeping appeal to the heartstrings.

It is interesting to note, in this regard, the rationale which Richard Nixon used in defending his veto of the child development program. In a statement released on December 9, 1971, Nixon argued that a greatly expanded network of day care centers would endanger the country by weakening its most vital institution: the family. "Good public policy requires that we enhance rather than diminish both parental authority and parental involvement with children, particularly in those decisive early years when social attitudes and a conscience are formed, and religious and moral principles are first inculcated." Nixon also expressed his concern over the expense of the child development program, but he capped his statement with a characteristic appeal to conscience. Such a program would be dangerous, he argued, because it would "commit the vast moral authority of the National Government to the side of communal approaches to child rearing over against the family-centered approach." This statement represents a refreshingly pointed application of moral principle to public policy. Unfortunately, most of the President's critics did not reply to the specific points raised in the veto message, but simply assailed Nixon's insensitivity to the problems of the poor.

In defending the "family-centered approach" against the allegedly communal system of day-care centers, Nixon relies upon traditional assumptions of the protestant ethic. He appears to assume that proper social attitudes, including religious and moral principles, are best "inculcated" by individual parents, and the correlate, that the availability of communal day-care centers would threaten the family structure and, by consequence, the values associated with family life. The question raised by the President's message is clearly fundamental. Will the protestant ethic continue to be a viable base for consensus, or adequate justification for public policy? It is precisely the exaggerated emphasis upon individualism and privacy that is so widely questioned today. A powerful brief can be made for the proposition that American society could be more justly organized around a system of values emphasizing community and cooperation rather than privacy and competition. As President Nixon rightly suggests, a major commitment to the public education of the very young could have profound consequences in this direction. Yet it is by no means clear that a more communal system of child care would represent a threat to the root assumptions of the Judeo-Christian tradition.

It is the more narrow phenomenon of an American civil religion that is at stake in the present context. It appears that the principal assumptions of Richard Nixon, that is to say, his peculiar blending of the protestant ethic and liberal-pragmatism, are not capable of transcending the divisions of American culture. Even his most creative offerings, which reflect his most liberal and humanitarian impulses, fall short. For his hopes are pinned to a liberalism that does not account for paradox or tragedy in human affairs. He recommends "faith in America" at precisely the moment when the faults of America are most glaringly apparent.

When Richard Nixon said that the crisis of this generation is a crisis of the spirit, he was quite correct. Yet in his response to that crisis, he has revealed himself as an outstanding symptom of the crisis rather than its resolution. In the final analysis, Nixon's failure results not from any malevolent impulses in his psyche or even the slippery tactics so widely regarded as the special hallmark of the mythical Trick E. Dixon. The tragedy of Nixon is that his most noble impulses are not equal to the trials of the time. In a very real sense, he is the political manifestation of the death of a national god.

72 73 74 75 10 9 8 7 6 5 4 3 2 1

CONTENTS

NOTE to IROQRAFTS Reprint:

This edition slightly reorganizes the first few pages of previous publishings of *Legends of the Longhouse* and compacts it by backing formerly blank pages with text. This consolidation, reducing by 18 the number of pages, has necessitated revised pagination, and should be acknowledged when citing this edition.

WGS

ILLUSTRATIONS

There are many things I cannot say due to
the fact that I find it hard to translate into
English my thoughts, if by trying to do so
you lose the beauty of the language. So as
you read along try to bear with the writer
and drift along in his Canoe of Thoughts,
but don't back-paddle; get into the stroke
and we will both be successful.

I have spoken

Wah Neh Hoh

I

LEGEND OF THE SKY-WOMAN
A CREATION MYTH

Tonawanda Reservation
October 13, 1936

Nya Weh Skennoh (Thankful you are well)

Dear Sah-nee-weh:

You have asked me for the story or rather legend about the origin of the world and the Indian in Seneca version. I am going to tell you in my own way, based from what I have been told or heard from old men who used to visit our home when I was real small. It is as authentic as I can make it, thusly:

According to the Iroquoian Mythology it seems that there was an celestial world above where man-beings dwell, where even animals and all living things today were all man-beings. It also seems that there was no sun, but it were lighted by the white blossoms of the great celestial tree standing in front of the lodge of the presiding chief. This chief had a wife and according to a dream he married this young woman. There was what is known as the Fire-dragon or Blue Panther who was supposed to have caused the jealousy of the Chief. It is said that in time the young wife was soon to become a mother from inhaling the breath of her husband but unknown to him; that from this he doubted her honesty to him so much that it cause him so much distress in mind that he got another dream which called for the Tree of Light to be uprooted.

It seems that in the olden times dreams were held in high regard in their everyday life, so much that their destiny were controlled by it to a great degree; so accordingly this tree was uprooted. According to the legend, the opening made from the tree being uprooted caused the light to shine through the opening; thus comes the light of the Sun of today. He managed to deceive his unsuspecting wife to look down through the new opening. In so doing while she was looking down, he pushed her down into the opening. It is said that from his anger, he also cast down through the opening all man-beings, such as Corn, the Beans, Squash, the Sun-flower, the Tobacco, the Deer, the Wolf, the Bear, the Beaver and all animals and growing things. He transformed them into their forms and size as they now appear, and when his anger has cooled down he had the tree of light replaced. Thus the great change was brought about because no one could divine his dream. It was the beginning of the present world and all the living things as they are now.

The Sky-woman, then falling through the hole of the upper world, was seen by the water-animals and water-fowls of the great sea. These beings are likewise like man-beings who at once took up the task of making ready a

THE BEGINNING OF THE PRESENT WORLD AND ALL
THE LIVING THINGS AS THEY ARE NOW

place for her to live. All the larger Birds flew up to meet her and with their wings interlaced received her and brought her down. While this was being done, the best divers among the water animals tried their best to get some earth from the bottom of the sea, until the Musk-rat succeeded in bringing up a mouthful of wet earth from the bottom, which they placed on the back of the Turtle's Shell. It was the Great Snapping Turtle who volunteered to hold up the earth, who at that time was also a man-being like the rest of them. This wet earth placed on the shell soon expanded in size in all directions, and on it the Sky-woman was gently placed. At once she began to walk about this tiny earth which by her action began to grow in size; she even took handful of earth and cast it all directions, which also caused it to continue to grow until she could not see the boundary. Then the Red Willow, shrubs, grasses, and all kinds of vegetation began to appear.

In time the Sky-woman gave birth to a daughter, who according to all legends attained womanhood and was courted by various man-beings and other beings who assumed the shape of man-beings as of fine-looking young men. But her mother advised her to reject all suitors until a young man of the race of the Great Turtle who sought her for his wife. He was accepted and invited to stay in the lodge of her mother. At night he came bringing with him two arrows, one of which was tipped with flint. (Now

I am quoting my father's version; some says that it was three arrows, but we will stick to our own regardless, as it seems everyone who knows about this has his own version which differs with the others.) This young woman laid down and the young stranger placed the two arrows in the wall just above her, then went away saying he would return the next day. Next day at about the same time he did return again and took the arrows with him, saying he would not return again. This I think will do for the present; remember where we left off, as my next letter will continue.

Just a few words of explanation of some of the subjects we have mentioned. The story-teller says in Seneca when he tells of this, he says, "Neh nih Che yonh en ja seh," which means, "When the world was new." The Chief is called "Ha sen no wa neh." About dreams they say, "Oh eh sen dah" or dream, which plays a great part in their daily life.

I have included a drawing of the Sky-woman as she fell through the hole, showing her clutching the corn that the Fire-dragon or the Blue Panther gave her; he also has with him a Corn-Pounder and Mortar which he gave her for her to use when on earth. It also show the Birds with locked wings ready to catch her, and the Turtle with the Musk-rat and earth in his mouth. This is to be your illustration to the legend, as I am anxious to have you know our myths and legends of olden days. Dah-neh-hoh, Sah-Nee-Weh, I have spoken, as we say in Seneca.

Your Seneca Brother,

Ha yonh wonh ish

Jesse J. Cornplanter

CORN, BEANS AND SQUASH

II

LEGEND OF THE EVIL-MINDED
AND GOOD-MINDED

Tonawanda Reservation
November 4, 1936

Sken-noh Sah-nee-weh:

I am writing again to continue our legend of the origin of the world as the Seneca tells it or as my father tells in his days. Starting from the last letter it goes like this:— In due time the young woman bore twins. Just before their birth she was so surprised to hear them talking while still within her. One was saying for them to come out by the nearest way while the other kept saying to come to the world in the proper way; so after a while they were born—the first came out as in the usual manner while the other came out through her arm-pit, which caused her death.

According to the legend, the old woman was so much angry at the death of her daughter, that she asked them which one caused her daughter's death, and the Evil-minded spoked and accused his older brother, the Good-minded. The Old Woman grabbed the supposed offender and threw him out amongst the shrubbery, and instead of dying he grew rapidly and soon developed into manhood.

15

THE EVIL-MINDED POURS ASHES ON THE CORN TO SPOIL IT

BAD MIND

GOOD MIND

The Old Woman liked the Evil-minded and hated the Good-minded who went about the place. He found his father during his wanderings, who told him that he was the West Wind. He taught him how to build a lodge, how to start a fire, how to plant and take care of various plants, giving him seeds of corn, beans, squash and tobacco. He also warned him of his Evil-minded brother's intention and jealousy, of his intention to spoil all good things that the Good-minded would create or cause to grow; that the Evil-minded would try to make all sorts of trouble in the future.

So he went back and started to work in his duty of making all good things in preparation for the man or human-being whom he was to create. The Good-minded did create all streams with double current for ease in travelling, which the Evil-minded spoiled by causing ripples and falls in the rivers and streams. He (the Good-minded) created all sorts of fruits to grow and also made all sorts of animals and birds, also creating fishes in the streams which the Evil-minded spoiled by throwing many small bones into them as to do more mischief for the man that is to come later.

Going back to the time of the death of the daughter,— the old woman buried her in a shallow grave. In due time there grew out from her head the Tobacco plant, from her breast the Corn, her abdomen the Squash, her fingers the Beans, and her toes the Potatoes. While the Good-minded sat and watched them grow his grandmother cooked the corn soup. (This is the way it is made as told by my Sister, Anna.

For 2 ½ qts. of shelled white corn use about 1 ½ qts. of sifted hard-wood ashes. First let kettle ¾ full of water boil for few minutes, then add ashes; when it has boiled about 5 minutes, then the corn. Boil corn in this until the corn turns red and the hulls are loose, about 1 ½ hour. Be careful not to stick in the bottom. Then take it out and rinse it in hulling-basket in water. Do not rinse too well.

Then boil again until corn gets soft and the hull comes off the black ones. Now rinse again; this time rinse many waters until water is not colored. Then cook it with small pieces of meat; cook until done, about 2 to 3 hours. This makes good soup. While getting this ready have about ½ qt. of colored beans ready and parboiled, and add to the soup; in the corn soup cook all together.)

After the efforts and evil work of the grandmother and her Evil-minded grandson had failed, she challenged the Good-minded to a Game of Bowl and Counters to decide who would rule the world and all that it contained. The time set was ten days to get ready. Upon the time set, the grandmother came with her Bowl and Plumpits. The Good-minded refused to use hers as they were very much under her control; instead he called upon the Chickadees to help him win. They came at his call, and he took six of them and used the top of their heads as counters, and asked them to use all their power for the sake of every good thing on

FROM THE BODY OF THE OLD WOMAN GREW THEIR FOOD

HA-YONH-YWONH-ISH
Jesse J.Cornplanter '36

earth. The grandmother made the first shake and did not score; so the Good-minded grabbed the bowl and called to all that he has created to his aid and made the throw. Behold! He made the score and thereby saved the world from the rule of the Evil-minded and his grandmother. So to this day in every Mid-winter Ceremony and the Green Corn Ceremony they have the Great Gambling Game of Peachstones and Bowl as memory of that great struggle when the stake of the game was the control of all that the Good-minded has created.

It is also told that the Evil-minded created all Monsters that devoured man-being,—serpents, and even caused the wind to create disease and sickness. All fruit such as briarbush were all smooth, and they were spoiled by the evil-minded jealousy. Also Pine-cones were supposed to be edible.

When everything was settled after the game, the Good-minded took a walk to view his work. While thus walking he met another man-being who asked him who he might be and all that. The Good-minded told him who he was and what he had done. This being doubted, they had a test, the one to make the mountain move towards them was the master. The stranger tried first, and the mountain did not move but little; so the Good-minded tried, and it was agreed that they must turn while he commanded it to move, then to turn around. But the stranger did not wait and turned quick to see the commotion; by so doing he struck his face against the side of the mountain, thereby causing distortion in his face. He was very sorry of his act, and asked to also be allowed to aid in the work of caring for mankind in the future, to be called the grandfather of the man-being. Thus was the beginning of the Spirit of the Faces who we call our medicine-man, our grandfather.

The Good-minded later created man, later making a mate and telling them to multiply. In all this is the substance of the legend of the origin of the world and mankind as told by our older men. They differ some to a certain degree, —who wouldn't when it is not written nor recorded? It is bound to be lost or forgotten soon or later.

Well, Sah-nee-weh, I am sorry not to tell the whole legend, but it will give you an idea anyway.

Dah Neh-hoh.

Ha-yonh-wonh-ish,

WOODEN TRENCHER
& STIRRING PADDLE
(WITH CORN MEAL)

III

THE GRATEFUL ANIMALS, A LEGEND OF
THE LITTLE WATER SOCIETY

Tonawanda Reservation
November 11, 1936

Dear Seneca Sister:

Now "Sah-nee-weh" for our subject:—in this letter it
will be the origin of the so-called "LITTLE WATER SOCIETY,"
why it came and all that. Take stock that I do not mention name of the Indian that was revived and helped by
the animals and birds.

According to our old story-tellers: There was an Indian
hunter who was very successful. He was an exception as
hunters go in those days,—it was his one good habit to
always remember his animal and bird brothers who eat
meat. Whenever he dresses his game, he always leave a
portion of the carcass for them, then he would call at the
top of his voice inviting all meat-eaters to the feast. He
spend good deal of his time in the woods, and it is said that
he never took advantage of any animal while in the act of
hunting, neither did he take any more game than his
needs called for; he was an unusually good man according
to the merits of hunters in those days.

But one day a War Party of Cherokees came upon him;

22

they took him by surprise that he never had a chance. They killed him,—at least, they thought they did; he was scalped and left for dead. It happened in one of his hunting trips; so there he laid in the woods where he had spent most of his life in the past.

A Timber-wolf happened along and came to the spot where laid our noble hunter. The wolf sniffed all over him and recognized him as their great friend, the Hunter. The wolf then set up one long howl of distress, a call (seldom heard in the great woods) that all animals knew. As each animal and bird heard that call, they knew that something unusual has happened, and straight away they came to the spot; in no time all the animals of all description and size were assembled. Likewise the birds, they too came in all their kind, both great and small, such a gathering of the animal-life as has never been known before, for they all knew that their good friend "The Hunter" had fallen, no more would he offer them their feast.

A council was held right then and there. It was decided that the Bear would take charge in caring for their fallen brother in their attempt to bring him back to life. The Bear was chosen because *he* of all animals stands next to man-kind in their relation, habits, and knowledge. The bear examined the fallen hunter all over and located a warm spot on the chest. They next held council as to how the scalp could be recovered from the Cherokees. They knew it must be a bird that can approach unseen and be able to get away so quick that there is no danger of being caught or killed. Now, Sah-nee-weh, my legend differs with other story-tellers in this respect: each has a different bird mentioned here. My legend, as told by my father "So-son-do-wah," says that it was the Humming-Bird. He volunteered, saying he can approach without being seen, and when he finds the right scalp, to dip down in one swoop and get away safe. So the volunteer went on his mission while the rest only wish for his success as they must not fail.

While he was gone, the bear started to revive the hunter; he kept on feeling the warm spot on the chest and noted that it was getting bigger and bigger. It is said that they all gave a portion of their flesh to make the medicine which must be the strongest in all the world. It is the white meat that is used as each one offered his share; it was cut out by the bear, then afterwards sewed up again and soon healed. They said as it was the white meat, it was pure. (To the animals, white meant Purity.) That must be compounded and given in small quantity at a time. While in the preparation of the medicine, in order to give the medicine full strength they all gathered in a large circle and started singing the strange medicine-song that is to be given to mankind later on, to be used in connection with this very sacred and unusual medicine that is to be used only in rare cases when all forms of medicine and all hopes is gone.

Now, SAH-NEE-WEH, let me again stress the point that this article now being written is about the most authentic as could be expected. But it was told usually by Indians that did not want to tell all they knew or either did not know proper English to fully describe as I am now doing. Of course I could do better if I had more education and ability. In this respect I expect to be properly reprimanded by those that are holders of the Packets of this so-called "LITTLE WATER MEDICINE." I do this for you, "Sah-nee-weh," knowing that it is in your heart that you really believe us and our ways and methods. That you really desire to know the truth and the mysteries of our strange and unbelievable manners, as we may call it. I would not try to tell this to anyone for any money nor no amount of coaxing regardless of who; it is not to brag to you in mentioning this here,—you no doubt realize the love and interest our people have in you, ever since you have been with us. You can only refer back to the times you were allowed to attend the periods of this "LITTLE WATER MEDICINE" as they restrengthen them every three months or given time, a favor accorded no white person unless the officials of the society are positive that the person admitted are not coming only for any purpose for their own gain or for publicity's sake, as they do not care to have this published by any means. They believe it is theirs and it should be kept secret and away from prying and curious eyes. We both, you and I, understand why I am doing this for you.

Now we will go back to our little volunteer, the Humming-Bird. He flew as fast as only Humming-Birds can fly

THEIR "GOOD FRIEND" THE HUNTER HAD FALLEN

in pursuit of the Cherokee War Party. He came upon them as they had camped for the night and were cleaning and drying the scalps that they had with them; so he waited and looked over at a safe distance unknown to the men. After a while he saw the scalp that he was after; it was being stretched within a wooden loop or Scalp-hoop over a fire to dry. So picking out a time when all were busy in their respective tasks, he flew down and in one swoop picked the scalp and disappeared in the night and flew back to the place where the All-Night Medicine Singing were going on.

The style or version as told by my father relates that the bear kept the spot on the Hunter's chest warm by his paws, while the wolf kept licking the place where the scalp was taken off. When the Humming-Bird returned, the scalp was likewise softened by the same manner and then replaced with care. The small dose was administered to the Hunter when he could swallow some of it. It is said that the Hunter seem to be detached from his own being and saw his body as it laid on the ground; he noted everything that took place, even learned and remembered all the songs and speeches that was used during the whole night. In the meantime the Hunter revived by small degrees, until about day-break he was himself again.

Now here is where my knowledge is vague, whether he was kept there for the duration it requires for anyone using that medicine to recover and be kept under care. But I am using this version, that when it was day-light, he was instructed to carry back to his people the secrets of this very strong medicine and all its requirements with its set of songs,—just the way it must be prepared and the restrictions. That they (his people) must give this ceremony every time it (the medicine) is applied. Failure to do so would result in the patient's death. That there must be certain time when Tobacco must be given to the sacred medicine to give it strength. That the Gourd Rattles must be used whenever this ceremony is given, that no unclean person or animal must be in the vicinity, that only those administering the medicine be allowed to see the patient. That there must be a feast such as the meat-eating animals are fond of, be made ready, with feast of Corn Soup and the Bears-head used when the whole ceremony is over. That no one be allowed to sing this song or any part of it at any time unless it is during the ceremony. That there will be given to man-kind portions of this sacred medicine in small bundles so they can be given whenever needed. The ones chosen to have these medicine-bundles be chosen for their ability to carry out its strict laws and methods,—to be used only when all other forms of medicine have failed and as a last resort.

This is about all I can tell. I am not allowed to tell how the dose is prepared or who are holders of the bundles. I must restrict myself according to the dictates of the society, because I am also member of the play-lodge of this society, known as the "Yaie-dose." This lodge or society, as may be called, are of members who were cured by this "LITTLE WATER MEDICINE" or else by the ceremony of the "Yaie-dose" songs itself. I am in position to know just what is to be told, and I want to keep within the limits. I have my faith in this medicine. The funny thing about this ritual of the "LITTLE WATER MEDICINE" singing is that in view of the fact that we are not allowed to ever rehearse or either to hum the tune at any time, yet we seem to know the very songs when it begins. To sing it at any time, they say, brings ill-luck, such as serious injury to the person violating its restrictions. You, "Sah-nee-weh," have attended the rituals and seen what little there is to be seen, know what is entrusted to you to keep secret on your word of honor as I am myself.

I have been told by my father and others now dead that in the olden days they used to have many members of this society that holds the packet and instructed how to administer in case they are called upon; that there were different varieties then in those days, as it came to us in the days when there were War-parties going out to different countries of the enemy; that they used to carry these small bundles to be used in short periods as an emergency treatment for wounds received in battles; that they were called "To-be-carried-along bundles." Now how true it is I can not say, as I have to ask someone more older and well-informed on this subject than I am. Another thing,—this is one matter seldom ever under discussion by any person, such is the belief of its potency and restriction. Again I will say that I am not allowed to tell where they meet and just when. In fact we never know until the ones instructed with its rituals always notify us just few days before it takes place, and we are not allowed to invite anybody unless they be members of either the "Yaie-dose" or the Medicine society itself. The singing takes place in total darkness, just like the Dark Dance, which will be written about later.

This is one medicine where the medicine-man who makes the dose will know before giving to patient whether it will help the patient or not,—that much I will say. We all believe its power to cure when properly prepared and administered. I will not try to contradict the medical profession on this subject, as I must take the view as an Indian of my tribe and keep on my side. It is our medicine, and as such we aim to keep it for us and us only. It is our belief that it was sent to us through our creator or our Great Spirit when he saw the possibility of serious injury to mankind in our daily strife to exist.

Well, "Sah-nee-weh," this is about all I can relate about this little discussed subject, and I feel guilty in doing so, but I know real well that you are not the type to come to pry into our affairs as many other white people has done in the past. There are too many would-be friends that come to us for all they can get out of us, or else for some other purpose more for their own gain, especially Newspaper writers who try to ridicule us or our ways and beliefs. I tell you these things because you want to know us more and is sincere about all you do for your adopted people the Tonawanda Senecas, your Brothers and Sisters. You hold an honor seldom accorded any white person; I know you rightfully deserves it. Enclosing drawing of the origin of the "LITTLE WATER SOCIETY." Dah-neh-hoh, (Now it is all) "Sah-nee-weh."

Your Seneca Brother,
"Ha-yonh-wonh-ish" the Snipe
Jesse Cornplanter

CLAN PHRATRY

WOLF

TURTLE

BEAR

BEAVER

IV

THE DANCE OF THE LITTLE PEOPLE

Tonawanda Reservation
November 13, 1936

My dear Seneca Sister "Sah-nee-weh":

According to the Pale-face superstition, this is Friday the 13th. I hold no faith in this idea; so I am writing you today. If I did believe in Jinx or whatnot, I would not write at all. It only shows that we, as Indians, are not the only ones that believe in the super-natural things.

For this time we will take up the origin of the "Dark Dance" or the Dance of the Little People as some people calls it. It is a legend very old and known only by few. My father used to relate to us, when we were small children, though lately I have heard Chief James Crowe of New Town tell it to a writer,—I was acting as Informant and noted the difference from my father's version. I may be somewhat mixed-up due to hearing many different versions of the same legend; at any rate, here goes:

Long time ago in the days when my people lived more close to nature and were able to converse with animals, when we were so near to being what the animals are that it was nothing unusual for a Hunter or traveler to be aided by some animal from being lost or from death; such were

32

the conditions of the times when our legend begins. There lived a small boy with his grandmother in their little lodge by the edge of a village. As was the custom of those days, this boy had a small Bow and Arrow to hunt small game as part of his training. He wandered here and there chasing after birds or trying to shoot squirrels, but one day he kept on going farther away from his home than usual; he was chasing a squirrel that he had wounded. He came to the edge of a cliff, and the squirrel he was after jumped to the top of a tree that was almost on the level with the top of this cliff. He was about to take another shot when he heard some voices down below the cliff at the base of the tree.

The voices were very strange; so he crawled slowly to the edge, forgetting the squirrel for the time being. Sure enough, there were two very little beings down at the foot of the tree. He recognized them as human beings like himself, only so much smaller than he was. They both had wee little Bows and Arrows each, and were shooting at a black squirrel, that he did not noticed on the tree-top, almost in line to where the Boy was. He also noted that their arrows could only come to half way to the top of the tree. They would pick up their arrows as it falls back, then would try again. They were encouraging each other to get their game, but instead of improving their efforts they were losing, the arrows falling shorter every time. He also noted that they were boys about his age, only they were so tiny, so much smaller than he was. It also seem to the Boy, that they were very anxious to get this black squirrel, judging from their talk as he heard them and understood everything they said. So taking pity of them, he took his own arrow and aimed at the squirrel that was so close to where he was.

He shot and it fell to the bottom where the two tiny boys were. They were so excited that they ran to where it fell, but they were surprised at the big strange arrow that was sticking right through the squirrel. They tried to pull it out of the squirrel and could not do it; then one of them happen to look up the top of the cliff and saw the face of our little Boy Hunter looking down at them. They were surprised, but glad to ask him to come down and help them, which he did with much joy, as he really was glad to see such strange small boys who seem very friendly to him. They asked him if he shot the squirrel that they had failed to get, and he told them he did; so he pulled out the arrow without much effort, and the two little friends were again surprised at the ease in which he recovered his arrow. One of the little friends then spoke up and told the Boy, that the black squirrel is the most desired of all meat for the Little People; to them it is like Buffalo meat is to our people in value of food; also that it is the hardest to kill of all animals to the Little People's opinion. The Boy told them that they can have the squirrel, that it was so common to him. The two little beings rejoiced at the gift and invited the Boy to come along with them, in fact he had to carry the squirrel for them,—it seem that they were unable to carry it themselves, it being too big for them. So he went along with the Little Boys carrying the squirrel with him; they led the way.

It seem but just a short distance from where they were, to their home; to him it seem that it was like any ordinary

J. J. Cornplanter
'37

home. They all went in. There was an old man and an old woman very much smaller than the Boy himself, which he understood to be the parents of his two little friends. The two little boys told their parents what took place and introduced their new friend. The old couple were very much delighted and welcomed their visitor to their home.

The old man said, "We are what you people must call 'Djonh-geh-onh,' the Great Little People." And motioning to the youngest of the two brothers, he continued: "This boy was born in the time when the rocks and stones rotted.

There are three tribes of us. We are the Hunters; it is our duty to continually be on the chase of the Great White Buffalo that travels under the ground and would cause great suffering to you man-kind if they ever come to the surface. In fact, we are watching all Evil-monsters that your Good-Spirit has taken below the ground for safety's sake for his people. The second group or tribe are known as the Stone-Throwers, and they are also powerful in their duties; some other time you may meet them. Then the last but not least are the tribe that wakes up the plants and causes them to grow in the springtime; they make the flowers blossom in their time, also paints the fruit red when it ripens. We are created by your Maker, and he has ordained certain duties to us which we must always be doing to help your people. We have been wanting all this time to get in contact with your people so our relationship would be made known to each other. This is the first time, and we will rejoice with our own ceremony, which will also be yours from now on. This ceremony is called 'Dark Dance' and really belongs to us, you must observe everything that takes place and remember everything so you can carry it back to your people, which will bring them good luck. They in turn will remember us and our relation by getting up the ceremony for our enjoyment. So I command you to watch now."

The old woman, "Djonh-geh-onh," started making ready a feast for the coming ceremony, making corn soup and using the meat of the black squirrel. When it was done and cooked, she then took a wee and cute little Water-drum (Tom-tom) and gave it three strokes with the little drum-stick. That seem to be the call to all the rest of the "Djonh-geh-onhs" to the ceremony, as it was not very long before they all came in. It was then night-time. The little mother of the two boys was the head-woman-in-charge of everything, as the Boy noticed. She then instructed a certain old member of this strange little people to do the announcing or what was later to be known as the "Opening Speech." He arose and started to give thanks to everything, then announced that this meeting was to be the beginning of the bond of relationship between the people of the earth and the "Djonh-geh-onh," and the purpose was to rejoice in the event by giving full ceremony; that hereafter they will derive much good from the introduction of their ceremony to the earth-people.

They all noticed the Boy, who was much bigger than anyone of this very strange beings. After all had partaken the Berry-juice that was passed around and had taken a few puffs of the sacred tobacco, the fire-light was covered up and it was then total darkness. The Boy sat next to the old man of the place. He was all excited and at a loss as to what was going on; he sat there and took notice of everything as it went on.

The old man of the place took the drum and started beating it, then started to sing, first very slow, then the

rest join in the singing. After a number of songs were sung,
then the time was faster. Everyone was singing until a certain song, then the leader gave one beat of the drum and
it was all over, and the fire-light was again uncovered, the
Boy then noticed that there were many of the strange

beings there, both men and women; many were old and
they were all types. After a short rest, then they had another drink of the Berry-juice and also another few puffs
of the tobacco, then it was again darkened as before. It
started as in the other period but of different songs which
the Boy seem to learn as it went on. After two more rests,
then it was over; then the feast was given out to all present
and they went home.

The old couple of the place showed the Boy where to
sleep, and he went to bed. He stayed there what seem to

him few days and nights. Every night the old woman would start the drum-beat, and in short time they would all come in, as in the first night. This same ceremony would go on again, and he learned everything as it went along. The two little "Djonh-geh-onh" boys were very nice to the Boy and made good friends and showed him many things that he never knew before.

Then one morning the old man told the Boy that he must now go home to his people, that he had learned everything now. So the two little boys took him back to where he first met them. They told him that any time that he wanted to see them, he can do so by coming to the same place bringing with him some sacred tobacco, called "Oh-yenh-gwah-onh-weh" (or The Real Tobacco) by the Senecas. That he must give a Dark Dance Feast in three days after he had been home and must tell his people that it is a gift to his people by the "Djonh-geh-onh" and that certain ones will hereafter belong to this sacred ritual. That it is the connecting bond of his own people with the "Djonh-geh-onh." That his people must remember the little people now and then by giving this ritual, and that it must be the custom to burn the tobacco before the ceremony, stating that the "Djonh-geh-onh" will hear the drum-beat at a distance of ten days' travel and will come right away to the place, wherever it may be. That there must be a feast of corn soup with Bears-head for them to feast on. That those that do respect this ceremony will be successful in the future, and the "Djonh-geh-onh" will help them and look after them, providing they live up to the binding ritual. That every time this song is sung the old-man who sang at the first ceremony and taught the Boy would be there and would help him sing unseen by others at the feast, as long as the Boy lived. That there will always be someone who will be the singer as time went on. That there will be certain members who will belong to this ceremony hereafter. That there are people who hold some secret bundle of Charm of some unknown animal or beast that uses it as good-luck for hunting purposes; these will be at once admitted into this new order, as the "Djonh-geh-onh" are so powerful on earth as any of the secret charm-animals whether it be dead or alive. That those who belong to this ritual will save their finger-nails trimmings and throw them over some rough place for the "Djonh-geh-onh" to use, as they like this very much,—being from the man-being, they value it much. That the secret-bundle of Charm shall be known as "Oh-che-nonh-genh-dah," and the holder must give Dark Dance every so often. That members are warned not to harbor ill-will against their own people, otherwise it may mean misfortune to the person against whom the ill-feelings were intended; as one member will, it may come true; and that it is not the intention of the "Djonh-geh-onh" to cause or create any trouble towards man-kind what-so-ever. All this the Boy was instructed to teach his people upon his return.

When they had finish telling him, they just disappeared before him, and he found himself back in the same place where he had met them, at the bottom of the cliffs. So he went home, and it was such a surprise to his grandmother that she really did not know whether she was seeing things, as she had given up all hopes of him being alive after so long a time since his disappearance. For really he was gone quite a long time, and his people had given up looking for him. He was quite a big boy then. It is said that they (the "Djonh-geh-onh") took him away to a distant place to their home among the rocky cliffs in their cave. His own grandmother asked him where he had been all this time, and he told her all what took place from the time he saw them. He told her all about his experience and the Dark Dance and his instructions about giving the feast on the third night after his return.

She went and told the people of the village that the lost boy had at last returned, and in no time there were all sorts of curious people coming to greet the lost boy, and all wanted to know just what had happened. He was a willing teacher and readily told his experiences and the promised Dark Dance. Everyone was excited and could hardly wait until the time set for the Feast. Instead of having only chosen ones attend, it was open to all so everyone can see what they knew to be the first mystic dance.

According to the promise of the two little "Djonh-geh-onh" boys, the old father of the two little boys did come and sat next to the Boy who was to sing. No one but the Boy saw this "Djonh-geh-onh" sitting there and singing with him when the ceremony began. They conducted it very much according to the advice of the Boy; he sang and the people of the village had never heard anyone sing so good as the Boy did, but it was the help of the "Djonh-geh-onh" that made the song so good.

Thus was the origin of the Dark Dance in those days when strange things could happen, when animals could talk to man-beings. It seems that this and other rituals were inherited, as it seem to follow down to the next generation until the present day; we still carry on these strange un-believable rituals, not knowing just the exact cause, only that we have to put on the dances in order to be released from the spell. It sounds very odd, but such is the case; as I say now, "Once an Indian always an Indian," so we must carry on with the customs that our ancestors did long be-fore we came to this world.

Sah-nee-weh, do you recall my last Dark Dance that you missed? My friend Carl Carmer was here and enjoyed it very much. I asked him how he like it. He told me he didn't see it, as it was total darkness. But he said the sing-ing was nice and weird in darkness. The soup, etc., were made by my wife "Yo-weh-sonh." My obligation to cele-brate this Dark Dance came from my great-grandfather on the father's side; his name was Henry Phillips, a Vet-eran of War of 1812. He was a hunter and used to carry some sort of a Charm in the gunstock of his rifle for luck in game, and it is said he never did release it before he died, so at last I had to be the victim. Now I have to put up this Dark Dance every year if I could afford it,—more like Health or Life Insurance, as it costs quite a sum to put a ritual like this,—we have trouble securing the Pigs-head to use for the feast. It seems ridiculous to have to do this in order to keep my health or well-being, but I am an Indian, so what?

Well, Sah-nee-weh, Sister of the Tonawanda Senecas, I hope I have made this clear for your information.

So I say, Oh-neh Nih-hoh, "This is all" (in other words).

Your Seneca Brother of the Snipe Clan,
"Ha-yonh-wonh-ish"
Jesse J. Cornplanter

CORN HUSK DOLLS: JJC

V

LEGEND OF THE STONE GIANTS

Tonawanda Reservation
November 14, 1936

My dear "Sah-nee-weh":

I will tell you the legend about the "Stone Giants" that used to roam about in this section and would devour people. You spoke of them the other day. I will relate the legend some writers have written about. As usual, this is my father's way of telling it.

Long time ago when this country was new, when there were all sorts of hideous beasts and monsters to be found in the great woods or forest, in those days many things used to happen that would scare the people; many of them were caught and killed by some of these man-killing things that were common. There were all sorts of strange incidents told by the people who travel from one village to another; it was their fire-side tales that the children were taught. (They gain their knowledge this way when still very small. Such was my training also in my boyhood days.) In one of the numerous villages lived this certain young man; he was the type that bragged about himself, that he was fearless and did not take much stock from other people's stories about what happened here or there. He always said he

44

would have to see it first before he would believe, and that if he saw any of the subjects mentioned (as the ones to cause the scare, or whatever it happen to be) he used to say he would kill whatever it was, even do it by his bare hands. Such was the way this youth carried on, and everyone knew that he was talking without thinking what it may mean in reality. His name was "Ska-nonh-wonh-dih" (meaning other side of the ripples or rapids); he delighted in his idle boasting. He boasted that he would either subdue or better kill any Ken-nonh-squah that he ever met.

Now it seem at this time the "Ken-nonh-squah" or "Stone-Giants" were the most feared of all man-killing beasts or beings that were common then. They are called "Stone-Giants" because their coats were of stone, and no kind of arrows nor spears were effective. They were very big and powerful, and were cannibals in habits; they love to eat human flesh, especially fond of little children. Their Seneca name for this strange cruel giants is "Ken-nonh-squah" (the translation is lost). Now moreover this powerful beings could hear any person who happens to talk about them, regardless who or where it may be; so they knew "Ska-nonh-wonh-dih" and his idle boasting, and were only waiting chance to prove, or test him of his courage.

One day a female "Ken-nonh-squah" volunteered to try this Braggart. She found him walking along the river-bank as unconcerned and as happy as can be. She was on the opposite side of the river; so she called: "Sken-nonh-wonh-dih, it has always been your boast to either subdue or kill any Ken-nonh-squah that you ever met. Is that true?"

Poor Ska-nonh-wonh-dih was scared almost helpless as he turned around and saw this great big image of solid rock in human-form standing just across the river from where he was walking, but just like his boasting, he thought a good joke would be played on this big man-eater. Anyway, he was a careless young man; so he bravely answered: "Yes, it is true and I can do it. Come on over here."

Then the bold and brave "Ken-nonh-squah" immediately started to cross the river, which was very deep. She went to the very bottom as she was very heavy, due to her stone garment. As she disappeared into the water, "Ska-nonh-wonh-dih" started in a hurry and ran up stream where it was shallow water and wade across to the other side. As he did so, he forgot his tomahawk on a big rock where it was before. When the "Ken-nonh-squah" came up the bank, she looked and was surprised to find "Ska-nonh-wonh-dih" across the river.

He called her over and said, "Here I am, come on over."

She did not know what to do. She happen to look on the big rock by her and She found his tomahawk laying on top of the rock. She picked it up and start to look it over; then she said: "Huh, just look at his weapon that he fights with! How would he do with it?" and She touched her mouth with her finger as if to feel the edge of the tomahawk, then brought it down lightly and struck

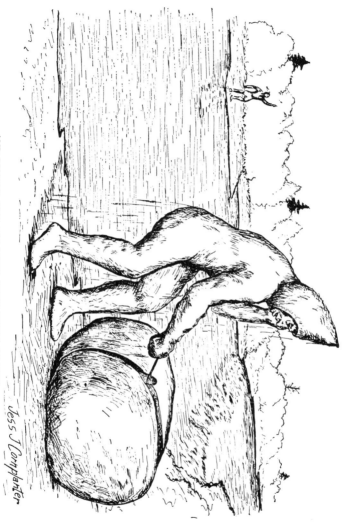

AND BEHOLD, THE BIG ROCK SPLIT RIGHT IN TWO

Jess J Cornplanter

the big rock as if to split it,—and behold, the big rock split right in two!

She was so surprised that she shook with fright, and she begged of him to spare her life. She said: "Please let me live, and I will promise you that I will never harm you or your people any more. I will also tell all the rest of my people to do likewise, and we will leave this country and go out west where we will never be seen again; our deeds of the past will only be as legends in the future. You are indeed more powerful than we are, and could easily destroy us if you so desire without any effort. Furthermore, I will make terms with you, so in the future you will be known as the most bravest man alive and will be able to do wonders in the days to come, if you only permit me to live and not kill me as you intended." Now she did not realize that it was herself that made the tomahawk very powerful, because she did touch it with her own saliva, thereby giving it her power.

Then did "Ska-nonh-wonh-dih" feel very brave and important. He told her thus: "I will let you go providing you carry out everything you said,—as I have a mind to destroy you and all your kind for all the evil you have done towards my people; but I will take you at your word, because if I find that you have deceived me in the least, I can easily locate you and all your kind,—so beware!" It is said that that was the last of "Ken-nonh-squah," they never have been seen since that day.

So it came about just because this young man could brag and could carry joke farther than anyone else, really at heart he was not as brave nor bold as he pretend to be. To this day when anyone makes idle talk or brag about one's own self, the people just laughs and point to the party saying, "Ska-nonh-wonh-dih is back." Now, Sah-nee-weh, this is my version of that legend as told me by my father.

This is another legend about the same mythical beings: It would seem that this strong and fierce race of Stone Giants had very bad feelings towards the Senecas, and always wanted to war on them, but somehow the Senecas were always successful in finding some means of protection from this continued warfare. This one story deals about the time when the great Chief of all the "Ken-nonh-squah" decided to put an end to this tribe; he had gathered all available men and started on a great march to the Land of the Senecas. It seem that the country of this great fierce warlike giants was in the great North Country. So on this day, on they came all prepared to wipe out forever this tribe of Senecas.

On their way they had to pass through a long deep ravine. (As they were intent on destruction of human race, they were very bold and even defied all to stop them.) While they were going along within this deep ravine, they started to sing their marching War Song. The Great Spirit looked down and saw what is about to happen to his own people, the Senecas; then he had a compassion and called on the "Spirit of the Wind" to stop the march of these giants by causing strong wind to blow on this big group of beings. The land of these Stone Giants were in the frozen country, and just south of that it was all rocky and full of deep ravines. It was in this country of ravines that these strong war-like giants were marching, singing their war-song, intent on taking the Senecas unaware, and exterminating them entirely.

So the "Spirit of the West Wind" he, the master and supreme of all Wind-Spirits, heeded the call of the "Great Spirit," and the wind did blow as no wind ever blowed before. (It was later termed "The Flying Head" or "Dagwa-nonh-enh-yen.") It blew so hard that it scraped the surface of the earth and rocks, leveling off hills and mountains as it went along. It came on, until it reached this certain ravine where these Stone Giants were then marching. With all its fury, it blew so hard that the sides of this ravine caved-in. First it started by taking off the tops of this big ravine and throwing the rocks into the ravine and burying the Stone Giants alive. On it came in its work of destruction; it levelled off everything in its path. Gradually the song of Defiance and War of these Stone Giants grew less and less until after a while it was all quiet; there was no sign of the Stone Giants and the force of the wind died down. Then Great Spirit was satisfied, because he love his Seneca Children. So today we have amongst our masks, long-haired weird Faces to show in remembrance of the

"Wind Spirit" and of the Stone Giants who did not accomplished their intention to destroy my people.

Sah-nee-weh, I hope you will be pleased of this legend as I tell it. It is very old legend.

Dah-neh-hoh, Your Seneca Brother,

Ha-yonh-wonh-ish,

SENECA BOW & QUIVER

VI

RABBIT AND PUSSY-WILLOW
A SENECA JUST-SO STORY

Tonawanda Reservation
March 30, 1937

My dear Sah-nee-weh:

It has been quite long while since you last heard from me, and our legends has been held up due to too much activity in our home life on the reservation in winter time, such as tribal dances in our homes, meetings and social activities. Last Sunday being Easter, we had with our Salt Creek Singing and Mutual Aid Society a delightful meeting and supper at our home. We ate all the eggs we could; then we had invited everyone in our neighborhood; then we had two chosen chiefs gave us good speech, thanking the Good-Spirit for all things he has given us. And after that we sat down and sang our "Women's Dance" songs. All winter long we had meetings of this nature, where we sang and enjoyed our companionship to each other. In this way we maintain social life to some extent.

For our legend this time, nothing is more appropriate than to tell about the legend of the Rabbit or the beginning of the Pussy-willow as sign for spring. More than this, it also shows that we have legends similar to your Animal

52

Stories. So, as the Story-teller says, "Open your ears, listen, and you shall hear about the Rabbit and his short tail."

Long time ago, when animals were still in their natural form as the Good-Spirit had created them, our friend the common Rabbit, often called "Cotton-tail" looked like all other animals: he had a nice bushy tail, and his fore-legs were just like any other animal. The only peculiar habit of the Rabbit was his love for green leaves and buds, or the tasty inner-bark of the Black-birch, and his desire or love for running. He had an idea, in his own way, that he was the fastest runner of the animal world. Thus it goes:

One fine night this certain Rabbit came out as was his custom, and being in good spirits he started to run around in one large circle in an opening near a swamp. The soft downy snow-flakes were falling softly like some feathers. As he started to run around, he sang his song thusly: "Ah-gah-nee-ya-ah-yenh, ah-gah-nee-ya-ah-yenh, Da-ken-da-donh, Nah-ga-nee-ya-ah-yenh," in other words his song went like this: "If it would snow, if it would snow, how I would run about, if it would snow."

Thus he ran in his own tracks round and round singing as he ran, and sure enough it began to snow so much more, —then he was so much pleased and ran that much more. He kept up his song and running until quite late in the night, when he began to feel tired. Then he noticed that he had all the snow he wanted; some of the smaller trees were buried in the deep snow; he was very high in his track, as the snow had packed while he ran around. So he ceased his singing and started to look for a place to rest. He finally found a crotched limb of an old Willow-tree near-by, close enough for him to jump to, which he did, and as he was

J. J. Cornplanter '37

very tired, he fell asleep. When he had settled down on this limb, he slept all night and quite late in the next day.

In the meantime the weather got warmer, the spring thaw came, the snow melted very fast and was all gone by morning. In its place green grass and other plants were growing, spring had come, snow and Frost-Spirit had gone back to their North-land. There was our friend the Rabbit, up in a tree asleep. As we know him, he never was a tree-climber of any sort. So, what was his surprise when he found himself way up on a tree! We also know that he never was very bold nor brave. He was timid by nature. Always let well-enough alone. But he had to come down or starve up there on the tree. He tried to reason as best he could; he wanted an easier way to get down; and to make matters worse, he felt much more hungry when he noticed the green things growing all over. He wanted to jump, but lack the courage to do so; so there he sat and worried for the first time in his life. He sat there and looked down. The distance was so great to risk jumping, but there seem no other choice. He did not dare to move around much in his little nest, as it seemed otherwise he would fall down. The more he looked down at the new growing things, the more his hunger grew,—still, he was afraid to jump.

Thus it went on for quite a while until he could not stand it any longer; then he gathered all his courage and, with his eyes closed, he fell off more than jumping. And by doing so, his bushy tail got caught in this crotch where he sat. As he fell, his own weight caused his tail to break off, and there it hung on the limb. When he landed on the ground, the force of his jump caused to drive his fore-legs to his body, thereby causing the two legs to be much shorter than his hind legs. As he landed so hard and his fore-legs being driven in his body, he struck his upper-lip on a sharp stone, thereby cutting it deep and causing him to have a Split-lip. And as the legend goes, he has never climbed any tree since, and all his tribe have to this day been tail-less, with short fore-legs and a split upper-lip. Every spring we see those tiny catkins on all willow limbs to tell us that spring is here again. Remember that it really

was the tail of a Foolish Rabbit. I have now come to the end of my rather short legend. Dah Nih-hoh!

This legend has been told me when I was but a little boy. I have heard the song that goes with it so often that it seems but only yesterday when I last heard it. Most of our winter-time legends dealing with animals had a song or two with it. They used to say never to tell these legends only at winter time; otherwise some snake or worm may crawl into your bed. Or a bug or bee might sting your lip. I could close my eyes, live over these days, when life was just one round of childish enjoyment. During winter time the story-tellers would be going house to house; they would come in; the wee children are gathered around the Fireplace or stove as the case may be. We would fill his pipe with tobacco and light it for him, so he could smoke as he relate his stories of the animals or the mighty beings and beasts that used to roamed. When I was the age of fifteen or about, I used to go out myself and tell some of the legends that I had heard earlier in my life. So I know it is told here as it was told me about forty-odd years ago. This legend is intended more for children.

"Sah-nee-weh," I'll say, "Dah, Nih-hoh."

Your Seneca Brother,

Jesse J. Cornplanter

WOODEN BOWL & SPOON

VII

THE ORPHAN GIRL, A LEGEND OF
THE HORNED SERPENT

Tonawanda Reservation
March 31, 1937

Sken-nonh, "Sah-nee-weh":

While reviewing the legend I wrote you last night, this one came to my mind, and while it is still fresh in my memory I will write about it. In this legend it shows that the things people looked with fear, in those days, were also their benefactors in many cases, as this will no doubt show. And from this, was borned many cases where families had in their possession different bundles of so-called charm, supposed to bring good fortune to the holder of the bundle, also the beginning of our various Semi-medicine rituals or lodges, often called societies. This "Djo-nih-gwa-donh" or the Great Horned Serpent in one of the main members of the Great Dark Dance, where it is intended to renew the bonds of friendship and contact to the mythical beast that once owned the charm they may hold sacred,—it is a feast of songs with invocation to the mythical beings, such as the one you and Carl Carmer witnessed year ago at my place. Now bring up your chair and be attentive as I will relate of this monster horned serpent that saved this poor girl.

As the legend goes:—long time ago in a certain village of Senecas, there dwell among them a young girl who was an orphan, she had no relatives; though nice-looking and trying to be industrious where she may be staying, she was despised and treated mean. She stayed here and there, until forced out, then went elsewhere. Such was the hatred the people bore on her.

It was in the summer, when the Huckle-berries are ripe. As was the custom with the people in those days, they decide to go to the great island to pick the berries for the day and return in the evening. So they made the preparation and started out one fine day. They had canoes to travel with, as this place where the Huckle-berries grew was an island located way out on a large lake. It was pre-arranged that they were to leave this poor girl there and get rid of her in this manner; so she was invited to go along, which pleased her much, as it was an honor to be thus invited. Had she known the main intention, she might have taken second thought, but she was then accustomed to the rough treatment accorded her.

All went well; they arrived at the island and then started to spread out, but to return at a certain time. Our poor friend then went all alone and started to pick berries. She did not notice the time so much, she was too busy picking, but it was getting dusk when she thought about going back to the place where the canoes were,—it then was the time set to all return. But Lo! Everyone had gone, there were not a single canoe left. She could see the spot where the canoes had been; she noticed the wet tracks as they got in to leave. She then realized that she was doomed to stay and die on this island, as it was never visited but only once, just at berry-picking time.

As it was then getting late, she just sat down and ate some of the berries, as she was very hungry. She wanted to cry right out and give vent to self-pity, but she realized that it was all pre-arranged and could not be different. So she just sat there by the water's edge and kept looking towards her people's village, the main land. It finally got dark; so she laid down and then gave in to tears at her sad plight. She dropped to sleep at last but was awakened when someone spoke to her. Some man was calling her name. She sat up but could not make out anyone, as it was dark. The voice said thus:—

"It was all arranged that you be left here on purpose to perish. The people did not stay very long; then they all came back and left for home. I saw it all. You shall not perish here as it was intended, but shall return home, providing we have luck. I will take you back in the early morning. You will gather twelve-year-old shoots of Red Willow; then I will come up to the edge of the shore. Do not be alarmed at my appearance, as I look very impressive with my horns. I am what your people calls 'Monster Horned Serpent,' but my real name is 'Djo-nih-gwa-donh' and not so bad as I look. All I am afraid is that the 'Thunder Spirit' might see me. If the sky is clear, we are safe. Now remember to have the twelve Willow whips. When I come out of water, you are to sit on my head between the horns. As we go along, I will go slower and will sink more; when you notice that, just give me one tap with one of the Willow whips and tell me 'Jah-gonh' (encouragement) and throw the whip away. Above all, do not be frightened when you see me, for I am your friend and will always remain so. Dah nih-hoh.''

After that, there was an awful commotion in the water; then she went to sleep and rested well. Very early in the morning she woke up and went to get the twelve Red Willow whips, and as she came back to the shore, there was an awful disturbance in the water, and in no time a great massive head appeared out of the water. It was a very large monster-snake with two horns. The snake rested its head at her feet; then without fear she climbed up on its head between the horns and holding the horns on each hand, being careful not to lose the bundle of whips. When she had settled down, then the snake pulled back and turned around and started to glide on. It seem to travel with ease and speed; the head was held up above the water.

After they had gone quite a ways, she then noticed that the snake began to slacken the speed and started to sink lower than usual; so according to her instructions of the night before, she took one whip and give it a sharp lash, at the same time saying "Ja-gonh"; then "Djo-nih-gwa-donh" seem to take new life, started out with its head up again and renewed speed. They went along in this manner for quite a long time, every time the snake weaken, she would take another whip and do the same as before. She could see the outline of the mainland. When she noticed one little speck of cloud come up in the west, then right away she

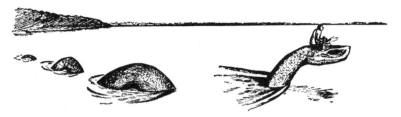

said, "Ah ha, oneh!" (Oh, now!) In no time the storm-cloud came up, and a real thunder-storm it was.

Then the snake spoke up for the first time and said: "At last they have seen me; now the question will be whether we can make the shore in time. However, I will do my best. I want to warn you one thing; no matter what happens, never tell anyone how you happen to return. In this manner, you will hold your position with the people, as they will no doubt fear you, as you are supposed to be marooned for good. Later on you will find with you, an article as charm from me. Keep it on your person all the time,—it shall be a token of our friendship, and shall bring you good luck and protection. After some time your people will have a dance and feast for the magic charm holders. When that happens, you too will observe a feast in my honor and memory; this dance shall be known as the 'Dark Dance.' You will do the invocation of thanks and everything, by throwing Sacred Tobacco in the fire. Let no one hear you. In this ceremony, I will have one song; my name shall be mentioned. So take heed and follow my instructions, and you will never see the same days as of the past; instead you shall be looked upon with respect by all the people. Some if not most of them will be afraid of you hereafter. Now bear with me and hope for the best. We may reach shore,—that is hard to say, as my enemy, the 'Thunder Spirit' is bound to kill me if he can."

Thus spoke the Great Horned Serpent, "Djo-nih-gwa-donh," all the while swimming as fast as he could, and the storm was coming very fast. It was more oftener that she was compelled to use the whip, as he was weakening much faster with the strain of the race. The shore-line was easily seen when she used up the last whip, and the dark clouds with lightning and thunder was fast approaching. In no time the storm arrived with much strong wind; rain and lightning was flashing all around them; she see the splashes as the lightning-bolts struck the water. Still she was not afraid but was more worried for the safety of her friend.

It was then little ways from the shore when the Serpent spoke again, saying: "It is the best I can do. I had better let you off here,—you easily reach land. Now remember everything."

So she jump off and the water was up to her waist. In

the meantime her friend had turned around and dove into deep water. As he did so, there was lightning flashes all over the spot; she was not sure whether they did kill him or not.

When the whole thing had passed, she made her way back to the village, which was not far away. She went into the first cabin that she came to, and what was the surprise, when they beheld her standing at the door-way,— she, that was left alone in that island. She was made welcome and was told to change into warm clothes, while food was place for her to eat. In a short time the news was spread, that she had returned. So a meeting was held in their longhouse, where there was rejoicing of all sorts for her return, but not a word was said about the manner of her return, and she did not venture to tell anything, remembering her instructions from her friend. When the celebration was about over, the chief of the village told her that a place had been reserved for her, as a gift of her people for her safe return, also stating which is her own home from now on. Everything came out as her friend had told her. Dark Dance was soon announced some other place, and then so on. She held a feast of her own, after she had discovered in her pocket a strange article,—she found out it was a scale, possibly from her friend. She directed the feast according to his directions. So the legend goes . . . Dah-neh-hoh . . .

In my old home town where I was born, they have this certain song dedicated to "Djo-nih-gwa-donh" as my father sang in his days long ago. You will find some morals to this legend. My father used to say that 'most all legends now-days were in the olden time a reality. It actually did happened, but in such a manner as to sound doubtful to us now-days. Most of our dances may have originated from some such event as this legend portrays. My people were living so close to nature that it was a sort of common affair to have someone get some help from some wild animal. All in all, I like them; I can listen to someone tell one legend after another, but who are they? They are all dead now, only few of us to carry on in our very limited knowledge. Believe it or not, as Ripley says.

Tomorrow we give thanks to the Maple for its sweet water. We give thanks for the things we enjoy, in forms of dance. I wish you would be here for our Maple Festival as I call it.

Will write when I have more legends in mind, it comes to me in a form of inspiration, as they were told to me when I was but a little boy. That is why I can not keep on every day. Some days I am unable to think of the simplest legend. It sounds funny.

My very best wishes to our White Seneca Sister.

Your Seneca Brother,

Jesse J. Cornplanter,

"Ha-yonh-wonh-ish"

VIII

MORE ABOUT THE LITTLE PEOPLE

Tonawanda Reservation
April 3, 1937

Dear Sah-nee-weh:

In our next legend, we will continue on the little people that we had written just the other day; it is something that must be included, otherwise it would not be complete. The accompanying pictures will illustrate this subject. The legend tells about the life and habits of the strange but powerful little people. Now we will begin here as follows:

In the olden times when my people lived more or less with nature's own way, when they were able to converse with animals, when strange things happened, when great beasts and birds were common, these little people lived in their various modes of habitation; they were very close friends of the "Ong-weh-onh-weh" our "Real Humans" as we are called. They made contact with our people in many different ways. To us, they are known as "Djo-geh-onh," and were considered more powerful even though they were very small. They had a way of making friends to little boys of our people, often taking them with them to their homes, which may be some place among the Rocky places or Caves.

66

One of the legends tells of an Indian boy about the age of seven was out hunting little birds. He had his little bow and arrow to shoot what he may see, as it was the custom in those days, to teach their growing boys all the sports of the hunt and chase as a major part of their early training,—

it was their school-time. This little boy was wandering on, when he finally came to a river to see if he could see some water-fowl to shoot. He had no sooner reached the edge of the water, when he heard a swishing noise to the direction of up-stream. Looking up, he was surprised to see a tiny canoe shoot around the bend of the stream at a rapid speed. In the canoe were two of the tiniest little men that the boy ever had seen. They came right up to where the boy stood and stopped. Both had a tiny bow and a quiver of arrows.

They both greeted the boy, then one of them asked him thus, "How would you like to trade your bow and arrows with one of us?"

Then the boy thought how foolish it would be to do so, as their bows and arrows were much smaller than his; so he

said, "How foolish it would be to do so,—why, yours are so much smaller than mine."

Then one of them took a bow and strung it and taking an arrow he shot it straight up, the arrow disappeared into the sky and did not come down at all. Saying at the same time, "That may be true, but all great things on earth are not always the biggest; you may live to learn that." Then they took their canoe-paddles and with one stroke disappeared around the bend of the river.

The boy was surprised; so he went back to his home, where he was staying with his grandmother. He told her all about what happened. Then his grandmother scolded her grand-son, saying: "You made a big mistake by your refusal to accept the trade. Had you taken one of their bows and arrows, you could take any game that you desired, as they are magic. Hereafter never be too hasty in judging people as you see them, for you never know who or what they may be."

That is one legend, then there are others. There are three different tribes of these "Djo-geh-onh," each living according to their type. There are the tribe who dwell underneath the rocks and caverns. It is their work to watch constantly the "White Buffaloes" that dwell underground,—if they came out above, they would cause much suffering to mankind. Then there are the tribe who live among the plants. It is they that causes the green things to come up in spring; they paint the flowers their colors and paint the fruit when the time comes; they also painted the corn all the different tints. And the third tribe are the ones who dwell along the streams and are called "Stone Throwers." They can throw big rocks long distance, uproot big trees, and are very powerful in every way, but are very friendly to the earth-children. They are mentioned in some of our songs, and the Dark Dance is especially dedicated to them. They are very fond of "Ong-weh-weh-onh-weh" and the "Oh-yenh-gwa-onh-weh," the sacred Indian Tobacco. Dah Nih-hoh. This completes all about "Djo-geh-onh." I know you have seen their dance at my place year ago last winter.

Dah Nih hoh, "Sah-nee-weh."

Your Seneca Brother,
Jesse J. Cornplanter,
"Ha-yonh-wonh-ish"

IX

THE FLYING HEAD

Tonawanda Reservation
April 9, 1937

My dear Sah-nee-weh:

This is another legend which came to my mind when the strong March wind blew so hard that I could not sleep at all, but laid in bed and thought of the wind and why it came to be. In this legend, it shows how the Flying Head was first seen. Though some others have different version than I have, it is all about the same in substance. In our language we call the Spirit of the wind, "Dah-gwa-nonh-en-yend."

Long time ago when my tribe was at war with our enemy of the south-land, the Cherokees or "Oh-ya-dah," the Cave-dweller and often called the people of the Red. This happened when a War-party was on its way to the land of the "Oh-ya-dah" to come back with as many scalps as they can. Now it seems that in those times they had a Head Chief in command in every War-party. It was his duty to give thanks every morning as they got up, before they ate their morning meal. In those days, long before they had any idea that there was a Supreme Being that created all living and growing things, before they knew that it was

71

wrong to kill human being, they gave thanks in their simple way for the day, the new light, and asks for success in their work of destruction of the enemies' lives. And when it was over, then the Chief would proclaim his deeds and gave his War Song, called "Ah-donh-wenh."

Now at that time, there was in this party, one very young man; in fact it was his first experience, so this man thought many different things besides war and scalps; but he was thinking that maybe there is some being greater than they are, who may have created the world; that this being made life and every growing things; that he ordained that people should love each other and be neighborly. Thus thought our younger warrior as he laid down before he went to sleep. He also asked any power that would help him to accomplish his intention to cease this slaughter of mankind.

It was the custom in those days to take their time in their march to the enemy country, to conserve their strength for the coming battle. So it took many days before they reached their destination. Every night, upon retiring, the Head Chief would cause warriors to stand guards at certain distance and there to give the alarm in case of attack. Now as this young man laid, looking at the numerous stars, he would meditate; he was an unusual man, as was the custom in those days.

They were just one more day's journey from the enemy's village, when as usual they had a few words of encouragement from their chief to be more watchful. They had just started, when a strong wind began to blow, such wind as one had never experienced before. So the party looked for some means of shelter, and in time found a shallow ravine or depression for creek-bed where they took shelter. There

they all huddled close to the bank of the ravine and just waited for long time. The storm grew more violent until they noticed what seemed like sparks of fire flying with the wind. They marvelled at the strange sight and wondered. The young warrior saw this sight and began asking the unseen power to make it more stronger so his people could change their minds. All at once they saw a monster Head with long hair in the storm. Now it seem that this monster head was the power of this wind-storm, as the trees of the forest just snapped in two before this head reached the tree. And they saw that it did have sparks of fire issuing from its mouth as it blew the wind. This monster Head with its long hair whirling all directions was the center of the storm. It would go this way, then would change its course. One could see its trail as the trees were levelled to the ground; many of the great trees were up-rooted and some snapped off at the strong force of the wind. There were all sorts of trees tangled up over the narrow place where the War-party had taken refuge.

The storm went as it came; all in a time, it was over. Then they came out from under their hiding place. So great was their fear at the super-natural sight they saw, that they were uncertain as to their next move; and the young warrior saw his chance,—he asked the chief for word. The Chief granted the request easily; so the young warrior said:

"It is my opinion that we are on a mission far from the pleasure of the Great Spirit who made earth and all living thing. It is also my idea that he intended that mankind should love one another, to help each other in time of distress, to give thanks for the many things that he has given us in return. That it was his messenger that we just now saw, and if we persist in going on with our journey, that we may all perish. If I had my way, I am sure we would all return, and we would give thanks to the great spirit for sparing us; also we would have a ceremony to the Big Head with the long tresses."

Thus spoke this young warrior,—it was the first time that a word of peace was ever spoken. As the Senecas were a proud and boastful tribe, they covered great territory, their word was respected to the neighboring tribes. Even their enemies respected them to a certain degree. So it was a thing most unexpected for a War-party to halt on its journey.

After a long period of silence, then the Head War-chief stood up. He addressed his party in the following manner: "Men of my party, I have given the whole matter a careful thought,—the manner of the wind-storm and what our young warrior has spoken, which carries much wisdom, and I should say truth if it were known and proven. Much as I dread the idea of retracing our steps, I think it is the only safe and sensible thing to do. But do not let me think for each and every one of you; so each one of you who thinks he is still yearning for the scalp and blood of our sworn enemy, in spite of the unnatural thing we had just seen, rise up now."

And not a single man stood up, nor as much as to move about, as they all sat upon up-rooted trees and the Chief was the only one that was standing as he gave the speech.

Then the Chief gave the following orders: "We shall return to our homes, we shall each carry back to our relatives a message of peace, and we shall celebrate the event of our close connection of this monster head with due ceremony, which I think is the reason we are spared; and more too,—we shall elevate this young warrior to that of head man in this ceremony and for all ceremonies to come. In the morning, he is to take my place as head man, I chose him for his wisdom. Let no man say that we retraced our steps by reason of cowardice. This I have spoken." So accordingly they all returned towards home.

In the following night as they slept, this young man had a dream. He saw this Monster Head; it spoke to him thusly:—"You are the man I have been looking for all this time. I am the Spirit of the Wind; my name is and shall be, 'Dah-gwa-nonh-en-yend' to anyone talking about me. I am to be your friend. You shall find a hair about your dress tomorrow; that is my own, it came to you during the storm. Keep it forever and it shall cause you to be lucky and be a great man hereafter. One thing you will do for me when you have told your dream,—just the one part where I am telling of my own name and who I am; the rest is for your own knowledge. Then you must sing for me my favorite song, what you people now call 'Ka-nonh-ih-o-wih'; and your people shall always sing this song as an offering to me in the future. Later on your people are going to observe what shall be known as 'Oh-che-nonh-genh-dah,' 'O-en-nonh' which shall be in total darkness, and shall be for spirits such as I am. We are your friends, you earth-children. But this part itself shall come from other source. But remember my instructions when it does come about in your village. No matter where you are, always keep the Charm, my hair; that is your Good-luck emblem from now on."

That was the dream he dreamt that night, and early in the morning, as announced, he took his place as leader of the party, and called everyone to meeting. After due thanks to the Great Spirit, he then related his dream of the night before. Everyone was surprised at the dream. When he had finished his talk, he started to sing this song which is to be set aside to the Spirit-of-the-Wind. According to the advice from the Flying Head, this young man soon arose to be a leader in all ceremonies and became a great and powerful man. In time his people did start a new ceremony known as "Dark Dance" which was supposed to be dedicated to the "Djon-geh-onh," the real small people. Then all the known animals and things not known were all included in this ceremony. Thus was the origin of the "Dah-gwa-nonh-en-yend" and also the "Dark Dance." This is my version of this strange being, that was seen but once. My people still talk about the "Dah-gwa-nonh-en-yend" to this day. It is included in our "Dark Dance" as one of the Charms. This is one of the most weird of legends, though my father says it really did happened long ago. Most legends are true, I supposed. Dah-neh-hoh . . .

Your Seneca Brother,
Jesse J. Cornplanter

X

THE GIANT LEECH

Tonawanda Reservation
April 26, 1937

Sken-nonh, Sah-nee-weh:

I had to write you again while I am thinking of the very nice time I had while visiting you and your folks, I enjoyed so much, and the fine dinners you served me just about evens up with the time you had at our place, and the Indian dinner we had, especially that "Oh-gonh-seh" or dried corn succotash,—you said it was so good. That is one of the old-fashioned foods we still use,—it is made in this manner: When the corn is green so it is still milky, it is made same as your succotash, then pounded in our mortar and pestle until it looks like Johnny Cake. It is put into pans and baked brown, then it is made into small pieces and then dried. When it is real dry, it is then stored away for winter use, real Seneca Food. We like it very much. While still on the subject of food, our next legend will be on animal food of olden times, it deals with ancient custom of our marriages and who picks out the wife or husband, so here goes:—

It was the accepted custom in olden times for the old people to choose the mate for their young people whatever the case may be. When the young boy or girl had reached the age to marry, it was the custom for the old parents to look about for a suitable mate for their young man or girl. If there is one found that is pleasing to the parents, especially the mother, then she goes to the mother of this certain young girl or boy as the case may be. They talk about the qualities of their young people in question and how a match of the two would make a good couple. If it was pleasing to both, then they set the date. Often the ones concerned are not aware of what is going on, until the time comes of the wedding, and if they do not get along smoothly after they are married, then it was the old folks' duty to preach to the couple and make up for the difference. If there was any love among my people in the olden days, it was only after they had been married and their habits and personal traits were all understood,—then love may be developed. Often it turns out just the reverse. Sometimes the man finds his wife hard to please, and it is the subject of this legend.

In those days there was a certain young man married like the custom just described, and as they lived together, he discovered that his wife was very hard to please. She was always finding faults with whatever game her husband brought home; it was always something wrong according to her idea, and she demanded the proper food. He tried real hard to please her, as he was very fond of her.

One time he brought home a deer, and to her venison

was too greasy and too tasty; so he went out in search for
what he thought would be the right food for her. He then
found a turkey and killed it. When he took it home, she
cooked it; she complained that it was too dry. So he thought
he would find other animal which may please her. He saw
a nice black squirrel and killed it, took it home. She
cooked it and ate it; she did not like it,—it had too small
bones. So again he went in search for an animal that had big
bones. He saw a buffalo, and he thought that it was the one
she would like. Then he killed it and took what he could
carry home. She cooked it and ate it; she found that the
bones were too big. So again he was wrong. Then he saw a
nice fish in a stream. He thought that it might be the kind
she would like as it had small bones; so he caught it and
took it home. She did cook and ate it, but she nearly died
when a tiny bone stuck in her throat. He had quite a time
taking the bone out of her throat. Now she was very much
angry at him. She claimed that he tried to kill her by giving
her fish that had such small bones and so many of them
that it was hard to find them all. She wanted something
that had no bones at all.

Now the hunter-husband was in a hard position; he did
not know of an animal that would not have any bones. Still
he loved his wife; as a good true husband he is bound to
please her. So went this way and that way, always on the
watch for an animal that had no bones at all. He wandered
far and wide, he saw all sorts of game, but they all had

bones. Then he went along the streams and lakes; maybe
he would find some other animal with no bones at all there
in the water-fowls and animals. Day after day he wandered
and still no luck, all he saw had bones. Then when he

found none that he wanted, he tried the swamps and all the
ponds and lagoons; maybe he would find the one he was
looking for in the swamps. He walked along the edge of the
swamps, often mired to the waist in muck and quick-sand,
but he was bound to find what he was looking for. He
spent much time among the rough brambles, getting
tangled up in devil-vines full of stickers or having cuts in
his face and hands by the saw-grass that lined the swampy

ponds or lakes. Still he kept on. Some way he knew that he would find what he was searching, providing he looked for it long enough or went to the right place.

He was a sight by now. His clothes was all torn into shreds, which made it hard for him to travel, as he was often caught in some brush or vine. He was getting thin and gradually losing flesh, due to too much hardships in his continual search; but such was his love for his wife that his condition did not matter. It went on in this manner for quite a long time. His wife would scold him when he returned home empty-handed, saying that he was not true nor good to her. He was in despair. But he only made up his mind that much more, that he would sometime find what he was looking for. So one day he went to another direction.

He had never been in this section before, and some unseen force seem to make him take this way. He went on quite a long distance until he came to a great big swamp located in the middle of a place what looked like a basin, surrounded with hill all around. In the middle of this big swamp was a large lake. It was surrounded by a dense growth of all known vegetation, and it was so hard to pass through. There were all sorts of Swamp-oaks, Poison-Sumacs, Swamp Nettle-weeds, crawling Devil-Vines, Saw-Grass and soft mud that seems to suck down anything that comes there, but this devoted hunter went into this swamp. He was cut all over, he was mired down to his arm-pits more than once, but somehow he always managed to get out and continue on his way towards the lake in the middle.

He finally reached the edge. He noticed that there were all sorts of birds flying around and dipping themselves into the water. He stood there and watched. He also saw that over on the other side from where he stood, that there seem to be some commotion every little while by the birds; so he went towards that way, working his way through with much effort. But after very much trouble he managed to get there; then he watched.

All at once he saw what appeared to him like a huge black thing shot out of the water as the birds came down near the water. This black thing, whatever it was, caught one of the birds and then went back into the water again. He could not see what it was, as it was too far out and the water was so smooth that it was hard to see anything from the edge of the lake; so he looked about him for suitable tree that he would climb, and at last saw one; so he went and climbed up, and from the top of this tree he could see the water and deep into the water. Then he waited to see what it was that was causing this commotion.

He had to wait just a short time, when he saw the birds came towards the spot again. He saw that they seem to know the exact spot, and they dipped into the water, and as they did so, he noticed a great big oblong thing came up from the bottom of the lake. It came very sudden, and as the birds were near the water's edge, this thing seem to stretch out and reached up out of the water and caught one of the birds and then returned into the deep water as it had came. Now this hunter wondered; he had never heard his people tell anything about such a thing as he saw. So he sat up in that tree and waited. Pretty soon the birds came back again, and sure enough this thing came up again and caught one more bird and disappeared again into deep water. He sat and watched this thing over and over again, until he thought he understood it;—this thing was actually a living thing, able to stretch into any length; it can swim along in the water by extending its shape and then drawing itself up again, like an angle-worm crawling. He saw and understood that it had no bones. Then he knew that he had at last found the very thing he was searching for, a fish or some water-animal that had no bones. So he drew his arrow and waited.

He saw the birds flying nearer again and then he strung his arrow ready to aim and shoot, and as this thing came up, he aimed quick and shot. But the thing just went back into the water like the other times without any signs of it being shot. Then our hunter made up his mind to keep on shooting until he had killed it; so he waited, and when it came up again as it had done previously, he shot again, and the very same thing happened,—it went back without any effect. He sat there and kept on shooting when it came up, until he had shot all his arrows. Then he was very much angry and determined to go home and get more arrows, which he did.

He came back and started shooting again. Still this thing kept on without any signs of effecting anything for all the

arrows he had shot into this thing. He used up all his new arrows. This time he was much more angry. He went home and found out that he had no more arrows.

Then he made up his mind that he will try to get arrows from his grandmother, who had a quiver full of old arrows that probably belonged to her husband. So he went to see her. He told her all about his trouble, everything about the thing that took all his own arrows; that he was determined to get this thing as that was the thing or animal that had no bones.

She told him in this manner: "Grandson, it is indeed very hard for you that you have this wife who can not be pleased at all; it is causing you lot of unnecessary hardships. If you don't watch out, you shall be killed by trying to please her. If something would only happen that would teach her the lesson, you would live. This thing that you are after is what we call 'So-gwah-dis-go-wah'; it is the monster bloodsucker like the ones you often see in water of all swamps. Surely it has no bones. It is true that it has lot of strong power. I do not think you can kill it; it has been tried many times before you. But that is your duty to please the sort of a wife you got, I will let you have your Grandfather's arrows. I do not know how good nor how much power they may have, but I do know that your Grandfather was no ordinary man when it came to doing things that others fail. So I hold some faith in your next attempt. If you should be fortunately to kill this monster, I am warning you not to eat any of it. Let her eat, her that desires."

So thus warning her grandson, she gave him the old quiver that was covered with dust of many years. He went back to this lake as fast as he could, and took his old position again and waited. He did not wait very long; then he saw it come up again. He shot. The thing acted as if it was hit and flopped back to the water and did not sink so soon, but as it was about to go down again. He took another shot; then it wiggled and splashed water all over. While it was thus struggling, he shot the third time. He knew that he had at last killed it, as it stopped struggling and just seem to float along. So he got down from his perch on top of the tree. He waited until it drifted to the shore where he could hook it with a pole that he found; then he brought it to shore. It was so large and so slimy that he can not even lift it out of the water. So he just cut a portion of it from the side, a size that he could easily carry home. At last he had killed a game without any bones.

He returned home and told his wife that he had brought back a part of an animal that had no bones at all. So she got ready and cut it up and put them on cooking. She cooked it all day and all that night, and by next day it was still tough and elastic. It just won't cook, that was all. But she was very persistent and she kept on cooking it. When her husband had all he could stand of waiting, then he went and told his people and her people also. They all came on the fourth day of her cooking. There they sat and watched her cook. Then when they saw that she was going to keep on and would not despair, then they got up one by one and told her her folly, her selfishness, and how she must be in the future; that this thing she was cooking was not for food, but if she ate it, it would kill her,—it was poison and was one of the most powerful of all monsters; that she must not tell her man what game to kill,— that it was a man's duty to hunt and that they all know what is fit to eat and what is not. I suppose if they had not stopped her cooking, that she would be cooking yet. Dah-neh-hoh.

I am not that type: if my wife don't like the things I kill for food, she can go without it,—and I love my wife, but not that bad. I think this is a good legend. Don't you? Some moral to it. This is one of the mystic charm animals and beasts that comprises our "Oh-che-nonh-genh-dah" ceremonies of Dark Dance.

Your Seneca Brother,
Jess Cornplanter

GAH-NIH-GA-TAH.
Corn Mortar & Pestle

XI

THE NAKED BEAR
A SENECA LEGEND OF PEACE

Tonawanda Reservation
April 15, 1937

My dear Sah-nee-weh:

I have been thinking about the next best legend to wrote to you and have finally decided on this one. It is like most of our legends,—based on facts, with a touch of morals to it. As you shall see. It deals with the first attempts at establishing peace, and the origin of the so-called Holding Hands Dance, also the fact that in those days the cry of distress as now used in case of the death of a Chief Sachem of the so-called Six Nations Confederacy,—as a runner is dispatched to notify the neighboring tribes, as he reaches the village, this call of distress is given every little distance to announce of the sad affair, and the runner goes to a certain Sachem's home. It is now used for this purpose. But in those days it was common, as mentioned in this legend. And last of all, the origin of the phrase of "Burying the hatchet or Tomahawk," believe it or not. Sit up close and you shall hear how the most dreaded monster that devoured people known as "Nyah-gwa-ih-heh-go-wah," the Naked Bear, was finally chased away and peace came finally to the tribe.

89

Long time ago, as they say, there were (it seems) a chief who ruled his people with such wise judgment that all his people like him so well. Now it also seems that in those days, they all lived in villages or settlements.

Each group of homes or village as we shall call them, are led and ruled by one man who is Chief. Now in this certain village there dwelled this very wise old chief, and it was then in the days when people did not know the difference of good and evil,—that it was evil or sin to take human life. They valued the human scalp more than anything else; in fact so much, that a member of the tribe was judged according to the number of scalps he has taken.

Now this wise old chief started thinking that there must be someone who made life and the earth and all growing things, that this man or being, whoever it may be, probably intended that there should be love and feeling of mutual welfare among people residing in villages or even among neighboring villages; that they were created as one family, all related to each other in some manner as to bind all people as one tribe or family. It seems that the more this chief thought, the more he began to see the folly of his people. He alone made his duty to study the sins of his fellowmen. He spent many days and nights meditating the wrongs of his people, trying to find a way to bring about peace to his village and if possible to his neighbor, the other village. So, after a time, he decided to call his people to council, to relate his decision and abide his plans with his people.

So a council was held in their long house. This chief arose when all had arrived, and started to tell his opinion, not leaving any little detail that he might accomplish his mission. After long discussions with his many War-chiefs and leaders, it was accepted that this Head-chief was right and should be announced as the new-thought belief. After all was quiet, the peace was thus established in his own village. He then wanted to let his neighbor know about it; so he arosed and made known his decision, that is, to have two men volunteer as runners and carry his message of good-will and peace to the next village. After a time, two very young men, who are very intimate friends, accepted the duty as runners. They were to start out the following morning at sun-rise. Then the meeting was over.

The two volunteers each went home and told his women-folks, whether it be a grandmother or mother, of his acceptance as a runner and everything connected with it. Then each woman made the necessary preparation for her men, as they were both known to be very good and brave men and such good loyal friends as was never seen in any place. After a good night's rest and a good sleep, they arose early and made ready, each being properly armed and equipped for war-path journey. They both arrived at the long house about the same time, and they were men to be looked upon as very outstanding and very fine physique. . So good were their equipment of war-gear, that the people marvelled at them. So the Chief made his speech to them, their mission, how to approach the village, and so on.

Then the oldest of the two volunteers spoke thus:—"We are about to start out on a mission, of extreme danger. Whether we will accomplish this well or fail all depends on our good charm-tokens and our ability, but if we are fortunate, then we will return at sun-set tomorrow." Thus speaking, they set out at an easy stride. There were an aisle or pathway made for them, people lined up on both sides.

In no time they were soon in the edge of the woods, and then they started to run at their own full speed until they had gone quite a ways, then they halted. The leader said that they should now travel in their own respective form of traveling for speed. So (according to the mode of

Jesse Cornplanter
37

traveling in those days) they each said as to what form he would resume his speed. The leader said he would be as a Wolf, and his partner that of an Owl, to fly on. It was agreed to travel thus and let each other know just where each were, by the Wolf barking and the Owl answering with a hoot. So, each assuming the shape of his chosen

Token of Charm, they both set out.

They traveled in this manner at a great speed; the Wolf ran on and the Owl flying at his top speed. Every little while the wolf would give a sharp bark, to be answered by the hoot of the owl. It was decided before thus starting out, that when it is noon, the wolf would give a long wailing howl as signal for the owl to come down for their mid-day meal or lunch. Sometimes the owl would be ahead when the wolf gave the signal bark, but they seem to be equal in their speed at the most. They had gone about midway of the distance to the next village when the wolf gave the long howling wail, and in no time the owl was down to earth and then each were once more in their human shape and ate their lunch of parched corn-meal sweetened with maple sugar (their regular traveling rations in those days), and drinking from a nice cool water of a spring. After a short rest they started again on their other half of their journey, each resuming his own Charm token, and both keeping track of each other in their own way, by the barking of the wolf and the hooting of the owl.

Thus they traveled until they reach the place where the activities of the other village can be heard,—as they used to say, within hunting distance of their village. Then the wolf gave the signal for the owl to come down, which it did. Then they both resume their own normal shapes, and each washed his face from war-paint and then they left their war-gear with the understanding that in case one might perish in their mission, the other would return and take back his partner's implements home as sign of his misfortune. Then after they had buried their war-gear and washed all war-paint, they started out. The leader gave the long wailing call of distress which sounds something like "Go-o-o Weh," repeated three times. They kept on towards the village of the enemy.

As they approached the village the leader kept on giving the distress wail as to assure them safety, lest they may be killed at the first sight. Such were the hatred in those days, that it was not safe to even go outside at night unless with some men with weapons escorting them; otherwise some lurking enemy may be waiting just by the door with his tomahawk ready for scalp. Very soon someone in the village heard the call coming nearer; so he gave the alarm, and when the chief had heard about it, he commanded his young warriors to make haste and see what might be coming. In the meantime, everyone was excited, waiting whatever may be that is coming to their village at this time. So the two volunteers were soon met with a big party all armed, but the one in charge of the party noted that the two men were not armed nor painted for war; so he soon subdued his men and warned them to refrain from any violence but to wait what may be the cause of the enemy coming to their midst. So the two men were taken to the home of the chief of the village, who received them with dignity and asked them what might be their mission, if any, for coming to his place at this time.

The leader of the two arosed and gave the following speech:—"Your neighbor, our Chief, has sent us to you, he has given us a message of peace to deliver to you. He has been thinking for some time back, that it must be wicked and a sin to take another man's life just for scalp; that there must be some supreme being that may have created life, the earth, about all living things; and that we are wasting them by not living the life that he may have intended we should live. That he may have intended we should be more friendly and visit each other, maybe help each other; that we may be all related somehow way back as one family that retains love. That he, our Chief, asks for your careful consideration as to your opinion regarding this idea; and if you feel willing to accept his terms, he will forget all ill-feelings and will heal his wounds with the salve of peace. He also says that it is entirely all up to you to say what will be done to bring about this bond of friendship and peace. All this we have spoken in his own words, Dah neh-hoh."

After they had spoken, they sat down. Then the Chief of this village called on his people for opinion, giving anyone who wants to speak a chance to voice his feelings on the question as it is brought to them. Some of the War-party leaders who are called War-chiefs gave speeches; many were bitter and more inclined to carry on with their warfare. Then many were in favor of accepting the terms as it was presented.

So, after quite a long discussion, their Chief arosed and made the following speech: "I and my people here assembled have given the good message of my neighbor as presented by you two, a good careful consideration, as you two are aware of, and it is my own opinion to accept every word. That I have been thinking of the very same thoughts many times, only holding back such ideas for fear that my people may mistake me for cowardice. Now you who are messengers may rest in peace with feeling of safety and free from any injury from my people, but you are now my visitors. This message I will send back to my friend; 'Hereafter, we are as brother, dwelling in neighboring villages. I, the Chief here, have accepted his words of peace and friendship, that we cover up the embers of hatred and bloodshed with the cool ashes of peace, and at a given time, shall put out the fire entirely; that in fours days' time, we shall meet all together, half-way between our villages, at the open field across the river, and there in one pit dug for the purpose we shall hold each other's hand in friendship and peace, my neighbor and brother. Then into this pit we shall cast all weapons of war and then will bury all hatred in one grave, then live as brothers henceforth. The only weapons allowed will be the ones we use for the hunt. And the War-cry will be a thing of the past, to be used only as such times as we may dance our old dances of the past, to remind our young people what we have done in the past. This meeting will be

at high sun; then all people must gather at the place mentioned. In closing this meeting we shall indulge in few
dances of pleasure to celebrate this great event tonight, then
we shall retire. My guests will be taken care of in my own
household and will depart early next morning; so anyone

wishing to see them start will come early to my place. This
I have spoken.' " Thus spoke the chief of the village.

Then accordingly, they had few dances of pleasure, and
then it was all over and everyone went home quietly. The
two messengers went back with the chief and were treated
with all respect and slept well after such an ordeal of the
day. So very early the next day, they woke up and were
each given a good meal and a carrying lunch of parched
sweetened corn-meal, and a pair each of new moccasins for

traveling. After bidding farewell and thanking the chief, they went out and were very much surprised to find the people of the whole village all assembled by the house, and a pathway or opening lane for them to take. Then after the leader making few parting words, they started out on an easy pace amid cheers of good words, and in no time were in the woods again at their travelling speed. It seemed but a short time when they came to the spot where they had changed their mode of dress, where they had left their war-gear. They soon found everything and made ready again for their long journey towards their home. Each resumed his own mode of travel; the leader turning himself into a wolf and his friend an owl, they started again as they had done on their way coming over. Every little while the wolf gave a bark, and the owl returned reply with a hoot, sometimes ahead and other times in the rear. Thus they travelled until they reached the spot midway of the distance; there the wolf gave a long wailing howl and in no time the owl came swishing down, and once more they were the two runners, who rejoiced at the success of their mission and ate the lunch given them, washing it down with the cool water of the nice spring nearby. After a short rest, while they talked about the events of their trip, they resumed their supernatural forms and were soon on their way homeward. Everything went on as before, so it was like no time when they were approaching their own village and the day was getting towards dusk; so again the leader, the wolf gave his cry of signal, and as before the owl came down again. They soon were in their natural forms, then they started to travel the remaining distance towards home, then the leader started to give the distress call, "Go-o-o Weh, Go-o-o Weh, Go-o-o Weh," three times every few paces as they ran. And it was then getting dark, and they soon saw gleams of light coming towards them, and they were met with a big party to escort them home, all bearing burning pine tinder torch well armed.

They were led direct to their long house where the whole village were all gathered waiting for their return and the news they would have. They were placed in the midst of the place, and after they had little drink of some medicine, then the chief of the village arosed and thanked them for their safe return and for fulfilling their mission. Then he said: "I now listen with ears wide open for what message you may bear, tell every bit of what happened." Then the chief sat down in his place, while the leader or the older of the two volunteers arosed and told his story.

The chief next responded with praise and thanks to the two men who accomplished their important and dangerous mission. Then he warned everyone to be ready to leave on the third day at high sun to the spot chosen as the place of gathering, also to take all weapons, leaving only such as used for the hunt. Then he said that they would cover up the fire with ashes (as was the custom in the early days, meaning that the council is ended) with few of their pleasure or social dances as they were called later. So they all enjoyed some dances as symbol of their success in thus bringing peace to the village and its people at last; then after it was over they retired to their homes with joy in their hearts.

Everything was quiet in the village the following days and nights with only the preparation for the coming trip to the place where the tomahawk will be buried. It was such times that it was never known before, where everyone was happy with no thought of danger. Such were their joy to be thus freed from this constant fear of the enemy that may strike at any place and time, that they had the pleasure of staying out evenings, singing, laughing and shouting. They even had parties all over,—the older men did this. They all wondered at the new form of life in their village. Some spent the evenings in singing some of their numerous songs or recounting their deeds or experiences in the days just recently past. Thus it went on until the time came when they all left for the place that was selected to gather; the chief with his leaders, men who were War-chiefs in the past, but now known as secondary chiefs, then the rest of the people.

They travelled very slowly, camping for the night about half way to the place. It was an unusual sight to see campfires in all directions as each family chose certain spot to camp for the night. There were much laughter and singing as the older men gathered some camps and started to sing their different ceremonial dance songs, until quite late at night when they all retired; then everything was quiet, not even a guard to watch over them but the twinkling stars above and the few night birds.

Very early next morning the air was full of the odor of cooking as each family made ready their morning meal. Then the chief called them to his camp, which was in the center of the whole camp. There the people came at his call to come forward. When all had taken seat in a circle, he then gave a short speech of thanks to this unseen or unknown being that made life, earth, and all it contains. That was the beginning of the opening speech that came to be adopted later as a custom for all meetings or dances of all sorts. And the camp was over, and travel continued in slow stages, always waiting for the older or the weak.

They reached the place just little before the sun was south, as they called at that time, and camped at the near side of the field to wait for the time set. It was but a short time that the other party from the other village came. So the people made ready and moved up towards the middle, being led by their chief. The other party did likewise. They met right in the middle of the great field. Each chief extending his weapon or right hand as signs of peace and friendship, they met face to face for the first time. Each had the look of joy as they approached towards each other, in the crook of their left arm they carried their War-club. As they met, they grasped their right hand and then greeted each as brother; they dropped their weapons as they held their hands. Then their leaders came up and each met some other man of the other village. All seemed well pleased; there was no sign of any ill-feeling nor any looks of doubt at any place, as the rest of the people met and shook hands, and there was the pit dug previously near the chiefs. They went and threw their weapons into the pit; then the former war-chiefs came in their turn, all throwing their weapons with a last look as they cast it into the pit. Thus was buried the tomahawk or War-club together with all hatred and warfare.

When all had cast their weapons, then the chief who had begun the idea, made this speech:—"Brothers, Relatives, and Friends, today at this place, in this pit we cast all weapons of warfare. With it we bury all hatred, all sorrows for the relatives who are gone ahead of us, who may be looking at us now,—we mourn for them silently. We find that we are all related as one family, and as such we shall stand hereafter. Instead of War, Scalp, Blood, or Glory from Warfare, we will replace in each and every one this feeling that we are but one people, that there must be some being that made us, the very earth we stand on, the sky above, the sun, the flowing streams, the animals, and all growing things for our enjoyment. Why should we want to forget them, why should we want to kill, to scalp? We now bury all weapons, never to dig it up again. All we keep is what we need to hunt with. Let

no one ever mention about the past. We all have lost someone; so let us not bring back the things that hurt us;
those that are gone will not come back. Beginning today,
we find we are one people only that we live apart in different villages, but let us keep up that relationship alive
within us; do not let distance interfere with our own relationship. This Being that may have made us, may have
ordained that we should visit each other, even help one
another. In case we find some of our younger people who
happens to see a mate in another village, let them go ahead,
let them decide which place to make their home. In the
future let us remember this Being who has been so good
as to give all this for our use, by having periods of ceremonies; let us thank the different things as they happen
by a speech or dance; let those that were called War-chiefs
be made into head-man of ceremonies, to prepare all feasts
and take charge of all dances and so on. So in closing this
event which will be remembered as time goes on, let us
hold each other by the hand in one single-file dance, this
dance what shall be known as 'Holding Hands Dance.' I
will lead, and my brother of the other village will follow,
and the rest according to their rank."

So saying he grasped the right hand of his neighbor
while in his right (the leader) he held a rattle to use
while singing. When all had taken their places, he started
to sing and it was a song that seem like everyone knew
before. So the dance started. First they dance all over the

field, curving about, then going into the woods, and they kept it up until the singer had sung all the songs he knew. Thus was started the song and dance known as "Holding Hands Dance," and peace was declared at last.

After that big day, they all went home with the feeling that peace was at last declared, that the war whoop and its terror amongst the villages had gone forever. It had reached to such a state of war individually that neighbor was against neighbor, even among their own villages; the desire for scalp had been so great, that it was even rated as means of gauging a man's ability and class. It had been also the accepted custom that whenever a warrior scalped he must give a war-yell, then announce his name, no matter where nor how dangerous the situation. All this the story-teller would relate as he goes on with his recital, more to acquaint his listeners with the real conditions as it existed in those days. So the people was almost like living in another sphere; they were like as if they were dazed, it was so sudden to them; they had lived through the period and were accustomed to its condition. You would see them in groups hereabouts in their villages talking in subdued tones as if afraid someone might come around and change it back again.

Then gradually the new mode of living seem to come to them, more through their young men, who took advantage of this life and its quietness or inactivity by indulging in games of manly sports, such as foot races, jumping, wrestling, and their most valued of all sport, the game of lacrosse, which to them meant almost as great as warfare. In fact more than once after peace had been declared outbreaks of slaughter arosed from a game of this lacrosse, maybe between villages or even tribes. And then later the older people gradually came to realize what it means to live the life of peace and quiet. That was the beginning when many new dances were introduced for pastime or even for curing some sort of sickness. Many of these dances were brought into the Senecas by the custom of adopting captives from the war-time enemies, who were considered one of their own once the adoption had been observed. Everything about their life and habits had to be changed; their meetings and the speeches all had to take different system,—they had to make new everything. It was strange how men that were rated as famous war-leaders were looked upon as ritual-holders. Such was the times as it existed when this great peace was declared.

It had been quite a long while since the great peace that two young men, both good friends to each other, made known to their chief their desire to go to the next village for a few days' visit. So a meeting was called by the chief, and announcement was made as to the intention of the two. Then the chief send a message to his brother-chief of the other village and then to the sub-chiefs and last to the common people and the children. Such was the new mode of friendship as it now existed, started all by this great chief, who had great vision of his people for the future; and it is even to this day carried on but in little modified forms. When the sending of messages were all over, then they took to dancing as means of sending them off on the long journey to the neighboring village. Just before they departed, one of the two made a short speech, stating the time that they would return. Then they left amid much laughter and enjoyment, as it was the first time that members of this village went to the next one.

Life went on in this village as was the custom, men doing some sort of work, some playing, others singing. Then came the appointed time that the two should return. Everyone seem tense, expecting some unknown ritual, news, or whatever it may be, but they failed to come back. Then the chief told his people that maybe they were detained on some good reason; why, they were all one people, —both were young and were both good in their appearance, —they may have made some good impression on someone. Or the people may have asked them to stay little longer; nothing was said to the contrary.

That passed, and quite little while later, another man made known his intention to go on a visit to the other place, and as was the accepted custom, a meeting was called in their long house. The same routine system was gone over again; the message of the chief, the sub-chiefs, and so on were sent. He also mentioned the time he should return; then the dance of sending him off was started to the great enjoyment of all until the man called out aloud that he was now going; then all was over. The same routine was evident, but as the time came of the set date for the return of this lonely visitor-to-the-other-place approached, then the same feeling of anxiety, unrest, a tense feeling felt by all. The time came and all were assembled in their meeting place; they all waited, he did not return. Still the chief just shook his wise head and dismissed the meeting.

Then just few days afterwards that another group of three young men who wanted to go on a visit; they too were sent away as was the custom, after a set of dances and speeches; they left. But one could detect a sense of mistrust, or more like bidding the men farewell for the last time on earth; the feeling of enjoyment were not so pronounced as those other times had been. They left, and the relatives even made signs of grief as their kin departed. They were then aware of something that must have kept the others from returning. It was the chief that was affected hard. He pondered and wondered if his brother had deceived him after all. He did not dare tell anyone his thoughts; his people's welfare depended on him, and he felt it. He knew that he was responsible for the lives of all his command. It was laying heavy on his mind, but he was a good chief, he could be counted to use and apply good sound judgment.

After quite a while a couple of nice young girls made known their desire to go visiting to the next village. They said they rely on the good promise made by the other chief, that if there is something wrong somewheres, they would know of it or else perish if necessary. Such was the extent of minds of the three of the most prettiest maidens of their village. They were determined they should go, in spite of the warnings of the relatives, the chiefs, and everyone. They said many people had gone. They were willing to find out what was wrong or else pay for their lives. It was to no avail,—people used and tried all arguments trying to prevent them from carrying out what was then considered foolish venture. So it was to be. They had a big time in their long house, a sending-off party never before seen of its kind. There were much gaiety and there were much grief, especially those of the relatives of the three. The old chief made the last attempt to help out the situation by offering to send along an escort of trusted young warriors, but it too was refused by the three. So after much dancing they finally made their departure. And what was the feelings of the multitude? As was the custom, they too promised to return on a certain day if all is well. The next day was like as if everyone had gone away, there was no games,—none about the village,—everyone was thinking of the same thing.

Time went on like this. It seems that there were plenty of deaths in the village, as there was no activities of no sort in the village, no signs of life whatever. Then the time came when it was the day set aside for the return of the three girls. Again there was plenty of excitement within the place; they all gathered in the long house expecting the girls to return. Time dragged by. They are so down-hearted that there was no dancing, as was the usual custom. They waited until quite late, then gave up; then there was much show of grief by those relatives of the girls. The meeting ended without any formal way of any sort; every-thing was upset, everyone was now worried. People went home with heavy hearts, because they knew that the feel-ing of peace about their homes were now doubtful. There was only one answer;—they all thought that the other had gone back on his word of promise, that warfare was again the accepted routine. So the next day found this settle-ment very quiet, it was as if everyone was dead, there was no signs of life nowheres.

The chief was the one that did most of the worrying, because he was responsible for all this condition,—he started on this plan of peace. He had no one to lay the blame to; he alone faced the outcome as it now existed. What was he to do? Who did he have to go to for aid or advice? No one; he was alone. For days and nights he pondered, often passing the night with no sleep, until at last he could stand it no longer. He then called a meeting. Everyone responded. He got up and told them in a few words all the things that might be and everything.

He started out in this manner: "It is my one opinion that my so-called friend and brother of the next village has deceived me unjustly. But if not, then there must be something that is causing the disappearance of our people who had gone to visit and failed to return. There is only one thing to be done now. That is to send out someone to find out, and we are going to do that tonight. Now before I begin, I want to impress the one who accepts the duty to go, that it is a case of death or great danger. One must then volunteer to assume the risk; but I have noticed my people here in our own village,—we have plenty of brave men; so I am not worried at all."

Then he produced out of his pouch, a string of wampum beads strung, a few strands as it appeared to them. Holding it up so all could see it, he said: "Whoever takes that wampum strings, it is the token that he has volunteered to go on this dangerous venture. I will now start."

He went around holding the string in front of him and offering it to all the men-folks in the long house. As it was presented to each man, you could see each man looked down and never at the chief as it passed the man, and thus it went clear around. Each man avoided the wampum the best way he could. And no man ever accepted to take the string.

Just as the chief had finish his round, a certain young man entered, and he stood by the doorway leaning and looking around. This young man was the sort of person that everyone makes fun of; no one seems to pay any attention outside of joking about his lack of this and that. Such was the way the people made fun of this man or youth, he never was at any of the sports as indulged by all youth of his age. He live with his grandmother in a small cabin or shack at the outskirts of the big village. He was an ordinary, no-account, poor youth. They all looked at him as he entered; then someone more bold than the rest made the remark to try this string on the young man, more as a joke than anything else, saying, "Why not try this brave man? He will no doubt do it."

Then the chief answered in this wise—"That can be a joke and I am not in joking mood at this time, everyone must have the chance." So saying he went up to the youth by the doorway and held out the wampum and explained what it is all about. Looking at the chief the youth reached out slowly and grasped the string of wampum.

Then the chief was thoroughly aroused with wrath. He said: "Men or poor excuses for one, listen to my speech at this time. I hereafter forbid anyone from any yelling of war-whoop by anyone here inside. You are not the men I thought you were,—even made fun of the only one that has a right to be called man. Now here is one whom you all made fun of. Now look at yourself, each and every one of you, all afraid to die or go near danger, even for your own people's sakes. If you all died, no one would miss you at all. I would not, myself. Now here again I will command respect to this one man whom you always looked down on."

Now then the youth made speech thus: "I did volunteer of my own free will; first, because I am of no account. Should I die, no one would miss me. If I were successful, which I hope to be, I may regain some respect from my own people, and be classed as man among men. I will start out early tomorrow before sun-rise from here."

Then the meeting was over without any ceremony or speech. All went home with a better frame of mind. Our hero, the poor young man, went home to his grandmother. As he entered, he laid the wampum string on the bench that was used as a sort of table, where they ate their meals. His old Grandmother, noting the string, asked him what it meant.

Then he told her thus: "Grandmother, I have volunteered to go and find out what it is that is causing the disappearance of all our people who went to visit the other village all this time. I am to leave early at sunrise tomorrow. I need your help if you can do so."

Then his grandmother spoke saying: "My grandson, it is as you say. I will try to assist you in your one mission. We are not as poor or bad off as the people thinks we are. But far from it,—I have great power. I can do wonders, no one knows that. Your old Grandfather was also a great man, but he never boasted nor bragged about it. I still have his things that he wore and used in his days of glory and skill. That I will gladly let you use now. No one has ever seen these things before. In fact, no one ever saw you

as you are. Now they are going to see the real *You* as we
should be by rights. I am so glad to see that you know
your duty to your people, my dear boy."

Whereupon she went up the loft to a shelf the youth
had seen, but did not know what was up there; and there
she pulled out an old bark-case all covered with dust. This
she put on the floor. Out of it she drew out an old Head-
gear as used by the Senecas, just a crown with one big
feather but trimmed with many small eagle-plumes of
downy feathers. As she put it on their table, the small soft
plumes seem to wave as if a soft wind was blowing upon
them. Then she also got down from the rafter-beam a long
bow, black with age, it was so thick and strong that no
one could ever bend it to string up. This she gave to him
to try, saying, "If you can string this bow, then you are
good enough to use it."

So he took it and with what seem no effort he bend it
and did strung it ready for use. Then she rejoiced to note
that he was the man she often wish him to be as he grew
from boyhood up. She told him to go to sleep and rest up
for the ordeal that is ahead of him in the morrow; so he
went to sleep while his grandmother busied herself in preparing for her grandson's big event. She made ready the
carrying rations, which composed of parched corn-meal
sweeten with maple sugar that is always carried on any
expedition of any sort. She also made for him two new
pairs of moccasins and the kilt that he was to wear.

She woke him up just when it **was getting** bright up in the eastern sky as signs of coming dawn. He ate his light meal for traveling, made ready all the things she had ready for him to wear. Carrying the great bow and also a quiver of poison arrows, a tomahawk that had been hidden with all his grandfather's belongings, thus attired he bade his grandmother farewell. He left for the long house where the people had gathered already to see him start. As he strode up to the place near the doorway, he recognized the great chief standing near the door. He went up to him, and the chief himself did not recognized him at all, but only took it for granted that it must be the man they were waiting for, as no one had ever beheld such a man before. He stood erect and tall as a pine tree, also big and broad on the shoulder; with his raiment, he was a man to behold.

Then he addressed the people assembled thus: "I am about to go on my first mission. If I succeed, I will return by sun-set tomorrow." So saying, he with few long easy strides sped out and in no time had disappeared into the woods. Thus left the man whom everyone always made fun of.

Now it seemed to him that he ran as if he was being carried along with the wind. He went straight towards the direction of their neighboring village, where a pathway could be easily seen. He ran and kept an open eye for any-thing that might be strange or new. Just when he was reaching a big ravine or hollow that is nearly halfway between the villages, he began to note that the trees are bare of limbs up to a place above his head, that also the bark of the trees were smooth as if something had been rubbing itself there. Then there were some mud on some of the trees; so he sort of slacken his pace and observed more closely. All at once he saw a piece of a thigh-bone of a person laying there; it was bleached white by now. So he knew then that there must be something close by that is doing all the work of destroying his people, and he also knew that whatever it is, it must be an immense size, judging by the height of all trees and the limbs. He kept running along, ever watchful for signs. He saw them and saw plenty of it; the more farther he went the more bones he saw laying in all directions,—some were still fresh with the flesh still on them as if it was left in a hurry. He was surprised at the amount of bones that he saw,—more so as he reached this big hollow or ravine. There he further noted, that whatever it was that was living off from his people lived or else came down in this ravine. This ravine extended East and West, —and it was from the direction of sun-set that the big trail could be seen. So he stopped there and stood there just a moment.

Then he thought that it would be a good idea to go towards the other village a little way to ascertain if there are any signs of people coming from that way; so he went on. He was much surprised at the amount of fresh bones scattered about all over. So he was satisfied that they (both villages) were all having the same trouble. Then his anger arosed in him, and he retraced his steps to the ravine. When he reached this spot, he was so much angered that gave a loud War-yell, saying also—"Whatever you are, that is destroying my people, I will soon kill you. The world is so small when you are in my path. You might as well give up now."

Then he took the trail with renewed speed, because he knew then he was on the tracks of some large beast, whatever it may be. He was determined to kill it at all cost. All along this beaten trail he saw more sign of fresh bones, some with the blood still on them. There were heaps of bones as he went on, showing that this beast had the habit of taking it along and eating it nearer its place. Then he finally came to the place where it had its lair or pen. It was a great big place amid tall trees and vines that offered some shelter and protection; there it showed where this thing used to lay, like a huge nest of a large bird. There were signs of new slaughtered flesh and parts of a human body laying where it had left as if in a great haste. He saw the great big tracks made as it took to flight. Then his anger was renewed, and he again shouted his call of defiance and told this thing that he would soon overtake it. He then went after his quarry, as the tracks were easily seen and it was made recently. He kept on with renewed speed.

He went on for a time,—it was then getting late in the

day,—then he thought he saw straight ahead of him in a distance, what seemed to him a very large beast running in great long jumps. It seemed to look almost white. Its back was seen above the timber of the country as it ran in its flight. Then again he gave the cry of challenge for the thing to stop and then fight it out like a good warrior

would. Now it would seem that he was slowly gaining on this race, a race never seen like it since,—that is, for speed on foot. Man against beast.

It finally got dark, night came on them; so the man decided to wait until the next day before he killed his quarry. Do it in broad day-light, he thought. He rested by a running stream to drink with his meal. And as he took out his pouch of Parched Corn-meal Samp, what was his surprise to see it was all full of worms and not fit to eat; so he threw it away, and made this remark, "So you have power to spoil my food. Just the same, I will settle with you in the morning." Then he made a little fire to keep small animals from disturbing him. He laid down nearby and was just about to sleep when he heard a great commotion towards the west; it was coming towards where he was. Then a man's voice spoke, the voice came from out in the darkness and sounded as if it was meant for him.

The voice said: "Are you asleep? I am the one you are after to kill. It is the one whom you people call the 'Nyah-gwa-ih-heh-go-wah,' and I have caused lot of trouble to you and all the rest of the people. It is I who have killed and ate all your people that came my way, I knew when you people formed peace, to end all strife; then I knew that there was chance to do my work of destruction. I thought that there was no one greater than I am; but the moment you volunteered to kill me, then I knew that my match and my end had come at last. You are truly a great man and able to do what you set out to do, but I came here to see if we could come to an understanding and make peace so that I could be spared. If you would consider letting me go away, never to harm you or any of your people after this, I will promise to leave the country and go out west where there are no people. My name will be mentioned in the future as stories. To make my terms more binding and as proof that you had accomplished your mission, I will give you one of my teeth to take and keep as token of our friendship and pact between us. It will always bring you luck; and to the one who keeps it after you have gone on, it is just the same as if I was killed, and I will leave this country right away." Thus spoke the monster known as "Nyah-gwa-ih-heh-go-wah" to the man.

This great man did consider the offer and then said: "You did not show any mercy to my people when you went and ate all that came your way; in fact, you were about to bring about another up-rising, to start out anew the war that was recently stopped, and that is one reason that makes me want to do my duty to my people."

Then this monster kept on and made more stronger appeal; so after a while, he consented to accept the terms. Then he heard the noise as this monster broke off its tooth.

Then it said again: "Here is my own tooth as a token of peace and friendship. Always have it with you and you shall have great power in the future. I shall put it on this log. And I now thank you for sparing my life,—I am leaving now, 'Dah Neh-hon.' "

Then he could hear and feel the rumble, the trembling of the earth as it went on away towards the setting sun direction. Then all was quiet; he went to sleep.

Early the next day he woked up, and there on a log laid a large tooth of this monster. Taking it with him, he then retraced his steps to his home, taking easy strides as he knew that he will be home by dark. As he approached his village, he started to give the distress call, by shouting "Go-oh-weh" three times every little ways, and in time he was met by a party of his people bearing torches, as it was then getting dark.

He was taken to the long house where the whole village had assembled. After he was given some medicine to drink and he had regained his breath, he then arosed and related all that took place and what he did to this monster, and produced the tooth as proof that what he said was true. All the people came and looked at the tooth that had been eating their people. Then the chief was greatly pleased, and he announced that this man shall be his successor, that he was the man to rule the village, also saying, that he forbid anyone to give the war-yell hereafter, as a punishment for the lack of proper spirit when condition called; that the one they always ridiculed as a man of no account was the one that had the good requirements of a brave warrior and leader. Then they all passed by him and shook him by the right hand as signal of their great respect and appreciation for his deed and his new position as their chief. After that they danced to rejoice the new victory that peace had come again at last. Then it was over.

The very next night the new chief called a meeting. He announced his plan to send some runners to carry the news of this new peace to the people of the other village, that the one that was causing all the trouble between the two villages has been removed for good. So two strong young men were found who were willing to go on the mission, to leave early the next day. The next morning they left and travelled like the other two that had carried the first message, and they found the conditions worse over there, that it was very much like war-fare to the people. Nearly every family had lost someone by this monster, and there was much rejoicing to know that peace had finally come to the two villages, and they were treated with due respect and courtesy. Thus was the beginning of the Hand in Hand Dance; the ending of war amongst people, the taking of scalp; the new form of chiefs as assistant to the old chief. And my father says this actually happened long, long ago. Thus ends the legend of "Nya-gwa-ih-heh-go-wah," Dah Neh-hoh. . . .

This is one of the longest and most complete legend dealing on early conditions of my people as they lived in those days and what they did, and how they did it. I have not omitted anything but have given little detail for the sake of better understanding of the people who is listening to this legend. You will see here and there that you will recognize something that is still done at the present time. I like this legend the best of all.

I have given you my best legend, and I feel you will appreciate it, as I seem to live over the very days that deals with this recital, it is so realistic to me. Again I say, Dah Neh-hoh. . . . In sunshine or shade I remain as ever,

Your Ong-gweh-onh-weh Friend and Brother,

Jesse J. Cornplanter

"Ha-yonh-wonh-ish,"

the Snipe Clan

XII

THE TWO FRIENDS
A DEVIL-LEGEND

Tonawanda Reservation
May 8, 1937

Dear Sah-nee-weh:

Now comes the next legend. This is about the dead man who was flayed by the Evil-minded so he could use it in his work on the earth-children or men. It also portrays the beginning of Oh-kee-weh, individual feast to the dead, and all dreams of the dead. It has many versions told by different ones, but this is my own.

As they say, this happened about the time when the white-man came in contact with our people; when there was much wickedness going on, due to the introduction of the white-man's rum; when the Seneca was not as reliable as he had been. So it is a sort of a modern legend compared to the ones that we have been telling in the past. This legend goes on and tells about the two young men who were real good friends; as we might say today, they were Chums or Pals in every respect. They were together all the time. The only difference in the two was their habits, or conduct. One was a sort of a quiet fellow and has no bad habits, while his friend was just the opposite,—he was

bad,—in fact, he prided himself and boasted that the Evil-
minded was his best friend, his God and Informer. He
seemed to enjoy doing the most wicked of all things. He
drank much and was constantly getting into fights with
his own fellow-beings. He took pride in running around
with other men's wives when he felt like it. Such habit in
those days were not tolerated, but this particular man did
and bragged about it. He stole things. He was a chronic
liar, made lot of trouble amongst neighbors that were of
his own designs, and then would laugh about it when it
reached to a point where friends were made enemies all
through his own evil work.

He used to tell people this: "I am working for the 'Ha-
nis-heh-oh-nonh,' the Evil-minded. Everything I do, no
matter how bad, he always protects me. He is my God,
and I am his obedient worker on earth."

Now his friend tried his best to discourage him from
his chosen work, but to no avail. Still it continued on as
before; they were both devoted friends, regardless of the
difference in their ways.

The good and faithful one told him once thusly: "How
nice it would be if we were both so good, where people
would both trust us; we would be respected. Then when
our life's journey ended, we would take the path to the
land of the hereafter. Whoever went first, would wait for
the other. It is so much nicer to both be doing good work
on earth."

Then his friend just replied in this wise: "What you say is true, but I have already chosen my God and advisor. I have taken the step, and to change now would not be so good to me or my own God. Anyway, our friendship is just as good and strong as if we both felt and did the same things. You need never worry of me ever doing any bad thing to you. I am your friend; good or evil as I may be, we shall remain so until our paths divide on this earth."

So it went on thus; both were true to each other,— where one went the other was sure to go, they were always together. People marvelled at the way the two remained friends when they were so different in their habits. They had made a vow between them, to remain as real, good, true friends as long as they lived; and to the one whoever happen to be the survivor, to fulfill their one duty,—pay his last respects and keep the three-day *grave-watch* which at that time was the custom; to have some one or two men stay and keep a small fire at the grave for three nights after the funeral. Such friendship was never seen since, as the two were in those days. They both kept their friendship up good.

The one who was good often tried to coax his erring friend to change his ways and be like he was. But this evil-minded one was always ready with the very same answer, that he had made the one choice, that he intended to be so and see what it is when his end came, that their friendship would not improve if he did change. So it always ended the same manner, but this good-minded man is always trying his best to convince his friend the difference in being good from bad; in fact, he felt sorry of his friend being so determined to remain in his bad ways,—he always thought that maybe some day his friend might see his error and change his way of living. Thus it went on for a long time. He (the evil one) even tried to teach his good friend the art of being a witch, to transform himself into some sort of animal, to be able to make Witch-light as the witches were seen to do when travelling at night. And he wanted him to know how to brew poison draughts or make incense for love-charm; in fact, he tried his best to make his good-minded friend follow his evil habits; but each one clung to his own belief and remained good friends at the same time.

Then came a time when the strong claws of sickness clutched the evil one. His good-minded friend came to the bedside and did all he could to help his friend. He went on little errands, brought some nice things to eat; he sat up nights just to be with his fallen Pal. Conditions changed from bad to worse; still the good friend remained by the bedside. When the patient was conscious, he tried to tell him some stories to cheer him up, or else relate some funny incident that had happened to them when they were together in the past. Different forms of medicine were tried, and all failed to help the sick man. He was then nothing but skin and bones; then he started to have convulsions and acted like he was a maniac; then he talked about the Devil, his so-called God. He was then a pitiful sight to see. He was suffering very much. Between times, when he was able to talk, he was telling all about what he did during his time on earth, all the wickedness he had done to others. He even asked his friend to help him out of his suffering. He asked him to do all he could to save him from this demon that was already after him. He realized then that he was mistaken by not listening to the good advice of his good friend. Then he wanted his friend to keep his promise of keeping the night-watch after his death and burial.

He said: "The Evil-minded Spirit is after my body. He is going to skin me, and make a human form with his own breath in it; then he would use me as means to come back to our people in disguise, to represent someone that had died some time ago. So please do what you can to help me out. Stay by me as you have done; and after I am buried, keep the fire burning and stay there for three nights. Do not let the Evil-minded Spirit make you change your mind. The very minute that you leave me, he will then dig my body out and skin me; so do not give me up at all,—this is my last request as a friend. I have made my mistake, and now I realize it; but it is almost too late. Still, you can save me. If you can keep him from getting my body for the three nights, then I am safe and will not do the harm to your people as he wants me to do. It is as important to you people that I be kept from this Evil-spirit until I had gone on to my resting place, if there is such. I have been so wicked that I am not sure just where I will go after my departure from this earth. Remember our pledge, our agreement, and do not weaken to his coaxing, as he will use all his force and cunning to make you give my body up. I am sorry that I am going to leave you now; we have been such good friends while we were together. If I had only listened to you in the time that you tried to save me! Now I am leaving you, but please remember our promise and stand by your friend to the last. Dah Neh-hoh." And the man took his last breath. Thus ended the friendship of the two men.

Then they made ready, as was the custom of the times, but the good-minded man was there to help out whatever way he could. He sat by the remains during the two nights before the funeral, and followed the body to the grave. When it was night, or about dusk, he went out to the burial place and made a little fire at the head of the grave of his lost friend and sat there all alone. It was not very long time when he heard a noise like a log-chain was being dragged on the ground, and it came towards him; so he stirred up the fire and made it more brighter and listened at the noise.

Then a man's voice spoke out in the dark; the voice said: "My good friend, I have come for the body of your friend, which is mine now; so please depart and let me do as I please with it."

But the man just replied: "That may be as you have said, but he is my friend, and as a last request of him that lies beneath I have promised to stay and keep the fire lighted so he can rest well in his grave. Thereby I can not very well leave as you asked me to."

This being, whoever he may be, just kept out of sight from the firelight, but he was very much determined to get the body of the one in the grave.

So the voice spoke again: "That is all very good of you to do so. In truth, you did more than your share to help your friend while the chance was there; but he is no more, he is gone, he is now mine. He had all the chance to amend his wrongs, but he always said that he was my friend, that I was his God. He never did listen to you, no matter what you said. So, as I said before, I merely want what actually belongs to me, and you are only in my way, you are keeping me from it. You had your chance to do everything to help him, and you did your best to no avail. He has lived the life for me. You have lost your power to help him now, —your time was when he was with you on earth; so just leave the place, and I will do my work."

Then he again heard the noise of the rattling of log-chain as if the being was coming nearer. Still the good-minded friend stayed on, and answered thusly: "I will stay as I had promised, regardless; that is my last chance to do anything to my friend."

But the other voice just replied only in more pleading tones, always with the idea to let the grave-watch be dropped. So they kept up arguing back and forth until the signs of dawn showed towards the east. He, the one that wanted the body, retired, and the man could hear the noise of the dragging chain as it went away, and then it was quiet; so he knew that he had won the first night's fight.

The next night was about the same as the previous night. As the night settled and the good man had taken his place near his little fire, sure enough there was the sound of chains rattling again, approaching the place; then again the same voice spoke and demanded that the night-watcher leave the grave. Again the man held his own and argued back and forth. The Evil-minded was more pleading than the night before, but the man kept up his word and the night soon passed into morning, and when the Evil-minded was about to leave, he told him that he would return again the following night.

So the third night, the last one, soon came, and as in the previous times, the Evil-minded lost no time coming and making his demand, sometimes pleading and then at times demanding in more stronger terms, but that availed him nothing. It was then close to midnight when the Evil-minded made the best terms that he could think of.

He made this offer: "Now it is useless for you to sit out longer. You have shown your friend that you did your

duty by him, him that would not listen to you in his
living days. He is now my property; it will not help him
if you stayed out all night. I will make this offer to you:
I will leave my Silk Top Hat here where I am. It will be
full of gold coins; I will pay you to leave this place and

Jesse Cornplanter
37

let me have what is mine. He whom you are helping will
never come back to earth any more; you have lost him.
You stuck by him long enough. I will eventually get him;
so why delay longer. Think for yourself now,—I am repay-
ing you well. Not only that, but you will be lucky hereafter, as I have power to do wonders in this world myself
if you only knew me better. I will give you power so that
you will be successful in whatever you will wish in the
future. No one will never know the secret agreement between us. Promise that you will go, and I will leave you

a hatful of money. Come back in the morning, and you will find it here."

Now it is said that the man who wanted to keep his promise to his dead friend now really realized his folly for trying to save his friend that had failed to believe him while he had the chance.

So after a long time of thinking, he finally answered: "That I will do. I have tried my very best all the time we were together to do him good, to change his ways and be like I am. He was your man. He told me time after time that he was working for you and he was your servant, that you protected him and helped him along. So I am going home, and not keep you waiting nor interfere with your affairs any longer."

So saying, he arosed and covered up the little fire that was burning by the grave, and started towards home. He had no sooner got away, when he heard the rattling of the chain, and then the noise of someone digging. And the voice of his departed friend was heard, it was more like an appeal, or as if in an agony or mortal fear.

"Come back and stay with me, my friend,—please be with me,—do not leave me now. He is going to skin me. You have sold me to him. Don't do that."

He stopped where he was and listened. It was just a little while, then the crying voice turned into a scream of pain, and in little while it was quiet. Then the man went on home. He was very sorry for his friend, but he could not see any reason why he should try to interfere any longer. Sure enough, the Evil-minded was right. His place to help him was when he was alive, and not when he had died. But no matter what he thought about, he just cannot rest in his mind, thinking how he had betrayed his best friend in the end, and more so, because he was going to get money for it. He went home and found out that he could not sleep; he just laid awake and thought about all that took place.

The next day at daylight he went back to the grave, and sure enough, the ground had been disturbed, but it was covered up again. And in a little distance there was the Silk Top Hat, and it was full of gold money. So he took it home and hid it so that the people would not know that he had sold his friend's body for money. He was a rather quiet man after this, but he was thinking all the time. So in the following night, he slept very sound, as he was very tired after three nights of watching the grave. Just when he had slept good, his dead friend came back to him in a dream. He was just like he had been when he was still alive, only he was in different mood.

He seemed sad, and spoke to him in this manner: "My old and trusty friend, it is as you thought when you submitted to the offer of my chosen God,—that you were powerless to help me any longer, that our time was when we were both together. It was my own folly, my own mistake that brought all this trouble to us both. You are indeed my true friend. It was me that was wrong. You did more than your duty trying to save a fallen friend. I am not angry at you at all. I am still the friend that I had been. Only we cannot see each other any more, but I will be with you all I can. Never be afraid, no matter where you are. I will always be near you as we had been during our time together on earth.

"I want to tell what my so-called God did to me when you left the grave that night. He dug me out and then started to flay me. I died the second time. It was very hard for me, but what can I do? He was my God, and I belonged to him. He skinned me and saved the skin. It is now drying, and as soon as it dries, then he will breathe into it and then it is my human form. That is what I meant when I told you not to be outwitted by him, to keep on with your grave-watch. Now as it is we will have this human shape, my form but with the breath of the Evil-mind, to come back to our people hereafter in a form of dreams. It will be just as if some of their own relatives had come back to them and wanted maybe something to eat. And always it will be with something to drink with it, such as a sort of a death-feast, only this will be done in night-time. It will only be the work of this Evil-mind and his working tool in the shape of human being.

"This will continue on as long as our people exist. The one main ceremony that will come from it will be the Chanters for the Dead, which will be known as the 'Oh-kee-wey' all-night ceremony. Then there will be the other individual-dream ceremony, that is for someone who had died to come back to someone who is alive, to demand food and also drink of liquor. It is a fact that our departed friends are all earth-bound. It is just their spirit, their material being that we saw when they were alive. They are with your living people. You only do not see them. They are powerless to even ask for anything. But now since you sold my body to the Evil-mind, then all this thing will come to pass. It will always be me who will represent who-ever it may be. But to you I will remain as ever your guid-ing spirit in death as we were when we were both together. All this will come to pass as time went on; so all this to your people; that since we were such good friends, you will have to remember me by observing this feast, and the others will follow as time goes on. Do not tell how it came to pass, that you had something to do in this. Otherwise your people will blame you for it; and you are so good,— tried your best to keep me out of my bad ways,—that it is my wish to keep you from all blame. It is all my own choosing. This you will tell your people,—*I came back and demanded food be set aside with plenty of drinks for all. In order to be free from the one that asks for food, the living must observe this new ritual to the dead. Then the sacred tobacco must be thrown in the fire, to ask the spirit of the departed to release their relative,—that they had ful-filled the request. That I came back to you because we were such good friends, and not from any fault of your own.*

"Please do this much. Then I can rest better. I did you people wrong by choosing my own God. Warn your people in this speech that will be announced at this feast and drinking, to never let anything like this happen again in the future. Any time anyone calls the name of the Evil-mind, he is then right by her or his side at the moment. His real name is 'Ha-nis-heh-oh-nonh,' the tormentor. And he likes his name. Tell your people never to repeat what I had done during my living days. It was a great mistake that I made. Let my mistake be a warning to our people in the future. This is all."

Such was the message that came back to this man from his lost friend. And it is said that sure enough there were plenty of similar feasts or ceremonies after that. All were supposed to be from some dead relative, but this man knew different but said not a word about it,—he was respecting his dead friend's warning. My father says that this was the beginning of "Oh-kee-wey" or the Chanter-for-the-Dead Ceremony, also the numerous cases of some dead relative calling for food to be set aside for them. It must be so, because we still carry on with this and other ceremonies that may have sprung from this source. We believe that the dead are with us; we feel their presence at times. Strange.

I will tell you what actually happened year ago, or repeat this Chief's narrative. He was a co-worker or Cousin

Chief to my own father,—what we call "Ho-nenh-sis-henh" (they are cousins aside); and he told this to few that were at his place one night years ago. It was when we used to hold singing parties to this man's place back in New Town on the Cattaraugus Reservation. This is his story:

"It was a night when we had The Great Oh-kee-wey to all that had died (a community affair, it seems); and as was my custom, being one of the singers on my side (Clan), I waited until it was about ten o'clock when I started towards the Long House. It was quite clear night (moonlight, I mean) as I went along, walking slow and not looking around. I heard someone coming from behind as if in an awful haste; so I stepped one side to let the party pass. There was a tall woman dressed as we are in the habit of dressing people when they depart this world. She was one of the Dead, and more than that, I recognized her as one of my own Cousins that had died quite long ago. She stopped where I stood and greeted me as if she had been alive. She asked me if I was going to the All-night Oh-kee-wey; and I said yes, that I was going to sing, as it was being held for the other phratry.

"She acted very glad to see me; so she said: 'Well, I will walk on with you. I came back to you, to show you that we who are long dead do come back to this All-night Oh-kee-wey, as you shall see.'

"So we went on towards the four corners. She said that

I will see what takes place every time we have this all-night
sing to the dead; so she told to me to look about as we approach the four-corner and then could see the big open field
or common, and what was my surprise to see the great
multitude of people all over the field. It seems that they
were all heading for the Long House. I watched real close
and then noticed that the living people were few as compared to the ones that are dead,—and one could easily see
the few that are living, they are more heavier, casting real
shadow, while the dead were more of an outline, but they
were all there.

"We went along. She was talking all the time; she said
that she had picked me out to show me that the dead actually came back to take part every time we have this ceremony. We came close to few that I knew were of the departed, judging from their dress, I saw that they were not
actually walking on the ground, but seem to be suspended
little above the ground. As we went on, we came to this
four-corners and as we did so, a man that was still on earth
came along from the other direction, and he called me as
a salutation. The minute he did, everything disappeared.
My own dead cousin had fade out like that. Then I saw
that the people that I saw before were all dead, that there
were only few people in reality. This happened to me, but
I have kept it a secret, as I was afraid people would mis-
understand me and call me liar."

Now, Sah-nee-weh, I have told you this, but did not

mention the person,—he is now dead, like all the good old Chiefs,—so what? I trust this legend will enlighten you again to our mysterious habits and ceremonies. I have spoken. Dah Neh-hoh.

Your Seneca Story-teller and Brother,
Jesse J. Cornplanter
"Ha-yonh-wonh-ish"
the Snipe

"GUS-TO-WEH"
SENECA HEAD DRESS

XIII

THE VAMPIRE SKELETON

Tonawanda Reservation
May 29, 1937

Nya-weh Sken-noh, Sah-nee-weh:

I have promised you another good legend when I sent you the last one; so I am sending you this one. It is about a man who is said to have been a witch and had died. He was not dead in some manner, according to the legend, and caused more trouble later. Why I think it is good, is because of its weirdness. I think all such legends are very rare, because the people lived different in those days, almost together with nature, thereby many unusual things used to happen, which is beyond believing now-days. If it is possible, bear with me as I relate this legend, so you can get the full value of the whole legend as we go on. This is one of the oldest legends told me when I was a small boy. So as the Story-teller says, "Draw up your chairs, folks, and you shall hear about this strange story, that is said to have actually happened, long time ago, when the people used to put their dead on trees or scaffolding, or even keep them in their own lodges."

There was a certain old man that lived in the deep forest where the game was plentiful. He was a very strange sort of a man, as his people knew little about him or his habits. He lived alone far away from the rest of his people. The people were afraid of this man, as he was noted to be some sort of a witch. When he got sick, some of his people came to help him, as was the custom in those days. So, while he lingered in his death-bed, he made known his last wishes as to the manner of his burial. He wanted his remains to be kept in his own lodge, that part to be partitioned off. That anyone hunting in that section, could use his place without any trouble, but no children nor even woman must ever stay there,—it would not be safe if they did. That was the wishes of the old man.

When he died, it was carried out as he had directed. His remains was carefully placed in an elm-bark coffin and placed in the middle of a partition made in his shack. All cooking utensils were as he had left them, to be used later by any hunter who care to share with the late owner of the place, so it is said.

In this village which was a day's journey from this man's hut, lived a young hunter who had a wife and a small girl. This village was an unusual large one as villages goes in those days, and this man have not heard about the last wishes of this dead hermit-witch. So when the hunting season came that fall, they went out together; he took his wife and their little girl with him. Upon coming to the shack and burial place of the hermit-witch, they thought it was so good and everything so handy that they decided

HE DID NOT GIVE REPLY

to stay there and make it their winter quarters during the hunting season; so they did stop there. They noticed the dead man in the adjoining room; but as that was a common custom in those days, they thought nothing of it.

As they arrived late in the afternoon, the woman made ready for the evening meal. She noticed that there were corn braided strings in the place, and started to bake what is call Unhulled Corn Bread. It was made by just grinding the corn into meal without using the hulling process with ashes. She baked them in the ashes of the fire in the center of the room. In the meantime her husband layed down by the fire with their daughter, saying as he did: "I think I will lay down for our baby to sleep while you are getting the meal ready."

It was then getting dark,—the only light was from the fire. As she went about her work, she thought that she heard a noise like some animal eating or gnawing on bone. She looked at her husband laying there by the fire and asked him: "Are you really asleep?"

He did not give any reply. Then she noticed that there was a stream of dark color issuing from where he was laying. At the same time as she did ask her husband, she thought she saw in the faint light the dead man sneaking back into the other room, and then later again she was certain she had heard him returning into his bark coffin. Then she knew that her man was no longer alive, that the so-called dead man had killed him and was eating him up.

Then she did some fast and deliberate thinking as to how she would escape alive without being suspected by this beast in the next room. It was lucky that their little baby was laying next to the fire and thereby was safe.

So she pretended that she had not found out all about it and spoke to her man thus: "I am going after water to rinse the bread, which is nearly done. I will take. our little one with me so she won't get into the fire, as you seem to be asleep. As soon as I return, then we shall eat."

It was all she could do to refrain from showing her grief as she spoke, as she was much affected with sorrow of her beloved husband's death. Her fear for her life was uppermost in her mind, and her little daughter also. So she picked up her girl, and taking her blanket she took her little daughter on her back, tying her blanket across her back, then it came over the front (It is called "Wa-enh-nih-gonh-soh-dah-ah"). In this manner her arms are free; so taking a water pail she went out with her daughter on her back with the intention to try and escape if she could. As soon as she had gone a little distance from the place, she broke into a fast run. She ran as fast as she could and merely threw the water-pail when she reached the spring. She then headed for their home, running at the top of her speed and telling her little girl to be brave,—that if they are lucky, they may reach home yet.

She had ran quite a distance, when she heard all very plainly the angry shout of the so-called dead man. He had now found out that she had escaped him by deceiving him; or else he may have finished eating up the husband, then seeing that she has not returned from her trip to the spring, he came out and made such a yell that she heard him.

He threatened her thus: "You think you can yet escape me. The world is small and I shall soon overtake you."

At his outcry, she got so weak that she thought she would fall down; but thinking of the possibility of escape, she renewed her attempt and continued on. In little while, she could hear his running after her. She took off her blanket and hung it up on a limb by the trail. As he came up to it, she could hear him rejoice, thinking it was her. He tore it up, and then finding out that it was not her, he began to cry out again that he will have her in time. She kept up her courage, but she knew that he was gaining on her; so she took her head shawl and hung it up by the path; then she went on. Very soon he came up to it, and again started to tear it up. He came on again with more fury, judging from his remarks. Every time she would find something to hang up, and that would occupy his time for a while; thus she is allowed more time to keep ahead of him. She had taken off nearly all her clothes and that of her little girl, but she was getting much nearer to her home. Thus she went on, carrying her child in her arms.

Now as she had thrown off all her things,—she was almost now without clothes,—she realized that it was near enough to the village to be heard; so she gave the cry of distress by shouting "Goo-weh! Goo-weh!" Every little distance she would give the cry. The dead man was just little ways behind her now and was about to overtake her, when she noticed a band of warriors with flaming torches coming towards her from the village. They came up to her just before this dead man caught her. They (the people from the village) opened up their ranks, and she fell in their midst; and the dead man just stopped at the edge of the glow of torch-light and said to her, "You were fortunate that they came as they did, so you managed to get away from me."

Now it happen that they were dancing in their long house that night; so when she started to give the cry of distress, young boys were out in the dark, having their sport of chasing each other and other game of sports, having for light big bonfires of stumps of pine trees, when all at once someone heard a distant cry of distress. As all knew in those days just what it means, they rushed in and told their Head-Chief about someone out in the distant woods coming and shouting the cry of help. He right off ordered his young braves to form a party with a torch of pine-pitch knots and armed with weapons to meet or see what person is coming. And they did form a good-sized party that met this woman just in the nick of time.

They took her back, wrapped her up in blankets of skins, and took her child to the long house; and after she was revived with some hot drinks, she was asked to relate in detail all about what happened to her and her husband, as they already had recognized her.

The Chief of the village then arosed and made this speech, "Tomorrow morning very early, we shall go to the place and take care that such event shall not happen again. You, who had this thing happened to you, will stay home and rest up. I ask all you women, who have any spare clothes, to give it to this woman." And the meeting was over and all went home.

Early the next day, there was a big gathering about their long house, all anxious to go to this cabin 'way out in the woods. When their Head-Chief arrived they all started out. The party was so big that travelling was rather slow; they had to camp for the night about half way to the place where they were going. The next day very early, they were all called by their chief to start out, and they did. It was late in the afternoon when they arrived at the place. While they were going along, they noticed every little ways the place where she had hung her clothes of some sort. There was a space about it, all trampled down, as if there had been some commotion; then her garment are scattered all over, torn into small pieces. They saw everything as she had explained in her story of her experience. They saw many places where her clothes were all scattered about. (Both she and her child were almost without clothes when they were found.) They also noted the water pail at the spring when they got to the place.

Inside, by the fire place, laid the husband, with a big hole in his side, where the dead man had sucked all the blood. They also found a badly burnt bread, still in the ashes. In the adjoining room laid the dead man, with his face stained with fresh blood. For some unknown reason his body had kept from being badly decomposed, as compared to the length of time since he had died.

The Head-Chief then addressed the dead man thus: "We have came to prepare you much better. We know you are not satisfied the way it is. We will do our best to make you well-pleased."

Then they went out, and the chief directed his men to gather all sorts of dry wood and bigger logs. When they had gathered quite a pile, then they closed the door of the cabin; dry wood was placed all around the building; then heavier wood was piled on. When all was completed, then the chief told his men to circle around, to start the fire all around; and when it had burned down, to watch out that nothing escapes from the fire,—to be ready with weapons. So at a signal the fire was lighted at different spots all around the cabin. Then all retired to a safe distance with war-clubs ready.

The fire made a quick start; in no time the flames had entirely covered the place, what looked like a huge wood-pile. Then it was settling down in the middle; it had burned down the cabin within. In the din, the rattling of the flames and crackling of the tinders, there came up the cry of the dead man.

He was exclaiming aloud: "You have promised to take care of me. You have fooled me. If I ever get out of this, watch out!"

He kept up yelling in the middle of the flames until his voice got weaker and weaker. As the fire seem to die down, when it was but a huge pile of live coals, then all at once a loud report was heard. It was the man's skull bursting open, like a thing exploded. The chief exclaimed to stand by and not let anything get away from them. At the report, there, out of the fire came a big Jack Rabbit. They all started to swing their clubs at the animal, but in spite of all their efforts, the Rabbit got away between someone's legs and was soon lost in the woods.

That was the end of the great witch, that was as bad in death as when still living. His orenda or "Ote-gonh," that was the evil-spirit in him, got away in the form of Jack Rabbit, so they say. This is the end of my legend, and the evil-spirit may still be alive somewhere. Dah Neh-hoh.

Now, Sah-nee-weh, they used to say that in the olden days everyone who was of any account had with him some sort of Ote-gonh or a Witch-token or charm. It was commonly practiced but seldom if ever spoken about openly. Even to this day, who may still have it? The very substance of this weird legend seems unreal, but that was considered common in their times. This is one of the best, according to my opinion. Put that in your pouch of legends with the

rest. This is all for the time being, until I have another one
to tell. In Sunshine or Shade I am

Your Seneca Story-teller and Brother,

Jesse J. Cornplanter

"Hah-yonh-wonh-ish,"

Snipe Clan

"GA-AHS-HEA"
HULLING BASKET

XIV

THE BEARS THAT ADOPTED A BOY
A LEGEND FOR HUNTERS

Tonawanda Reservation
May 15, 1937

My dear Sah-nee-weh:

We shall now resume with our legends. Now comes the one about the Bears that adopted the little boy. This particular legend was told me when only a boy of six or seven years of age. It appealed to me to an extent, because of the manner it reveals all the mysteries of the animals as compared to mankind, the Hunter. . . . This is another story that is modern in its scope as compared to the rest. It deals with the time when white-man's firearms were introduced to our people. So, Sah-nee-weh, as the story-teller would start, draw up your chair and listen attentively and you shall hear about the Bears adopting a little boy:—

In the olden days there was a certain man who had recently lost his wife. They had a little boy about the age of four or so. This man, being a hunter, thought best after a lapse of time to remarry again, more for necessity than anything else. So he did succeed in finding a mate which pleased him much. He wanted to have someone take the place of the wife he had lost, to take care of the boy while

151

he is absent on his hunting trips. So it was agreed that when the time came to hunt that they would go to the hunting grounds. All went well at first. She took good care of the little boy, as it seemed, but not so well, because she really detested the very sight of the boy, due to the fact that he so much resembled his dead mother. It really hurt her to see him,—she was a very jealous woman,—but she tried her best not to show it. She was very anxious to go to this hunting trip, as she knew the time would come when she could work her plan to get rid of this boy that was causing her trouble in her heart. She meant to get rid of him, to kill him if necessary.

When the time came, then they set out on their annual hunting trip. After they had settled down to the routine camp life, the hunter said that he would start out early in the morning, that the two were to stay home. But the woman spoke and told him she wanted to go out in search of fire-wood after they were alone, and she meant to take the boy along. The man just warned her not to go too far away from the camp unless she could easily find her way back. On the morning, the hunter went away very early, to be gone all day. So the woman stayed at the camp with the little boy, her step-son.

As soon as her work about the camp were done, she then took the little boy and told him that they were going out to get some wood. They went out into the woods. The boy really enjoyed being in the big forest. He had never

seen such big timber. They went out quite a ways. At last
they came to a mountain side; there were all sorts of rocks.
They wandered about along the edge of this steep side of
the base of this mountain. All at once they came to a hole

on the side of this mountain. It was a large hole, big enough
for anyone to crawl in. Then this woman who had wicked
ideas saw the chance to fulfill her desire. So she told the
little boy to crawl in and see what is inside. The little boy
did not know fear, nor had no idea what it was all about
but to mind what he thought was his own mother; so he
went in on his hands and knees.

He went little ways. It was dark there, but she told him
to keep on till he reach the end and see what he could find

there. He then kept on going forward. Often he could not see at all; but that was what his step-mother wanted him to do, so he just kept on going until he reached the very end. There were what seem like a sort of a nest, the home of some animal, but it was just the boy's luck, the owner of the cave was not there.

In the meantime, when the boy had gone into the cavern, his step-mother found a huge rock loose, which she rolled to the entrance of the cave and closed it entirely, thereby imprisoning the boy. She was then very satisfied, knowing that at last she had succeeded in getting rid of the boy she hated so much. So she went on back to the camp with an armful of wood.

When the hunter returned at night, she met him at the door and started to act very sad. She told him that she had lost the boy in the woods; that when she was busy gathering wood, he wandered off all by himself; at first she told him that she did not know that the boy had gone away until she got ready to come on back home; then she told him that she had missed the boy, that he was nowheres to be found, that she started to call by his name at the top of her voice. She said that she went here and there calling for him, then when she could not find him, she came on home with a heavy heart. That was her story to the father of the boy. And the man just took her story as truth. He felt grieved over the loss of his little boy that he dearly loved. That was the end of the boy. He was given up for lost. And they went back to the village after the season of hunting was over. The news spread all over that the boy was lost during the season.

When the boy found that there was nothing but the empty nest or home for some animal, then he went back towards the entrance, it was a slow process, often stopping to find his way back in the darkness. When he came back to the entrance, he saw or rather felt that it was closed tight with a big rock. He tried to get out some way, but it was hopeless; then he just sat by the big rock and started to cry. He was then very hungry. He called for his step-mother, but there was no answer. Then he settled down to sleep. He did not know whether it was daytime or night, as it was dark inside.

He lay there for some time, when all at once he heard someone call his name outside. It sounded like some woman's voice. She called again. When she called the third time, then he answered. She asked him if he was asleep.

When he told her that he was awake, then she told him thus: "It was the very intention of your wicked step-mother that you perish here; she had been thinking about destroying you for some time. The moment you went far into the hole, she placed this rock so you were imprisoned. When your father returned, she told him that you were lost, that she tried to find you. But do not worry, because I am going to save you, and you can go home with me and play with my two little ones. I am what you people call 'Nya-gwa-ih,' bears."

Then the rock was removed and he saw that it was night by now. Then he saw a woman standing there who took him by the hand, and they went back to her place. They returned home and sure enough he found two little boys that were very glad that he came. (Now it is said that in those days the Indians were living so close to nature that it was common to see animals in the form of human-being. This legend is one of these strange events. To the boy, the bears were like anybody that he was used to see,—he did not know the difference. And the place where she took him back was a hollow tree.) He found the place a very nice home, the two little ones were about his age, and they got real friendly and played all the time. The mother-bear warned them (her own) to be careful and not to touch him so rough nor strike the boy, due to their sharp claws. They went out all over the woods, and he saw many things that boys were never taught. Time went on, he stayed with the bears.

When winter came, they stayed in and he was told many things about the ways of the bears. He lived as good as anyone would wish. They had big stores of all manners of dried fruit, nuts, and honey in combs. He used to eat dried huckleberry or blackberry cakes, which answered for bread, and the mother-bear used to hold her palm upwards, and in the cup formed there would be oil, and he used to dip his dried bread in this grease. He liked it very well. They spent much time in winter-time by sleeping. They were kept warm, as their house was nice. She would wake up in time to give him food, as she realized that he was not like the bears. Thus it went on until spring; then they were all ready again. He spent much time playing with the two bears, who treated him as if he was their own brother. He never was lonesome. Time went on and then summer came; then they went out to pick berries when they were ripe. Blackberries seem to be the main food. They would pick many berries, and as it was picked, the mother-bear would make them into cakes, by making it into pulp,—then she would take the large leaves of the basswood tree and put the cake of berry juice on the leaf and then dry it out in the sun. She make many such cakes; they dry fast. The huckleberry they picked was dried in the sun, and that was stored for winter use. Then the cold weather with its frost of the fall came on and they went out in search for all sorts of nuts. These they also stored like the rest for winter use. So the routine life of the bears were full of all sorts of amusement to the boy. Life was about the same the year around; they went to the same place to pick the berries, or gather the nuts; they also observed about the same time to go into their winter's rest. . . .

He had been with the bears now three years; he had learned lot about the animals. It was season for the fall hunt again; and as usual they were on the alert for hunters, lest someone would discover their home. The mother-bear had a long pole with a sort of a fork at the end or tip, which she uses when some hunter with a good dog comes near their home. She would reach out with this crotched pole. As the dog approached the tree, she would hold it to the dog, and he would be caught between the tips or crotch; then she would swing the dog around and off to one side.

The mother-bear called the boy to her side one day and said:—"It is now three years since you had been with us. I imagine you must be about eight years old now. I want you to learn few more things that you people never knew existed at all. I feel as if some day soon or later we shall be separated for good. Your people may yet find you, though they have given you up for lost or killed. Now remember what I am going to show you. First of all, it is now time to hunt. We shall see all sorts of hunters, and I want you to see the different types and the habits of each, and what they appear to us animals. We can see far more than your people; in fact, we can see into the minds of all hunters as they came towards us. We, the bears, are the most closely related to your people. Our habits are almost the same as your people. Some people says that it is the dog that stands next to man. But if that is the case, why is it that dogs cannot help mankind like we can? You cannot eat the food that dogs live on, nor can you live as they do in winter-time. For this one reason I want you to remember hereafter.

"We will give you a series of songs for our own enjoyment. Observe that sort of a dance whenever you happen to think of us. We shall be there even if you do not see us. Every time you hold this dance, which shall be known as the 'Bear's Song Dance,' you must follow our custom and manner of living, by having for feast berry-juice drink; and as the ceremony is about to begin, you must do this thing;—have you or someone give this invocation to us, by burning the sacred Indian tobacco, asking us to enjoy our own group of songs, and to bring the sponsor luck and happiness. There will be more members as time goes on. For the beginning, anyone may dance that feel thankful to us for taking care of you in time of distress. We will teach you the songs and everything that is to be done. Most of the members that will carry on will be admitted into the society by some form of illness that will be cured by having our dance and songs take place of medicine. All this I command you to remember and teach your people whenever you get back to them. I feel something is going to happen soon; that is why I am now telling you all this. You are now old enough to remember this." Thus spoke the mother-bear to the boy.

It was now the "Moon-of-falling-leaves," the time to hunt. So they were all expecting to see hunters coming for the annual fall hunt. They kept inside of their home lest some hunter would see them. Then one day, the mother-bear called the boy to her side. As he reached her side, she pointed to a place and told him to watch. He did watch and he saw a hunter coming towards them in a distance. He noticed the man was carrying a good-sized limb of a tree in his mouth, and it seem that he was having trouble in making his way, as the limb was getting tangled up with the trees and other shrubbery that grew by the way; moreover he was making quite a noise as he went on. The mother-bear asked the boy what he saw.

Then he said thus: "I saw this hunter coming slowly. He has a limb of a tree in his mouth and seems to be having trouble with it."

And she told him that it was as he saw; that it was the habit of this man as he walked along the woods to break off a limb or a twig and chew it as he walked; that it was the way he appeared to all animals and he will not get any game.

After a while she called his attention again. She said, "Here comes another hunter; now watch him"; and the boy watch the coming hunter. This man had a big wooden bowl in his mouth. It was like wearing a mask,—he could not see where he was going,—every little while he would run into a tree or else stumble on a fallen tree.

She asked him what he saw, and he told her this, "This hunter has a big wooden bowl in his mouth, and it is bothering him so that he cannot see his way; and moreover, he is making quite a noise by the limbs hitting against the bowl."

She told him that it was the habit of this man, when

he eats, that he always want to drain to the last drop by holding the bowl to his mouth instead of using a spoon; that was his manner of appearance to all game animals, thereby he will never kill anything.

Soon she told the boy to watch again, which he did. He saw a man coming; as he walked he sang at the top of his voice, which echoed all over the forest. Again she asked him what he noticed.

Then he replied, "This man coming is singing at the top of his voice and is making much noise."

She answered: "Quite true. It is the habit of this man whenever he is walking alone to always be humming a tune or else thinking of a song. To us of the animal-world, he is singing out as loud as he can, he will never be a good hunter."

Then she saw another one coming and told him to watch, which he did. He saw a man coming, a hunter, and the man acted as if he was blind; but he kept on going, only every little while he would go against a tree or into a thicket, then he would back out again. And the man looked very young. She asked him what he noticed.

He told her thus, "This hunter is a young man; he act as if he is blind, often going against trees or in tangled brush, but he would back away and resume his way."

She replied: "It is true; he is a young hunter, too young to hunt. He is as you saw him, often getting tangled up or running against trees. The reason is that he is not of one mind; he is not thinking of game or of hunting, but has many other things in his mind, thereby he is not going to be a good hunter until he forgets his other duties, or whatever he may be thinking of."

Then she pointed to another hunter coming, and he watched. He saw this man coming, and there seem to be a great cloud of vapor or steam issuing from his mouth. It was causing him to lose his way, and it could be seen from a distance. Then he told her that he saw this man with steam or vapor coming out of his mouth which seems to be bothering him. She told him that it is the habit of this man to eat and drink very hot food and drinks; that he is not such a good hunter.

Then he did noticed that every time a hunter came with a dog, that she uses the pole with the crotched ends to guide the dogs away from the place where they lived. Then all at once she exclaimed, "Ah-hah! Oh-neh wa-ih (It is now)." Then she showed the boy; a hunter was coming with no outward signs of anything but determination. He had a dog, and the dog had four eyes. (To the bears, the dog that had two spots over each eye was a dog with four eyes and could see more than ordinary dogs.) Both came direct towards the tree where the bears and the boy lived. In no time the dog started to bark and scratched at the base of the tree. He had found their home. And then the hunter came to the tree and right away he saw the bark of the tree all scratched (what the Indians called "Oh-eh-dah" or claw-marked). Then he proceeded to cut the tree down.

In the meantime the mother-bear called all her charges to her side for final words and told them thus: "When the tree falls, we must all go out. I will lead, then you older, then the younger; and lastly you, the boy, will go out. Now remember this."

The man kept up with the cutting down of their tree, the dog running in circles around the tree and barking all the time. Then the tree fell with a noise. After everything had quieted down, the hunter came to the opening of the tree and tapped with his gun and called out for them to come out. So the mother-bear went out. The boy saw everything clearly. As she went out, the hunter had retired to a distance to wait for the bears, and as soon as the mother-bear came out there was a loud report. Then the boy saw his adopted mother throw down a big bundle of meat and ran towards the setting sun. (To the boy it appeared that the bear threw down the bundle of meat and continued on; but it was her spirit that went on, as her material being was laying there where the hunter had shot her as she came out.) Then the next older cub-bear, as he went out,—there was the shot and he likewise threw down a smaller bundle of meat and then followed his mother's direction. And then the youngest cub went as the other had done. He also threw down a small bundle and went on. Then the boy came out. As he came out, the hunter stood little ways off ready and aiming. But what was his surprise to see the boy come out of the tree. And the boy then saw that, instead of bundles of meat, he saw on the ground the three bears,—one big one and two small cubs. He then saw for the first time that

he had been staying with the bears; he had always thought that they were like any other people instead of bears. He felt sad at the sight of the dead bears; who had kept him all these years; and who had taught him so much wonderful thing to remember.

Then the man came over and said: "Why did you come out last? If you had came out first, then I am duty-bound not to touch your adopted mother and brothers. We had given you up for lost or killed. They had kept you all this time. I shall not take the meat back home; they are your kin and I am a murderer. We shall bury them in as decent way as we can. Then we shall go on home."

So they dug a shallow pit and buried the remains of the boy's adopted mother and brothers. Then they went home, and what a great surprise it was to the people when they heard that the boy who was lost had come home alive again to his father! It seems that the wicked woman had died little while after they had returned from the hunting trip; she never seemed the same woman after she lost her stepson. She just seem to waste away, then in the end died. But his father was so pleased to see his son, who had been known as dead all these years. Now he was a large boy. It was decided to have a regular feast of enjoyment, and to hear all the boy had to tell from his experience with the bears, and how he came to live with them. So at night it was announced to all the people of the village to gather in their meeting house. Then the boy told everything from the beginning. They ended the meeting by dancing the "Bear's Song Dance" for the first time. Thus was the beginning of the Bear Dance and the end of my story, Dah neh-hoh.

Your Seneca Brother and Story-teller,
Jesse J. Cornplanter
Ha-yonh-wonh-ish,
the Snipe

XV

THE SPECTRE WIFE
A LEGEND OF LOVE

Tonawanda Reservation
May 8, 1937

Sah-nee-weh
Penn Yan, New York
Sken-nonh, Sah-nee-weh:

Spring is here again and what a day it is today,—one cannot help but admire the work of Our Great Spirit, the Good! Everywhere you look you see growing things; life itself is taking fresh start, it seems. Such a day that I will tell you another legend which deals with the dead and how we believe they do come back to us. My father says that they are with us but we don't see them. We are separated by the thickness of maple leaf. And in this legend it will reveal the idea that there was love, that we had respect for our wifes in a sense almost bordering on love. So many writers has given the reading public that we do not know live, in our daily life. Why is it that young men went out to war? Why is it that they always left some men back at home to defend their women? Why? Do you know, Sah-nee-weh, that it is with great pleasure to me to be able to write all these legends?

166

If we could only go back to those days, to live over the days as they lived it, do away with all worries, but live entirely as the Good Spirit has willed that we should live. To be free from the everlasting slavery from the almighty dollar, and the computation of time into minutes, seconds and hours. To the Red Man, day was summed from daylight to sun-set and so on. I say again that the life that my ancestors led were far better than the present, regardless of all luxuries and inventions. No wonder they lived to an old age in those days, nature took care of the very life's need as it were. There were no bakeries, stores or any of the modern day luxuries. One could not live by using a can opener nor even the use of money as we do now days. Life, in the olden days, seem more to my opinion as worth living.

The legend for this time deals about the belief, that the dead are with us unseen, and in this case came back to this world. Now bring up your chair closer to the fire as I start to relate this legend; bear with me, and do not fall asleep as I tell it.

In the olden times, when the dead were not buried but are kept wrapped up in skins and placed on trees or scaffoldings, such was the time of our subject. There lived a young hunter whose young and rather good-looking wife had died, leaving behind her with her devoted but sad husband, a little girl about the age of one or two. When the necessary time had elapsed after her death, funeral and its custom of Death Feast of Ten Days was over, the sorrowing widower with his little daughter wandered about their village,—very much demented, as he loved his wife. After a while, he decided that a trip to the hunting grounds would be much better than to stay at home; so packing up for hunting, he took his only love, his little girl, with him and departed for the big timber. As this happened just before the regular hunting season, he went about at the hunting grounds, wandering aimlessly, reviewing everything of the past when he had been there before, when he had his wife with him and everything was all very good then. In fact, he went about talking to himself, or else went about calling his wife's name, even to hoping she would hear him and take pity and return to him and their daughter who was alone in his hunting lodge. Day after day he went about, ever asking her return, even if in a dream.

It went on for a long time, until the season came for hunt. He left his little daughter at home. After talking to her and telling her to be a good girl and stay at home,— that the kind mother would be near her while she was alone,—then he would go out on his daily round of hunting. During the regular season when he was more or less busy with game, he was surprised to find his little daughter well taken care of. When he return home one day, the fire was burning as if someone had just made the fire, and his daughter acted very happy. It worried him at first, wondering what might be the cause. He could not find out anything; as his girl was so small, she could not talk yet.

So the next day he went out as was the custom. He wondered what would be like when he returned at night, as he really sensed something unnatural had taken place. He asked his Maker to make his beloved wife come to them once more; he wished it would be her that had been back to her own daughter the day before. So the day passed, and he went back to their lodge. Sure enough, he found his little girl's hair had been combed and her face washed; moreover, the little girl seem very much delighted. As before, the fire was going on nicely as if someone had recently made the fire. He was very much pleased and hoped that he would be able to just get one glance at his wife, for he was sure it must be her that has been coming back to her daughter when she is alone. He was much pleased to think that at last his pleading to his Great Spirit had been heard.

The next day he went to hunt again, but came back little earlier than usual. He found that everything was about done and ready to serve evening meal, only it was still cooking, and the girl's hair was again combed. He did not say anything, but was very much pleased. The following day when he returned, he just saw a part of the wife's dress as he came around their hunting lodge, and he saw that meal was ready, waiting for his return.

Just as he came around the end of the shack, he saw part of her dress as she ran around the other corner of the building. Then when he went in, he knew that it was her sure enough that was coming back to them. Now he rejoiced much as he went about getting ready for the evening meal, which was nearly done by now. He and his little daughter

ate their meal with much better feelings. He told his daughter that very soon they will be reunited again, as he felt positive his wife will eventually return to them.

So again the next day he went out on his daily hunt. He knew it must be now that he will see his beloved wife again. Such was his love for her that the day seemed long, but finally it did came time for him to depart for his camp. So he went home. Sure enough, she was at home with their own daughter.

She told him thus: "I will stay with you. I have heard all the wishes, your desires to have me return to you. I am so much worried to have to leave you two, that I cannot rest; I have been coming back to our daughter right along. It is a fact that I am of the Departed Spirits. One thing I will warn you; that is, you must keep your distance,—you must never lay your hands on me. As long as you keep your place, we shall be together. Because I love you both so much."

Thus was the beginning of this person who had departed this world to come back and live like any normal being. They were very happy; they did live as any normal people. He went out every day, returning to see that home was like it had been before her death. They stayed at the hunting lodge all that hunting period, until, the very last days, they were at meal, eating, when all at once she gave one shrill scream. She told them that she had to go now, that her burial place had caught fire. She bid them both farewell and was gone like a flash of lightning. Thus ended this very unusual event in those days.

Now it happened in this manner. Her burial scaffold

had caught fire,—it may have been set afire by some person. And that was the beginning when they buried their dead in graves, often a shallow grave. So the hunter and

his little daughter did not tarry around their camp longer, but returned to the village. And sure enough, he found that her remains had burned almost entirely. Then they were at last separated in this world. And here the legend ends. Dah Neh-hoh. . . .

This is more of a modern date. As we say, mostly all legends actually happened. I think it is an unusual one. It shows that what we believe,—the spirits returns to earth sometimes. From this and similar legends, the creation of the Chanters to the Dead, known as "Oh-kee-wey," originated. No wonder the people of dead person's relatives often show emotions when this ceremonies are given. It was intended to ease some earth-bound spirit so that one or more spirits can rest in peace.

This is my idea of a good legend, always with a moral to it. My next one will deal with another legend of Dead and that of the living. So watch out for the next one. Neh-hoh. . . .

Your Seneca Brother,
Jesse J. Cornplanter
"Hah-yonh-wonh-ish"

XVI

THE WITCH GRANDMOTHER

Tonawanda Reservation
May 25, 1937

Nya-weh Sken-nonh, Sah-nee-weh:

What a nice spring day it is,—I just have to write you again. Last Sunday night we had our Annual Ceremony for blessing the seeds before we put them in the ground. It was very good. I think it is so nice to give thanks to the Great Spirit and ask for his care while it is growing. Just another of our numerous thanksgiving ceremonies. For my story this time I have been thinking about Mr. Carmer's book in which he mentions of our superstitions, that about witches and its effects amongst our people; he only mentioned of it, but did not go into detail. So I have been thinking all about it lately. Oh, yes, by the way, I am going to New York City on June the fourteenth to broadcast with Mr. Carmer. I know I will enjoy the trip and have the pleasure of meeting Mr. Carmer again.

The belief of witchcraft among the Senecas are so much that it has instilled fear amongst them; their faith is such, that you cannot go and tell them, it is only imagination. I will tell one legend and explain as I go on, because there are very few writers that have covered this subject and done

174

justice to it. In order to do so, one has to be an Indian, to live and believe as they do; so here it is, as related to me by old story-teller.

Long time ago, it is said, there lived a little boy with his aged grandmother in a little old shack at the edge of the village. This boy was about the age of five or six years,— at the age when their curiosity gets the best of them. But he was a good obedient boy, an orphan who had no other relative to care for him but this aged woman, who people looked to with a certain amount of distrust as to her honesty and kindness. And the boy had his feeling that his grandmother was doing something or else going some place nearly every night. He had seen her go out at night many times. Just as he goes to bed when she thought he had gone to sleep, then she would come to the bed and move him gently to see if he is really asleep. When he pretended that he was asleep, she would then go up on a small loft. Then she would bring out something, and then she would go out; then he would hear a strange noise, and she would return quite late. It would always be preceded by the same noise just before she would enter again; then she would climb up to that loft again. Then she would come to his bed and look him over to see if he was asleep. After finding that he was sleeping, she would laugh to herself and then would go to bed.

This thing went on for quite a long time. Then he really felt curious about her strange actions and decided to find out, if he could, at the first chance without her knowing it,—he was very much afraid of her, as she scolded him very much. So one night the chance came. She was notified to attend a dance of some sort, and just before leaving she warned him about being nice and not to touch anything while she was away. So when he was alone, when he was sure that she had gone, then he went up to this loft and felt around. He found a package all done up in skin of some animal. It was a good-sized package. He brought it down; then he went out to see that she was not anywheres; then he came in and started to undo the package. In it he found many strange things. He found an old dried-up owl's head. From being curious, he put it on. It fitted his head,— then he was turned into a Screech-owl, and it flew out and began to fly amongst the trees.

He was helpless to stop or to control himself. He felt so funny. The owl was a very funny acting bird and flew about from tree to tree until it flew to a certain home, where there was a young woman laying on bed sick. He saw the sick woman from the outside, but he felt pity on her. So he flew back to his place without doing anything at all. And when he returned home, it flew in; then he took the head off again. He was then a little boy, once more. He took the head right back as he had found and replaced it on the loft and then went to bed. He no sooner had settled in bed when his grandmother returned and again went to his bed and noted that he was asleep.

The following night she went out again, as she had done many times before; so he got out of bed and followed her out. He saw her going towards the deep forest; so he followed her at a safe distance, and when he was in the forest, he broke off a limb of the trees as he went on, so he would know how to find his way back. He followed her 'way into the deepest part of the forest, and there at a clearing she came to a little group of older people who were gathered around a small fire burning in the middle of the circle. Over it hung a bundle of snakes. Also there was a small kettle hanging over the fire, and the blood of these dead snakes were dripping into this kettle. He stayed back among the shadow and listened, but he could not understand everything that was said. An old man was talking to the small gathering.

He noticed that they were about to break up their meeting; so he was afraid to be seen and went back towards home. He found his way out by watching the broken twigs; and when he had returned home and in bed again, she came in and did the same thing again, by looking at him to see if he was asleep,—then went to bed.

Now this sort of thing went on quite a long time. The boy was getting to be a big boy now. He was thinking about finding out what it was that they did.

So one night when he knew that it is her night to go out again, he asked her this: "Grandmother, where do you go to when you go out? I have noticed you going out every other night. Tell me."

She was very much scared when he asked her this, but she answered him thus: "You are not as obedient as I wanted you to be; you have been deceiving me; you must have found out the very things that I have tried my best to keep secret. You are a naughty boy. I will not tell you where I go nor what I do when I go out nights; that is only for certain ones to know, and not for small boys that are naughty."

He answered her: "But, grandmother, I already know where you go to,—have seen part of it; but I want to find out more about it. I have followed you one night. You never saw me nor even knew that I had been where you folks gather. I could find that spot now if I tried."

Then she looked at him with a different expression and then replied: "There is only one way by which you can find out more,—that is by joining our group; but you must be in earnest and brave to be with this group,—it takes courage to do it. You must have your mind all set to join."

Then the boy spoke: "I am determined to join, no matter what it may be."

She told him that he could go with her on this one night, that they would try him out first. So that night she took her grandson with her when she went out. They went out to this same spot as he already knew, but he never told her that he had made signs so he could find his way out or into this place, because he did not fully trust his grandmother. They arrived at the place, and the rest had all arrived already.

Then she got up again, after they had been seated, and made this speech: "My grandson here have made up his own mind to join our group here. He has seen me come out before, all by mistake on my part. He is willing to try out according to our law."

Then the old man who acts as if he may be the head of this meeting arosed and made this reply: "If your grandson has seen you, then he must be admitted into our circle, or else it would mean trouble to us if he did not join."

So a meeting was held and different ones made speeches. It was decided to accept him and try him out, as it was their custom in their organization. Then he was asked if he really meant to become a member. He replied that he did. He noticed the small fire burning and the bundle of snakes over the small kettle. The tip of the tails of the snakes were cut off, and blood was slowly dripping into this kettle. Then the old man who seem to be the chief, made the speech as to their law or custom in this queer little circle.

He said thus: "In order to become a full-fledged member of this organization, you must pick out someone to pay for your admission. After you had drunk this brew" (pointing to the kettle that was brewing the blood of the dead snakes), "then you must go to this place where a person is sick and point to her, and she will die; then you are a full-fledge member."

Then the boy told them he was ready for what they asked him to do; so one of them went and dipped a small wooden spoon into this kettle and told him to drink it. He took the spoon and in the dim light of the small fire, he did another trick of deception,—he poured it on the ground; but he pretended to drink it, and made noise of swallowing it slowly. Then he was given the same Screech-owl's head and told to put it on and go to this certain sick person, and when arriving at the place to point at her and she would then die; that he could see through the wall of any lodge without trouble.

After he had made the motions of drinking this brew, he put on his grandmother's owl's head and he flew away straight to this cabin, the same one he had been to once. There, sure enough, he saw right through the walls; he saw this sick young girl laying by the fire place suffering; he felt sorry for her. So instead of pointing at her, he saw a cat that was laying by the fire. He pointed at this cat, and sure enough the cat suddenly got up and started to roll and squirmed all over the ashes of the edge of the fire, and then died without much suffering. Then the owl flew back.

So he returned to their meeting, and they asked him what he saw. He told them all that took place, but he did not tell about the cat; and then the meeting was considered a success, and they dispersed.

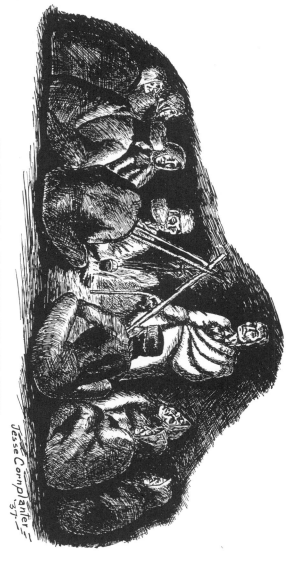

THE BLOOD WAS SLOWLY DRIPPING INTO THIS KETTLE

The next day one of this secret group of witches went to this place to see what the new member had done. And what was his surprise to see the sick woman still alive. Then he asked them what peculiar thing did they noticed the night before,—that he was ready to make medicine for her. They told him that there was nothing peculiar, but the cat had suddenly taken sick and died. Then this member came to the shack of the boy and his grandmother, and the man started to tell of finding the sick person still alive and that instead the cat had died; that the boy, as new member, had failed, that it would be the boy's own life instead, for failing such an organization.

The boy was outside when this member told his story, but the boy heard every word of it, and he ran to the chief of the village and called him out and told him all about it. He told him that he had tracked his grandmother to their secret meeting place, but he was afraid to tell about this before as he had no one to take care of him should his grandmother be killed for being a witch. This the chief told him: that the boy would be much better off without his grandmother; that he was welcome to live with the chief, as he would be aiding his community by exposing all the witches so they could be destroyed. He told him also to be ready to act as guide in the following night, as they were going to send a big party to surprise the witches at their meeting, but not to tell his grandmother about it or anyone else, to go back home and not let his grandmother find out that he had given the alarm.

So the boy went back as quick as he could, but in his absence they had discovered (that is, the member who told his grandmother, and the old witch or boy's grandmother). They had come out when he did not come in the house, as this man saw the boy outside when he came at first. So it is claimed that this one man has escaped the destruction of the rest of the witches at that time. When they found the boy was not home or near the house, this man knew that he had gone to give the alarm, and as the following night was the meeting night again, this man was not there. When the member of the witches had gone, the boy returned, but it was too late,—they had already found out he had been away. But the boy went in and told his grandmother that he saw the most beautiful bird near the house, and while the man had visited, the boy saw this bird and followed it from tree to tree and it took him far away, so he gave up and came back. This seem to please his grandmother as an excuse, and she never thought anything more about it.

So the next night she started to get ready to go to the meeting. She noted that the boy was not getting ready; then she asked him if he was going with her; which he answered that he would rather wait, as he have not yet fully developed to a full-fledge member,—he said that he had not had the heart to point at this sick person, so pointed to the cat instead. He was not sure whether the rest would like his membership, so he was not going this night, but for his grandmother to let him know what the decision of the rest would be. Little did she realize that he was to wait for the executioners that were coming at a set time, that he had volunteered to act as guide for them. She had no sooner gone out, when the party that were chosen to kill the witches came into the lodge of the boy. They asked him if she did not insist on him going. He told them that she took his excuse and did not suspect anything.

After waiting little while, they started out at the guidance of the little boy. They found the spot all as he had told them, right in the middle of a great swamp. When reaching at the edge of the opening, the head-man of the party told them to separate and surround the circle, and at a given signal of a certain bird-call or whistle that they were to rush right out and jump upon the circle and hit the first one that came in his way,—they were all well armed with huge war clubs. So they separated and worked their way clear around the group of witches.

During this time there were some members who seem to sense the presence of danger and often would tell others to listen, that there was someone moving about near the place where they were. But the more brave just laughed at those who acted so nervous, saying that it was only the small woods animals who had come near, maybe attracted by the small fire. As it was, it was the men who were working their way to their respective places and often step on some dry twig that would snap and make a noise.

The meeting was going on as usual; the Head-man was giving a speech about the new member who had failed to pass the test, who should be present at the meeting; and the old woman, the grandmother, arosed to tell her knowledge about her grandson's absence—when there was a very shrill whistle of a night bird that cut the stillness of the night air. And without any previous warning, there came men out of the darkness and with a loud war whoop,— came to the circle swinging their war clubs. Each witch were dispatched with a single blow on the head. In no time the work of the executioners were completed. They left the bodies as they fell; and after putting out their fire, they returned home. Thus ended the meeting place of the witches.

After that, the boy was taken to the chief's home and accepted as one of the household. The next day the shack of the old woman that was the boy's grandmother was set on fire and destroyed. But according to the legend there was one member who escaped the slaughter; he was the one who had come to the place of the boy's grandmother of the day before. He had an idea that there was something suspicious and had stayed away from this meeting. So the legend goes. Neh-hoh.

Now, Sah-nee-weh, this particular legend is one of the most earliest recollection of any. I should say about the age of five or six years,—I was so small that I could run under the table without my head touching the top of the table. There used to be an old man, a very old man who had no teeth, who walked with a cane; he used to come to our place often and would tell the most weird and mysterious legends,—I was really afraid of him as he appeared to be so old and full of wrinkles. He was one of the best story-teller that ever came to us. At that age, I was too small to recall his name. I never thought of asking my mother who he was. When he told of some legend that was full of excitement, I would get so scared that I used to sit close by my mother; then I would beg her to pick me up as I was too scared then.

Well, Sah-nee-weh, this much gained; so get set for the next one. I am just about getting ready for another good one. Dah Neh-hoh.

Your Seneca Brother and Story-teller,

Jesse J. Cornplanter
Hah-yonh-wonh-ish,
the Snipe

XVII

THE ORIGIN OF THE FALSE FACES

Tonawanda Reservation
June 1, 1937

My dear Seneca Sister, Sah-nee-weh:

My last letter has contained in it a legend that is different than the others. Still, this one I am going to tell you will be different in its nature than the others. This is about the creation or near that period; it is about Hawen-nih-yoh or the creator, and the man-being with the red face, the spirit of the hurricane, or Ga-gonh-sah,—commonly called by students and writers, False Faces, which is wrong. In our language, Ga-gonh-sah means "Its face" or just *Face*. I selected this one, as it is the one token that you are now carrying with you,—I mean the one that I had carved for you, and later had it blessed with the sacred Indian Tobacco,—what might be called "Invocation" made to this little token of the original spirits that, we claim, wanders all over creation. It is said to bring you much good fortune by wearing it with you all the time. It is your own personal Good-luck Charm. I will draw also with the illustrations to show the size as compared with the others. As I told you at the time, always wear it so you can have the good fortune from it, I know that you are wearing it

187

all the time, as I have seen you wear it around your neck in that little buck-skin beaded bag that one of the women here have made for you to use. I think this is fitting that we include something that you have with you, as a protector or guardian spirit. The origin of The Faces are different and many according to the tribe. The Onondagas

SAH-NEE-WEH'S SACRED TOBACCO

CHARM MASK
ACTUAL SIZE.—

calls it "Ha-doh-hih," or the Hunchback. We call him "Sca-go-dyo-weh-go-wah" or "Gah-gonh-sah" as a common name. So, Sah-nee-weh, here goes:

It was long, long time ago, when the earth was new, when the two brothers were contesting as to who would rule the world, just after they had played the gambling game of Bowl and Counters (on one side the Creator or Ha-wen-nih-yoh, and on the other side that of the Yeh-ken-sih or the older woman and the Evil-mind that is called Hah-nis-heh-ononh). It was with good fortune to all living things that the Ha-wen-nih-yoh won the Game by using the heads of the Chickadees. Then it was decided that the

Ha-wen-nih-yoh was to rule, as he had made all things then about, that the Evil-mind did all he could to overthrow the good in all the work of his good brother. It was then that the Ha-wen-nih-yoh took a long walk to examine all the things that he had created, and he was going about, when he spied another man-being going about.

When that being met Ha-wen-nih-yoh, it said, "Where did you come from and what is your name?"

Then Ha-wen-nih-yoh replied thus: "I am going about examining all things growing about the earth. My name is Ha-wen-nih-yoh." Then Ha-wen-nih-yoh reversed the question by asking the man-being, "Since you asked me, I will now ask you, who might you be and from whence did you come?"

Then the man-being answered thus: "I am Sca-go-dyo-weh-go-wah, the spirit of the wind in motion. I go about the earth from one end to the other. I have great power. I came from the direction of the setting sun."

Again this man-being asked Ha-wen-nih-yoh what he was doing on earth. This is what he replied: "It is I who have created and completed the bodies of all mankind going about, also created all things that are growing hereabouts. Since you have stated that you have great power on earth, we might have a test of power right now."

At this the man-being called Sca-go-dyo-weh-go-wah held in his hand a huge rattle made of the shell of a Snapping-turtle, which he did shake with much force, that made such a noise, it scared all the animals nearby. He was trying his best to impress Ha-wen-nih-yoh of his great power; he was also making such a noise with his mouth. That only made the demand for test more urgent.

So Ha-wen-nih-yoh said: "Whoever can make that yonder mountain move, is the one that has the power. We will face away from it and at a command remain so, while the one showing his strength will command the mountain to move forward. At the length of a person's breath, then we shall turn around. So you will now do so."

And they both stood facing away from the mountain; then the man-being said, "You, yonder mountain, move towards us."

Then they turned and noted that it had move little. So Ha-wen-nih-yoh said it was his turn to show his power. They done the same thing again. At the command of Ha-wen-nih-yoh for the mountain to move up to them, the man-being heard some strange noise and turned around quick, forgetting the agreement of the test. As he did so, his face was so close to the cliff that he struck it with such force that his face was distorted, his mouth was drawn up one side and his nose was twisted. By that time Ha-wen-nih-yoh had turned around, and he also noted that the mountain was at their back; and then he saw that his friend, the man-being, had his face all twisted out of shape.

It was then that Ha-wen-nih-yoh spoke: "It was I, who have made everything here about,—I am the master of this place. I can create life. What has happened to your face, that it is so twisted now?''

Then Sca-go-dyo-weh-go-wah did say: "It is true that you are most powerful here on this earth; you are able to cause the mountain to move up to where we stood. By that reason, I am now as you see me. As we stood thus, I thought I heard a noise at our back and something seem to brush against me; so I turned around quick, forgetting our agreement. The cliff was just behind me. I struck my face so hard that it has distorted my face so. It is all as you say,—you are the creator here, and it is my own opinion to ask of you to let me be one of your helper,—if you should have mercy and let me help you. As the human race will dwell on this earth that you have created, I will be able to help the mankind that will live here in the future. It will come to pass that in time they, the people, will be troubled with visions and dreams. As it is now, I have certain amount of power or Ote-gonh in my flesh and being. I have infected with this Ote-gonh to all places that I have wandered. As I have now been the first to traverse this world now present, it is infected with my own power as I went about; so when the people who will dwell on this earth will go about, they shall be troubled with some sort of illness,—they shall have seen me, in vision or in dream.

"Then the people will cause to be made an image with my likeness; then will I aid the people with my own ceremony of healing; then will people go in the woods and carve a face of my likeness out of the Basswood tree, and true enough, my spirit will enter into that mask; then will I help your people by my power to cure sickness, I also will have power to control all wind in motion on this earth hereabouts. Then will mankind say as they will address to me, 'Our Grandfather, the mighty Sca-go-dyo-weh-go-wah, the great medicine man or healer of sickness.' Because the people will be as my own Grandchildren in the future. To my Grandchildren, I will not only cure sickness, but will be able to drive away strange and serious disease; also will be able to warn them of coming sickness, which they can easily avoid, providing they will fulfill my directions. In case of coming sickness or plague of serious nature, they will avoid all this by having their community be visited by the spirits of the Faces of 'Sca-go-dyo-weh-go-wah' to drive away all forms of disease. This will be done by men wearing my likeness, each to be dressed according to my manner of clothes. They shall go to all places of dwelling and go through every part of each home. At that time, there shall also be stationed at each spring of water a person wearing the medicine mask, who shall act as one that purifies their drinking water and thus free them from all things poison in their daily use.

"The leader of this society of Sca-go-dyo-weh-go-wah as they marches from lodge to lodge will carry with him our pole of hickory staff also striped with red paint; on it will be hung at the top small specimens of masks. As they go about on this mission, the leader will also sing our marching chant or 'Gah-nonh-eh-oh-wih.' As they enter each home, this leader will announce that the Sca-go-dyo-weh-go-wah are going house to house driving all known and unknown disease; that if there be someone in the place who wish to have the party give her or him any ceremony of curing,

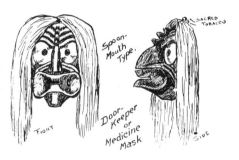

they can do so, if their own sacred tobacco is given as token for this ceremony; that there shall be the dance for the Faces alone, to be used after this curing ceremony, also another dance, which shall be called the 'Doorkeeper Dance' or 'Deh-yenh-sih-da-dih-ahs.' The dance for the Faces only shall be called 'Ho-di-gonh-sohs-gah-ah' or just their faces alone.

"In return for all these ceremonies, I will want as payment, a mush made from parched corn sweetened. Also at this big ceremony of driving the disease, there will be made a strong drink of Parched Sunflower Seeds boiled into strong drink for all to swallow as means of preventing sickness; this will be our own medicine to our grandchildren on

IN THE SMOKE THAT WAFTS SEND THEIR MESSAGE TO ME

earth. Every time anyone calls on us, we shall only hear through the medium of the sacred tobacco smoke and no other form. We are all over this great earth. As we travel all over, I have with me many other helpers who go about from one end of the earth to the other. I am very fond of 'Oyenh-gwa-onh-weh' or sacred tobacco; so every time your people desires my attention, all they have to do is to burn the tobacco, and in the smoke that wafts on send their message to me. I will hear their word every time.

"They must select out of their number one who will address to me. He must have this tobacco with him as he makes the speech,—the substance will be like: 'Now it goes up to you the smoke of the sacred tobacco. You who is fond of it, you of the Sca-go-dyo-weh-go-wah, you who goes all over the land from one end to the other, continue to listen as they direct their words to you. You have said that in the beginning you would be a Grandfather to the man-being on earth; that you would continue to help mankind providing they fulfill your wish; that you would always listen whenever they direct the word to you with the smoke of the sacred tobacco. Now also we give tobacco or Oyenh-gwa-onh-weh to your rattle of the Mud-turtle shell that you always carry with you. Now we give tobacco to your resting place, the giant pine tree with the limbs at the very top, where you rub your rattle as you go about,— this great pine tree which stands in the middle of the earth. Now we give tobacco to your staff which you use as a cane, the giant shell-bark hickory tree without the limbs. Now we give tobacco to your own song which you have said will be your own dance song. Now we ask of you to give your full power to restore to health one of your own grandchildren, by applying the hot ashes to the patient and then blowing the sickness away with your own breath. All this we ask of you with this tobacco which you value above all things.'

"This shall be the custom when mankind shall have societies of the Sca-go-dyo-weh-go-wah. All members shall compose of those who have been cured from sickness by the ceremony. This society shall be known as 'Deh-yenh-sih-dah-de-ahs,' the 'Doorkeeper's Dance' and the 'Hoh-dih-gonh-sohs-gah-ah' or the 'Dance of the Faces only.' I am going to be your helper in this work that is ahead of you. You will depend on my help. I will be coming to the minds of the people that will dwell on this earth. They shall see me, in their visions. Then the people will make my likeness, and I shall give them my full powers to cure those that shall be afflicted with my own method of illness. It all depends on how they shall respect me and my dance. I shall be their friend and helper to those that repeatedly fulfill all my desires, that is—to put on the ceremony every little while, so I can have what I value most, the 'Oyenh-gwa-onh-weh' for my own enjoyment."

Thus spoke this man-being to "Ha-wen-nih-yoh." Then "Ha-wen-nih-yoh" spoke in this wise: "It shall be as you have offered. Everything that you suggested to me are very good. I shall accept your aid, and shall add to your power, so that in the future, when the earth hereabouts shall be full of mankind, you shall watch over my creation, the living mankind and all things created by me, for their well-being. You shall be on the alert for all evil-spirits that may come about, trying to do harm to my own people, the 'Onh-gweh-onh-weh' of the earth. I have planted on earth your most valued of all gifts, the sacred tobacco, 'Oyenh-gwa-onh-weh.' They, the people, shall offer it to you as reward for your kindness to them, that the images of you, made from the Basswood tree, shall have as much power as I have myself. The people who shall carve my likeness shall give this offering at the tree, before the face is carved. Then the full spirit of the woodland, my spirit, shall enter into this mask. In case of any serious windstorm, you must watch for the signs of such storm. And when you see anything that may hurt or do harm to my own creation, the mankind, then you shall cause it to be made known to anyone whom you may choose, so they can comply to the proper precaution. You must ward off all elements that is capable to do them harm. All this I command you to do, to keep up as long as the 'Ong-gweh-onh-weh' shall live here on earth."

Thus was the agreement and acceptance of this spirit-of-the-Faces or Sca-go-dyo-weh-go-wah (often called Ga-gonh-sah as a common name) and Ha-wen-nih-yoh, later called the Creator or the Great Good Spirit, in the earlier days of this world, which is still functioning to this day. It is often mistaken by those that does not understand our belief, that this ceremony and the Sca-go-dyo-weh-go-wah is our religion,—which is a different thing entirely. He is our medicine man, but has no connection with our Spirit-world, as we call our Hereafter. Dah Neh-hoh. . . .

This, Sah-nee-weh, is the version of the Ga-gonh-sah dance or the whole belief, as to its origin, as told by my father who was one of the most well-informed Chief of New Town at Cattaraugus Reservation. Like all legends, there are different versions told, all depending on who is the narrator. I am enclosing a sketch of few of the most important types of faces as they are now and have been in the past. As you know, most of our dances in this order takes place during our Annual Mid-winter Festivities; we call it in our tongue, Nis-ko-wuk-neh Ga-nenh-yahs-onh.

This is one legend that I know will interest you very much. My supply of Gah-ga-ah is exhausted, as a story-teller will say. In Sunshine or Shade I am,

Your Seneca Story-teller and Brother,

Jesse Cornplanter

With Best Wishes
To "Sah-Nee-Weh"
Beaver Clan

THE GREAT FEATHER DANCE

OS TOH WEH GO WAH

Drawing By Ish
"Ha Yonh Wonh"
Snipe Clan
Jesse J Complanter
1936

XVIII

JESSE J. CORNPLANTER

One of the best known Iroquois personalities of the first half of the twentieth century was Jesse J. Cornplanter, whose Seneca Indian name was *Hah-Yonh-Wonh-Ish*, "He Strikes the Rushes". He was born into the Snipe clan of the Seneca Nation on September 16th, 1889, at the Cattaraugus Reservation, the son of Edward Cornplanter, *Soson' dowa*, "Deep Night", of the Wolf clan, and Nancy Jack, *Ga-Nen-Doah*, "Next To a Big Hill". There were ten children born to Edward and Nancy but only three lived to adulthood. The parents both died in the infamous influenza epidemic of 1917, as did several other members of Jesse's immediate family.

The origin of the Cornplanter surname has been a source of speculation for several writers. The best discussion of the topic is contained in the definitive biography of Jesse Cornplanter by the anthropologist William N. Fenton entitled "Aboriginally Yours" (1976). In addition, more data has come to light. It would appear that Jesse's grandfather, Moses Cornplanter and his brother Jimmy, were originally of the Joe family and may have changed their surname for theatrical purposes sometime during the mid-1800's. Genealogical search of the records of the Seneca Nation of Indians concerning the ancestry of his maternal grandparents, John and Mary-Ann Jack, and that of his paternal grandmother, Sarah Phillips, has not revealed any Cornplanter connection. His grandmother, Sarah, according to one Seneca Nation document, may have been among those Senecas who emigrated to Kansas in mid-century and then returned to New York State. Certainly, none of the individuals in this family appear among those officially recognized as Cornplanter heirs listed in the documents relative to the formal partition of the Cornplanter Grant in 1871. Today, the Cornplanter surname is extinct among the Seneca.

It is generally recognized that Jesse Cornplanter's greatest contribution to the Iroquois was his artistic depictions of Seneca history, mythology, and religion, and from his writings. It was from his father, a highly respected Faithkeeper in the traditional *Gai-wiio* religion, that Jesse received extensive training in history and ritual. Jesse, although he only formally attended school until the fifth grade, extended his education by accompanying his father on various Indian pageants and Wild West show circuits at least as early as 1906, including travel to

Europe when he was fifteen. By living in the traditional Longhouse community at Newtown, and participating in its daily life and ceremonial cycle, Jesse became intimately familiar with the scenes that he depicted in his art. It was this solid background in his traditional culture that established his credibility with the many Iroquoianist scholars who were to seek him out for his knowledge and advice in all areas of Seneca culture. He also became recognized among his own people as one who was very knowledgeable, including the areas of myth and legends. This store of knowledge became the foundation for the "Legends of the Longhouse".

Jesse's father had worked extensively with the young anthropologist Arthur Caswell Parker, also of Seneca descent and originally from the Cattaraugus Reservation, in the translation and analysis of the good message of Handsome Lake. As Parker's contemporary, Jesse, had done the drawings for the publication of Parker's "The Code of Handsome Lake, The Seneca Prophet" (1913). Interestingly, Edward Cornplanter had also previously published a brief article on an Iroquois story in 1917, the year of his death.

When Jesse Cornplanter was eleven years old (1900), he began a correspondence with Joseph Keppler, the editor of "Puck", a major periodical of the time. Jesse included examples of his art work with his letters to Keppler, in an attempt to begin sales of his work. Keppler's response was to begin to send Jesse art supplies and children's books. Keppler, and others of his acquaintance, were very impressed with the artistic potential of this young Seneca Indian child. It was this same year that Jesse, in conjunction with the Pan American Exposition in Buffalo, had the first of his drawings published.

Frederick Starr, who apparently was aware of Cornplanter's work before the turn of the century, copyrighted a group of Jesse's drawings of the games and dances in 1903, when Jesse was fourteen years of age. Starr eventually established, in 1904, the well known Cornplanter Medal to reward research in Iroquois studies, naming the award after Jesse's reputed ancestor, the great Seneca chief who was a leader of the Allegany River Seneca.

It was through the telling of his legends and the depiction of his art that Jesse felt that young Iroquois people, and interested non-Indians, could learn about the moral and intellectual life of the Seneca. An inveterate lette writer, the publication of "Legends of the Longhouse" was actually the compilation of his extensive correspondence in the form

202

of letters to Mrs. Walter A. Hendricks, *Sah-Nee-Weh*. He felt that the Seneca could provide an example for the rest of the world. With this in mind, Jesse Cornplanter did, to the end of his life, devote much of his time to the education and encouragement of young Iroquois people to acquire formal training.

Jesse J. Cornplanter died at the Tonawanda Reservation on March 18th, 1957. He believed that his art and "Legends of the Longhouse" would remain as a permanent record of him and his contribution to the world from the Seneca people. As he said, "This is for my people. I want it down so that those who wish may learn the old ways and keep them alive."

George H. J. Abrams
Horseshoe
Allegany Reservation
25 July 1986

BIBLIOGRAPHY

Bartlett, Charles E., "Jesse J. Cornplanter". *The Bulletin*, New York State Archeological Association, No. 10, July, 1957, pp 1-3.

Cornplanter, Edward, "The Turtle's War Party". *The American Indian Magazine*, Vol. 5, No. 3, 1917, pp. 195-197.

Cornplanter, Jesse J., *Iroquois Indian Games and Dances, Drawn by Cornplanter*. New York, 1903.

Cornplanter, Jesse J., *Legends of the Longhouse*. New York, 1938.

Fenton, William N., "Aboriginally Yours, Jesse J. Cornplanter, *Hah-Yonh-Wonh-Ish*, The Snipe". *American Indian Intellectuals*, Proceedings of the American Ethnological Society, 1976, pp 177-195.

Fenton, William N., "Frederick Starr, Jesse Cornplanter and the Cornplanter Medal for Iroquois Research". *New York History*, April, 1980, pp 187-199.

Ridley, Marius (Ed.), "Jesse Cornplanter: Chief of the Senecas". *The Saint Bonaventure Laurel*, Vol. XLII, No. 8, May, 1941, pp 6-7, 23-24.

Seneca Nation of Indians, "Census of the Cattaraugus Reservation". 1881, p 146.

Seneca Nation of Indians, "Census of the Cattaraugus Reservation". 1894, p 28.

IROQRAFTS Indian Reprint Series

IROQRAFTS Catalogue Number	Title	ISBN-0-919645-
24-00300	**Scalping and Torture: Warfare Practices Among North American Indians** Frederici, Nadeau, Knowles	-10-0
24-00301	**Hair Pipes in Plains Indian Adornment** J.C. Ewers	-11-9
24-00302	**Indians of Ontario** (Pending) J.L. Morris	-12-7
24-00303	**Wildwood Wisdom** (Out of print) E. Jaeger	-14-3
24-00304	**Indian Uses of Wild Plants** F. Densmore	-16-X